THE
HERB GARDEN

Sarah Garland first became interested in herbs
and their uses during her childhood in
the New Forest in Hampshire, England, and
in recent years has concentrated on growing
and using a very wide variety of herbs in her kitchen,
and to treat minor ailments.
Author of *The Complete Book of Herbs and Spices*
(Viking), Sarah Garland has also written
Wild Flowers of Britain, as well as 13 books for
children, illustrating many more.
She now lives with her artist husband and four
children in Gloucestershire, where she
cultivates a large herb and vegetable garden.

THE
HERB GARDEN

SARAH GARLAND

**PHOTOGRAPHS BY
PAT HUNT**

Published in co-operation with
The New York Botanical Garden Institute of
Urban Horticulture

PENGUIN BOOKS

PENGUIN BOOKS
Published by the Penguin Group
Penguin Books USA Inc.,
375 Hudson Street, New York, New York 10014, U.S.A.
Penguin Books Ltd, 27 Wrights Lane,
London W8 5TZ, England
Penguin Books Australia Ltd, Ringwood
Victoria, Australia
Penguin Books Canada Ltd, 2801 John Street,
Markham, Ontario, Canada L3R 1B4
Penguin Books (N.Z.) Ltd, 182–190 Wairau Road,
Auckland 10, New Zealand

Penguin Books Ltd, Registered Offices:
Harmondsworth, Middlesex, England

First published in the United States of America in
simultaneous hardcover and paperback editions by
Viking Penguin Inc. 1984

7 9 10 8

© Frances Lincoln Limited 1984
Text © Sarah Garland 1984

The Herb Garden was conceived, edited and
designed by Frances Lincoln Limited, Apollo Works,
5 Charlton Kings Road, London NW5 2SB

All rights reserved

ISBN 0 14 046.690 8

Library of Congress Catalog Card Number 84 42922
(CIP data available)

Set in England
Printed and bound in Hong Kong

Contents

Introduction

Why has the image of the herb garden changed so radically during the past ten years? It is certainly no longer thought of as a bed of rank greenery where mint and parsley straggle together and are occasionally picked to flavor potatoes, and it has lost any 'olde worlde' connotations.

Pleasure in food must have played a part. Cooking has become far more adventurous and fresh herb leaves, seeds and roots are used to give original character to a dish. A balanced diet has long been recognized as the basis of a healthy life, but with the new emphasis on natural high-fiber and vegetable foods, the enormous range of pot- and salad herbs is being rediscovered. There is, too, a growing disenchantment with artificial cosmetics and medicines. Although only simple herbal remedies can be employed at home, they can be used to treat minor complaints – headaches, insomnia, mild fevers, skin infections, minor wounds and burns – for which so many complex, orthodox medicines are usually prescribed.

Finally, there is the peculiar and special beauty of herb plants themselves, which seems to me to be heightened by some knowledge of their uses, and of their significance and importance in the past, and of their potential value for the future. (The scientific investigation of the properties of plants, their potent oils and active principles, is still in its infancy.)

Whatever the reasons, herb gardens are being cultivated again on a breadth and scale that hasn't been seen for several hundred years.

There must be many people like myself whose involvement and fascination with herb plants has sprung from different sources. I seem to have approached them from every direction in my life: as amateur botanist, cook, mother and gardener, and as a student of domestic history.

My favorite botanizing grounds were mere wastelands, trash tips, neglected roadsides and abandoned quarries. There I found many of the old medicinal herbs growing as outcasts – motherwort, greater celandine, deadly nightshade, henbane and black horehound – which seemed set apart from other plants and to have strong characters of their own. I looked them up in the herbals of Gerard and Culpeper, then found Parkinson's *Paradisus*, Walafrid

Strabo's poem 'Hortulus' written in the ninth century AD, herbal charms from Anglo Saxon times, and scraps from the herbal of a Saxon monk, written on yellowed parchment and preserved in the British Museum.

I have always found great comfort in a sense of the continuity of history; not the history of battles, kings and queens, but the lives of ordinary men and women, their preoccupations and beliefs, their domestic chores, their food and their gardens. The herbals spoke directly, in vigorous and expressive language, about living history, about plants that I could grow, taste, smell, eat and use to cure my indigestion and my children's coughs, as they had been grown and used for thousands of years. They made me vividly and movingly aware of the way that spiritual and earthly matters were bound together in the past, and how men and women wrestled to come to terms with and make sense of a world where disease, suffering and early death were commonplace. Plants, with their ability to heal or kill, were not only depended upon for food, medicine, clothing, fodder and fuel, but also for protection against much that was incomprehensible: the powers of darkness, elf-shot, thunder and the evil eye, which could be said to represent death, infection, natural catastrophes and mental suffering.

Herbal writers, who were usually priests and physicians, watched the responses of animals and birds to certain plants, drew on the vestiges of their own ancestral instincts, copied from the herbals of the ancients (especially from Pliny and Dioscorides) and searched for symbols and signs in the appearance and habits of plants to direct them to their uses. As the potency of plants fluctuates according to the season, soil and even the time of day, so the writers suggested harvesting herbs according to the movements of the planets, the birthdays of saints and the waxing and waning of the moon.

Reading these books and manuscripts, I wanted to grow the plants in our own garden. To our plot of culinary herbs, I added many wild and naturalized plants such as vervain, valerian, skullcap, houndstongue and viper's bugloss. I also found that many of the flowers we already grew had been used as medicines in the past. Lilies, roses, peonies

A bank thickly planted with many varieties of creeping and upright thyme, compact marjoram and a low form of wild sage. Foxgloves, primroses and cowslips have self-seeded among them and large-flowered calamint (*Calamintha grandiflora*) is on the left.

and monkshood, wallflowers, columbines and lily of the valley, for example, are able respectively to soothe, disinfect, spice and poison, to heal, to sedate and to regulate the heartbeat.

A trip to Greece made me aware that the herbal tradition is still part of daily life in parts of Europe. There I saw men and women park their cars on their way home from work in the cities, and walk into the fields and hills with plastic carrier bags collecting sorrel and mallow leaves for the evening soup, agrimony, yarrow and chamomile for tisanes and gentian root for use as a bitter digestive. Returning through Italy I saw market stalls heaped with the salad herbs I had read about in Thomas Tusser's herb list of 1577: purslane, rocket, borage, sorrel, burnet and corn salad. In France the drugstores were filled with herbal remedies.

At home, our garden became neglected as I wrote *The Complete Book of Herbs and Spices* and by the time I finished it the garden was a jungle. Invasive tansy, mint, soapwort and a beautiful but spreading white-flowered comfrey were suffocating the more delicate plants. Many herbs had grown unexpectedly large; others had vanished.

There had been no design to the garden, just a haphazard arrangement of beds crammed with the plants we liked best, with newcomers fitted in wherever there was a space. Now we began to divide and select, to plan the garden properly, contain it with low hedges and borders, lay paths and clear a bank for low-growing species.

I visited other herb gardens and discovered that the ways herbs are grown are as various as the reasons for growing them, and as the characters of the growers. I saw small yard and roof gardens, richly scented cottage gardens, commercial and private physic gardens and the National Trust garden of medicinal herbs in Cumbria, England; the gardens of chefs and herbalists, reconstructed historic gardens and the beautiful knot gardens at Hatfield and Cranbourne in England. Reflecting on these gardens and comparing traditional and modern gardening methods and designs, I began to write this book.

I very much wanted to include a *thorough* catalog of herbs and was faced with the difficult but unavoidable question: what is a herb? The dictionary definition is a plant that is used for food, medicine, scent or flavor, but this includes agricultural crops and excludes those used in the past. I have finally included all the species and varieties you would expect to find in a herb garden, and have added as large a personal choice as space permitted of less usual herbs and also some climbing plants, trees and shrubs with medicinal uses.

Apart from the support and encouragement of my family, I have had great help during my research. I went first to the Chelsea Physic Garden in London, England and searched their files and seed store, then to the Herb Society to look through their records and slides, then to the marvellous collection of books belonging to the London Library. Scores of gardeners have patiently given me their time and advice. I have been helped again by Michael Bull, particularly with the herb catalog, and I have been very fortunate indeed to have had the photographs specially taken by Pat Hunt, who is not only a professional photographer, but also a knowledgeable gardener.

Grateful thanks, too, to the owners of the four gardens which are shown on the next few pages. Each has approached the design and the choice of plants and cultivation from a different starting point and in a different way, and together they act as an introduction to the beauty and variety of the herb garden.

A FAMILY HERB GARDEN

This is a greatly loved and lived in herb garden. Rich and abundant, it is in a constant state of change and development.

The herbs are used and enjoyed by the family and the children know which they can eat and which they should avoid (really poisonous herbs are not grown). They play along the crisscross brick and turf paths, and their tree-house has the best view of the layout of the garden.

Before the existing herb garden was planned, there had been only small beds of herbs – a patch of flavoring herbs by the kitchen door, then two cartwheels laid flat by the front gate with herbs planted between the spokes. As her interest in herbs grew, Lesley Bremness began to design a far more ambitious garden in a grassed area running east to west beside the cottage. A big diamond-shaped bed and four outlying beds were cut from the turf, leaving turf paths; then these beds were divided again with narrow brick paths bedded on sand, which means that the plants can be easily seen and cared for. The soil, heavy unyielding clay, had to be laboriously mixed with quantities of compost, grit, pea shingle and sharp sand to lighten it. Her only regrets are that she didn't hire a machine to remove the heavy clay before digging the herb beds and that she didn't bed the brick paths in cement. The bricks are constantly lifted by a persistent though beautiful form of wall germander.

Soon the five new beds were overflowing with plants. As the largest herbs reached maturity they began to dominate the garden. A border was dug around the whole area, and the tall herbs moved there to act as an enclosure and windbreak: elecampane, gravel root, mullein, valerian, foxgloves, vervain and woad.

Recently four more beds have been added to hold sixteenth-century salad and medicinal herbs, and miniature knot patterns. Yet more recently, a yew hedge has been planted around the garden to provide a dark background for the herbs and a windbreak. It will grow very slowly but the owner says that she has become more philosophical about time.

Her pleasure in the garden increases with every year, and this year she is planting herbs that are at their best at dusk and by moonlight.

Above Looking west toward the cottage at the height of summer. Bowles' mint is next to towering mullein and purple sages. Behind are clary sage, white lavender and valerian.

Right Bright flowering herbs near the seat in the garden. The yarrow on the right (with a yellow *Helenium*) grows taller in cultivated ground than it does in the wild.

Below left A southfacing bench 1 is shaded by an arbor of honeysuckle, roses, jasmines and a purple-leaved vine, and a chamomile seat 2 faces west to catch the evening sun. The entrance to the garden 3 is over a mat of scented chamomile, flanked by two tall lavender bushes. Opposite the entrance, are two miniature knot gardens 4 with patterns in rosemary, dwarf box, purple sage and thyme. The corner beds 5 contain assorted herbs underplanted with primrose and violets with hedges of golden feverfew, curry plant and lavender. The central beds have collections of different species, sages 6, creeping thymes 7, marjorams, with German chamomile and viper's bugloss 8, and rosemaries underplanted with dianthus 9. Sixteenth-century medicinal herbs 10 include houseleek, self-heal, Roman chamomile, lungwort, thornapple and comfrey. Culinary herbs 11 include chervil, borage, rocket, anise, lemon balm, caraway and comfrey.

A MEDICINAL HERB GARDEN

At least three hundred species and varieties of herbs grow in this narrow garden behind a small terraced house in a run-down inner city area. Although some of the plants are very large and spreading – goat's rue, melilot, comfrey and tall mulleins – the garden has an atmosphere of order and peace. It is beautiful as well as functional.

From the back door to the large compost piles at the bottom of the garden, medicinal herbs are grouped according to their families, as they would be in a botanic garden, beginning with a raised bed for the mallow family (*Malvaceae*) by the concrete yard and ending with the rose (*Rosaceae*) and borage (*Boraginaceae*) families. The largest beds hold the most extensive herb families: the thyme family (*Labiatae*), the daisy family (*Compositae*) and parsley family (*Umbelliferae*), while many others are ranged along the fences and around the small lawn. The only herb family with strong medicinal properties that is missing is *Solanaceae* as it contains so many poisonous plants which might be dangerous for the children who play in the garden. (The flowers of white bryony are also pulled off before their poisonous berries develop.)

When the family arrived four years ago, they cleared the overgrown, southfacing garden of dock, brambles and elder and enriched the sour city earth with compost. All the materials for constructing the garden were collected

Right Medicinal herbs are grouped in beds according to family. In the list below, each Latin name is followed by an example of a plant belonging to the family. The families are:

1 *Rosaceae*, rose
2 *Boraginaceae*, borage
3 *Leguminosae*, pea
4 *Scrophulariaceae*, foxglove
5 *Labiatae*, thyme
6 *Compositae*, daisy
7 *Caprifoliaceae*, honeysuckle
8 *Crassulaceae*, houseleek
9 *Polemoniaceae*, Jacob's ladder
10 *Verbenaceae*, lemon verbena
11 *Caryophyllaceae*, carnation
12 *Papaveraceae*, poppy
13 *Apocynaceae*, periwinkle
14 *Liliaceae*, lily
15 *Mentha spp.*, mint
16 *Ranunculaceae*, buttercup
17 *Malvaceae*, mallow
18 *Rubiaceae*, bedstraw
19 *Polygonaceae*, sorrel
20 Mixed species, including daphne and sweet flag
21 *Umbelliferae*, parsley

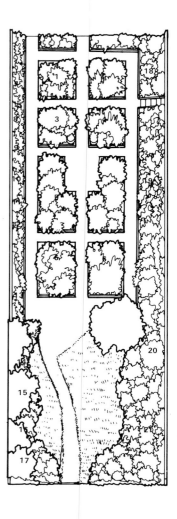

Left A view down the garden from the small courtyard toward beds of herbs that belong to the daisy family. Elecampane and hemp agrimony are in the right-hand bed, feverfew and sunflowers to the left. The beds are raised and the earth contained with wooden planks.

Opposite Looking up the garden toward the house with goat's rue leaning on the right. On the left are flower spikes of purple toadflax (*Linaria purpurea*), and behind them in the thyme family bed are Virginian skullcap and a tall plant of motherwort.

from demolition and junkyards: blue bricks for the paths, floorboards to edge the raised beds and abandoned doors and pallets for fencing and for containing the compost piles. (Here vegetable waste, collected from the city's markets, is converted to a dark crumbling humus.)

Sowing seed, taking cuttings and growing herbs in their own family groups has helped the owner, Paul Stocking, to understand their properties and characters and to train as a medical herbalist. In the same way, a knowledge of living plants was an essential part of the training of physicians who studied in the first botanic gardens planted four hundred years ago.

It is not necessary, though, to be an expert to take pleasure in this garden and to learn something about the relationships between plants. In the bed of the borage family, for instance, the leaves of all the herbs are bristly or hairy, often containing a healing mucilage, and their pink, purple or blue flowers are humming with bees. Powerful scents come from the leaves of most of the labiates, which are often strongly antiseptic.

Planted in this way, the similarities as well as the infinite variety of herbs are clearly seen.

A COLLECTOR'S HERB GARDEN

Set in the corner of a larger garden and protected on two sides by high walls laden with roses, the herb garden at Alderley Grange has been established for many years. The air is heavy with scent. Old prostrate rosemaries spread across the gravel at the entrance, woodruff and sweet cicely grow thickly at the foot of the wall, lemon verbena and balm of Gilead bushes are planted in pots, and rain draws a peppery scent from nearby shrubby curry plants.

Although many of the herbs are used for cookery and for their scent, the garden belongs to a collector who is prepared to travel a long way to find unusual scented and aromatic plants. There is a golden-leaved valerian, spignel from Scotland, a fine-leaved sage from Spain, and henbane with its pale, penciled flowers. A Carolina allspice tree with scented bark grows nearby; even the ivy which climbs through honeysuckle around a seat has scented leaves.

The profuse, lush planting is held together by the tight design of eight triangular box-edged beds, each with a pink

Below The scented herb garden at Alderley Grange contains eight triangular box edged beds, with the planting arranged so that low herbs are toward the center, and taller, larger herbs around the outer edges. Some examples of the herbs grown are:

Low plants
Allium schoenoprasum, chives
Calamintha nepetoides, lesser calamint
Fragaria vesca, wild strawberry
Galium odoratum, woodruff
Origanum vulgare 'Aureum', golden marjoram
Viola odorata, violet

Medium-sized plants
Achillea millefolium, yarrow
Apium graveolens, wild celery
Helichrysum angustifolium, curry plant
Hyoscyamus niger, henbane
Iris florentina, orris
Polygonum bistorta 'Superbum', bistort

Teucrium chamaedrys, wall germander
Tanacetum parthenium, feverfew

Larger plants
Allium cepa, tree onion
Artemisia abrotanum, southernwood
Ballota nigra, black horehound
Filipendula ulmaria, meadowsweet
Inula helenium, elecampane
Rosmarinus officinalis, rosemary
Ruta graveolens, rue
Salvia officinalis, common sage
Smyrnium olusatrum, alexanders
Valeriana officinalis, valerian

Opposite The garden in late spring with the pink flowers of a cultivated bistort on the right. Valerian and monkshood are coming into flower in the left-hand bed behind variegated lemon balm.

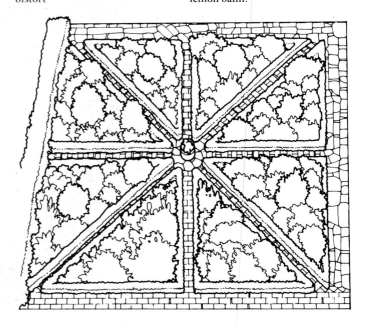

The pale penciled flowers of henbane growing with *Allium moly*. As the germination of henbane is so erratic, seeds are sown early under glass each year at Alderley and planted out when frosts are past.

damask rose at the center, and eight narrow brick paths that radiate from an astrolabe.

Both garden design and plants are associated with well-known gardeners. The previous owner, the designer of the garden, was Alvilde Lees-Milne who was given plants by her friend Vita Sackville-West (including the red-flowered Sissinghurst rose, found in the ruins of Sissinghurst castle). The present owner, Guy Acloque, was much impressed as a child by the garden of Eleanour Sinclair Rohde, a near neighbor and the author of many books on herbs. His plants reflect her influence.

During the past ten years Guy Acloque has added much to the garden, though always integrating any changes into the original design. Tall herbs, elecampane, lovage and bronze fennel, are planted around the outer edge of the garden to emphasize its enclosed and serene atmosphere. Toward the center are the lower herbs, wall germander, Welsh onion and bistort. Pots of tender balm of Gilead are sunk in the earth to their rims. Low-growing, sun-loving Mediterranean herbs were recently moved to a more open situation as they didn't flourish between the box hedges. Now they grow among other culinary herbs, including the owner's favorite, coriander, around a central

clump of white-flowering orris. In the nearby greenhouse are precious or tender herbs: a white-flowered rosemary, a variegated horehound, a collection of scented pelargoniums and trays of sweet basil.

A SIXTEENTH-CENTURY HERB GARDEN

In the sixteenth century, John Parkinson described his great herbal as a 'speaking garden'. The garden at Tudor House Museum has been planned as a 'flowering book', and is a celebration of the plants and garden features of the English Renaissance. With the old buildings of the museum to one side and the ramparts of the city wall to the other, a small yard has been transformed by the vivid colors and scents of herb plants which have been worked into traditional patterns and designs.

As it is part of a museum, there are more garden constructions here than would have been usual in a sixteenth-century garden of this size. Each one is authentic and is soundly based on contemporary records, and the effect is cheerful, uncluttered and complete.

By the door into the garden, a stone fountain plays. It is surrounded by a lawn of creeping chamomile, pennyroyal and thyme, bounded by hyssop and rosemary hedges. Striped rails enclose beds of perennial shrubby herbs and herbaceous peonies, irises and lilies. A tunnel arbor runs along the far wall and a smaller arbor faces the large central knot which is the main focus of the garden.

An interlaced knot, it is kept closely trimmed, showing the subtle variations in the colors and textures of the hedge herbs. A low rail encloses a hedge of silver santolina, with a square of dwarf box hedge set at an angle within it. Around and through the box run curving hedges of winter savory and wall germander, with bright bedding plants in the spaces between them and a rosemary bush at the center. Around the knot, which is slightly raised and enclosed with wooden planks, run sanded paths.

The designer of the garden, Sylvia Landsberg, faced many problems when she began to plan it. Although it was

All the garden structures and plants shown here have been recorded in designs and plant lists for sixteenth-century gardens. The low rails enclosing the beds and the striped poles topped with heraldic animals are copied from a contemporary painting of Hampton Court, England.

Above The planting plan of the reconstructed sixteenth-century knot. Only authentic species are grown.

Knot herbs
1 *Santolina chamaecyparissus*, cotton lavender
2 *Buxus sempervirens* 'Suffruticosa', dwarf box
3 *Teucrium chamaedrys*, wall germander
4 *Satureja montana*, winter savory
5 *Rosmarinus officinalis*, rosemary

Other herbs
6 *Rosmarinus officinalis*, rosemary
7 *Lavandula officinalis*, lavender
8 *Vinca minor*, periwinkle
Armeria maritima, thrift
Artemisia abrotanum, southernwood

A. absinthium, wormwood
Hyssopus officinalis, hyssop
Origanum spp., marjoram
Salvia officinalis, sage
Thymus vulgaris, common thyme
Tanacetum vulgare, tansy

Winter bedding plants:
Bellis perennis, double daisy
Cheiranthus cheiri, wallflower
Primula veris, cowslip

Summer bedding plants:
Borago officinalis, borage
Calendula officinalis, marigold
Centaurea nigra, cornflower
Matthiola incana, stock
Viola tricolor, heartsease

Right Colonies of lungwort and periwinkle are shaded by an old fig tree, with borage, rue and feverfew growing among them.

not difficult to find sixteenth-century plans and lists of plants, there was no way of finding out *how* plants were grown together. She felt that the sparse planting shown in early illustrations was probably a device used as an indication of species by the artist rather than an actual planting method, and so she spaced her herbs fairly closely.

The practical problem of access to the yard (through the polished corridors of the museum) had to be overcome. Tons of garbage, broken crazy paving and several Irish yew trees had to be wheeled out and much compost and topsoil brought in. It was often difficult to get hold of seeds and plants of the original wild or cultivated species. When a hundred cuttings of wall germander were eventually found, they had to be cut into three in order to give the three hundred plants needed.

For the maintenance of the garden, its designer and gardener have had to rely mainly upon their own experience. They found that the knot hedges have to be cut hard back during mid- to late spring and that new growth needs to be trimmed and neatened every three weeks throughout the growing season. In the late summer a final firm cut gives the hedges time to develop new growth as winter protection. Cuttings are taken each year so there is a steady supply of stock plants available to fill any gaps in the hedges.

It is hard work, but the garden is very rewarding, and many of the ideas here can be simplified or adapted by those who love early plants and gardens.

THE
HERB GARDEN
IN HISTORY

The idea of separating a garden of useful plants – herbs – from a garden of ornamental plants is only fairly recent. Until about three hundred years ago, all plants were grown for food or medicine, or used in a symbolic way as a protection against malignant forces. Even their beauty was thought to have a purpose, contributing to general health by strengthening the spirit and giving support and comfort to the soul. So, in the broadest sense, gardens were herb gardens for thousands of years. This chapter follows their development, beginning with records of early monastic gardens, up to the present day.

In pagan times plants had been used as part of every religious ritual and celebration for purification, decoration and incense, and they continued in this role in the early Christian church. As monks and nuns cultivated their gardens, their cherished plants symbolized the virtues while weeds were destroyed as the vices of mankind, and the germination of seeds reflected the mystery of the Resurrection.

It was only during the later years of the Renaissance that there came to be a marked change in the attitude to both plants and garden. Herbs had begun to lose their identity and significance. Gardens were filled with new exotic plants from foreign lands and with 'improved' garden varieties, and the properties of herbs were being questioned in the new spirit of scientific enquiry. The old rituals and traditions associated with herbs became suspect as they had been based on intuition and instinct rather than on rational research. Knowledge of herbal properties could even be dangerous: such knowledge was often associated with pagan religions and black magic (witch hunting and burning was at its height during the seventeenth century).

By the eighteenth century, herbs were generally grown separately away from the purely decorative plants in the ornamental garden. They were confined to the kitchen garden or to the large market gardens that were cultivated around the growing cities, or to the traditional cottage gardens of fruit, flowers, vegetables and herbs. Occasionally, ladies might be encouraged, in a condescending way, to grow herbs, as is shown in this extract from a ladies' quarterly journal of 1842: '. . . there is a neatness and prettiness about our thyme, and sage, and mint and marjoram, that might yet, we think, transfer them from the

In this fifteenth-century miniature of a medicinal herb garden, the herbalist points out a herbal remedy to his suffering patient while gardeners tend the plants and a lady in the foreground smells a herb. This is a typical medieval city garden.

patronage of the blue serge to that of the white muslin apron . . .'

Toward the end of the last century, interest in old-fashioned cottage garden plants revived and many scented herbs began to be grown in ornamental gardens. Now, gardens are again being designed specifically for herbs. This is part of a gradual reaction away from the emphasis on size, color and novelty in plants toward the old breeds that were first grown in a self-sufficient society and whose subtleties and scents are given a special emphasis by their ancient associations and virtues.

Monastery Gardens

From the earliest records, gardens have been associated with religious houses. Temples had their sacred groves, hermits their plots, monasteries their complex garden systems where they grew herbs for food, for healing and for religious festivals. As monastic gardens were likely to remain undisturbed during war and local violence, their account books, lists of plants and descriptions of gardening methods often survive, and one can assume that gardens of the ordinary working population were similar, though run along more basic lines.

Following the fall of the Roman Empire, classical villa and garden design, incorporating the atrium and peristyle, survived through the influence of the Byzantine church. The first European monasteries adopted a similar pattern, with the atrium and peristyle becoming the enclosed court-yard garden which was the monastic cloister. The internal structure of the cloister garden often showed an even more ancient influence, the simple design seen in Persian carpets with garden motifs and in the wall paintings of ancient Egypt. This is an enclosed rectangle divided into four beds by paths, or canals, in the form of a cross, with a fountain or water tank at the center.

From ancient Persia, too, came the name for the enclosed and often circular garden by the walls of the church – the paradise – which was a sanctuary for meditation and prayer. Here the sacristan grew flowers to decorate shrines and statues and for feast day garlands.

It usually fell to the monasteries to treat the sick, and the infirmarer's garden of medicinal herbs is usually shown in illustrated manuscripts as a small, neatly ordered area of

This detail, from a larger painting, shows a small secluded monastery with a simple garden plot of herbs and vegetables. A thick hedge of thorny roses marks the garden boundary, while a picket fence separates and protects the carefully tended plants.

narrow beds set close against the infirmary. Three sources from the early ninth century give a good idea of the plants grown there. Charlemagne's list of medicinal herbs, drawn up as part of his long *Capitulare de Villis*, includes poppy, burdock, marsh mallow, clary and houseleek. His plans of the physic garden for the enlargement of the seventh-century Benedictine monastery at St Gall in Switzerland contain, among other herbs, savory, iris, rosemary, fenugreek, sage, rue and lily. The German monk Walafrid Strabo in 'Hortulus', a Latin poem, adds agrimony, betony, wormwood and white horehound.

The kitchen garden in the St Gall design is larger than the infirmary garden, and is also planned as rows of narrow beds. Here were grown the basic pot- and flavoring herbs that are repeated in records of monastic and manorial vegetable gardens during the next seven hundred years: quantities of onions, leeks and garlic; several varieties of beans and peas, beet and parsnip; and large beds of those herbs that are especially necessary for the digestion of a heavy diet: savory, fennel, parsley, cumin and mint.

The orchard was an important garden in the monastery. It was often ornamental, with beds of flowering herbs and perhaps a fountain, and was sometimes combined with a cemetery for the monks.

Large monasteries would include a garden for the man responsible for alemaking, where he would cultivate the bitter or 'gruit' herbs: sweet gale, alecost, ground ivy, rosemary, yarrow and lovage; and a garden for the refectorer of scented, disinfectant herbs such as rue to be strewn in the refectory. (Other plants were needed for making ink and colored paints for illuminating manuscripts, and there might be an area for growing hemp and flax for rope and cloth.)

The early Benedictines were followed by other orders: the Cistercians, who placed an even greater emphasis on physical labor, horticulture and agriculture, and the Carthusians, who lived in separate cells, each of which opened into its own small, totally private 'paradise'.

The common Latin language of all monastic orders, their comparatively high level of literacy and shared interests in horticulture and healing led to much exchanging of plants and plant lore, and the histories and properties of herbs, and illustrations of them, were laboriously and beautifully copied by the monks into their herbals. Sometimes illustrations and stories would be copied unquestioningly from manuscript to manuscript until the likeness of the herb would be lost and myths would develop such as the Barnacle Tree from which geese hatched and the mandrake root whose shrieks would strike the harvester dead.

AN ALL-PURPOSE MONASTIC GARDEN

The narrow, intensively cultivated beds of herbs shown in early monastic plans were highly efficient and productive, and this system is being used increasingly today for growing crops of herbs and salads in a confined space.

With beds no more than a yard wide, there is no need to trample and compact the earth, and plants are accessible from all sides. Ideally, the beds are slightly raised and contained between boards or curbstones. (These should be inspected regularly for slugs, which tend to gather against their cool, damp sides, just below the surface.) Raising the beds helps give good free drainage and allows for the addition of manure and compost each year, and even a slightly raised bed makes seed-sowing and weeding easier, and brings the plants closer, both to see and to smell.

For close-growing annual and salad herbs the earth should be especially enriched, and it is helpful if the paths can be made wide enough for barrowfuls of compost to be wheeled along them.

Above Flowering fennel, with tansy in the foreground. Fennel was grown on a large scale in early gardens, especially by monks whose diet consisted largely of bean pottage and fish. Fennel seeds are an efficient remedy for indigestion.

Left and right Two views across the reconstructed monastic garden at the Cloisters of the Metropolitan Museum of Art in New York, showing the simple layout of beds around a central stone fountain. The famous fifteenth-century Unicorn tapestries are exhibited in the museum and most of the plants shown in the tapestries are cultivated in the garden.

The four beds in the center of the garden have an inner edging of thrift and hold herbs used as chaplets and garlands and as church decorations. Around them are beds of culinary, medicinal, strewing and dye herbs.

PLANT LIST

1 (top to bottom)
Artemisia vulgaris, mugwort
Papaver somniferum, opium poppy
Mentha pulegium, pennyroyal
Althaea officinalis, marsh mallow

2 (top to bottom)
Levisticum officinale, lovage
Satureja montana, winter savory
Coriandrum sativum, coriander
Origanum sp., marjoram

3 (left to right)
Anethum graveolens, dill
Mentha sp., mint
Salvia sp., sage
Apium graveolens, wild celery

4 (left to right)
Cuminum cyminum, cumin
Thymus sp., thyme
Petroselinum sp., parsley
Foeniculum vulgare, fennel

5 (left to right)
Trigonella foenum-graecum, fenugreek
Stachys officinalis, betony
Agrimonia eupatoria, agrimony
Portulaca oleracea, purslane
Achillea millefolium, yarrow

6 (left to right)
Rosmarinus officinalis, rosemary
Sempervivum tectorum, houseleek
Marrubium vulgare, horehound
Artemisia absinthium, wormwood

7 (top to bottom)
Anthemis nobilis, chamomile
A. sativum, garlic
Allium porrum, leek
Rosa sp., rose

8 (top to bottom)
Hyssopus officinalis, hyssop
Lavandula stoechas, French lavender
Iris sp., iris
Ruta graveolens, rue
Lilium candidum, madonna lily

MONASTIC HERB GARDEN PLAN

The herbs in this simple and practical design are those that would have been grown in an infirmary or kitchen garden in a monastery five hundred years ago. The taller, stouter plants are around the outer edges of the beds, where they give protection against the wind and emphasize the enclosed atmosphere of the garden. The setting could be a small yard or a corner of a larger garden, for example; size is not important but the situation will need to be quite sunny. The beds can be made longer or shorter to fit an existing space, but they should not be much wider. The main paths are wide enough to maneuver a wheelbarrow.

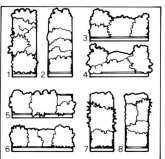

Medieval Gardens

As European society became more settled and secure during the twelfth century, so records show the existence of small pleasure gardens and garden walks among the fortified walls of castles, as well as the employment of gardeners among the castle staff. Gradually castles became less fortresslike, new windows of glass were put in, drainage was improved and vines and fruit trees were planted.

Palaces and the hunting lodges of noblemen and women during the thirteenth century were less fortified. The gardens of large estates were divided like those of the monasteries into many small areas, though without such specialization. Since the owners lived in such communal fashion, the privacy of their gardens must have been particularly precious. They were sometimes reached by steps leading directly from their own chambers, or from covered passages linking their private apartments, while the kitchen gardens, orchards and parks were often outside the main walls.

The walls enclosing these privy gardens were high and were ideally of stone, though more often they were of wattle and daub or wooden palisading or fencing, which was often covered in whitewash. The entrance was through a stout gate, well locked and barred with iron.

In contrast to the monastic layout, there was much emphasis on seats and arbors, sometimes referred to as 'roosting places' or 'playing places'. A bench was often made right round the garden by piling earth in a low bank against the walls, fronting it with stone, brick or wood, and planting flowering herbs in turf along the top.

The Virgin is shown seated on many variations of such a bench in numberless medieval paintings; sometimes the embanked benches stand free from the walls and are backed with a trellis entwined with roses. These lines about Hampton Court, near London, England, describes them well: 'My gardens sweet, enclosed with walls strong, Embanked with benches to sit and take my rest'.

Arbors were sometimes made by cutting a recess or low seat into the bank and building a protective lattice above to support climbing plants. Covered alleys often surrounded the garden and might be roofed and walled with a curving, open structure of wood, entwined with vines or roses, or with plaited, trained trees.

Tall irises and lilies are shown growing along the raised bench. Gilliflowers, columbines, lavender and rosemary grow in pots set about the garden, or are planted in very narrow border beds enclosed with low rails or little fences.

There is still an enclosed, fortified feeling about these privy gardens. They might be encircled by a path, the lawn

The Virgin and Child sit among the flowers in a garden enclosed by an elaborate tunnel arbor which is entwined with roses. Birdlike angels swoop, and a fountain plays in one corner, while in the foreground of the illustration St Catherine can be seen weaving a garland from the roses.

fenced with pales or more elaborate crisscross fencing, with yet another enclosure of railings surrounding the narrow beds.

Even the larger, more public gardens are likely to have had several enclosures, often with locked gates. These are usually pictured with paved paths and raised rectangular or square beds arranged symmetrically. The grander gardens might include a 'gloriette', an open-sided summer-house with seats and a table. The little trees and shrubs in the garden are often trained into ornamental shapes using wire or wood, or clipped into tiers known as 'estrades', while the planting in the beds is sparse.

Paintings of these gardens and poetical references to them are often based on allegory and symbolism, with special reference to the Virgin Mary. The primitive image of the closed circle against evil has become the *hortus conclusus*, the enclosed garden celebrated in the Song of Solomon: 'A garden enclosed is my sister, my spouse; A spring shut up, a fountain sealed'. Here the Virgin sits in her purity.

Other garden paintings from the twelfth and thirteenth centuries celebrate the courtly love of the troubadour that sprang from the love poetry of the Provençal poets. Closely allied to the mystical garden of the Virgin, the troubadour poet in his earthly paradise devotes himself to his virtuous lady with a pure, patient and selfless love. It is only with the increasing realism of the fifteenth century that there is a lessening in the romantic symbolism of sacred and secular gardens in painting and literature.

As society became increasingly stable, so gardening records multiplied. In the fifteenth century 'Mayster' Ion Gardener produced his practical treatise *The Feate of Gardening*, a guide to grafting, viticulture and the cultivation of herbs. His straightforward, obviously firsthand accounts of sowing and harvesting contrast with the folk-lore of contemporary herbals.

The plants Ion Gardener discusses are those grown for so many hundreds of years in Europe as flavoring and potherbs, medicinal and scented herbs: fennel, parsley, thyme and borage, orach and garlic, lilies, honeysuckle and lavender, wood avens, plantain and the toxic henbane. His list marks the last years of the Middle Ages. Already, Portuguese navigators had returned from the Americas with unknown plants, and through the Italian city states the Renaissance was spreading.

AN ENCLOSED MEDIEVAL GARDEN

The enclosed privy garden, close by the town walls or flanked by other buildings in the crowded, fortified medieval towns, can be adapted as a pattern for modern urban herb garden designs.

A raised bed or bench built along a boundary, or perhaps dividing a larger area, gives extra space and height for planting, and helps define a small area. Grow different varieties of creeping thymes along the top and they will form a close, multicolored carpet (an example is illustrated on page 99); or plant bushier chamomile or groups of taller flowering herbs, lilies and columbines; or make a turf top, either clipped short or left to grow long like meadow grass. Lay a large stone, or a group of bricks, at intervals for sitting places during damper weather, or as bases on which to stand pots of scented herbs.

The fountain that is always included in medieval garden paintings could be used to bring constant movement, light and reflections into a shadowed yard. There are simple pumps which circulate and spout water that can be bought for less elaborate versions of these fountains, but even a large terracotta bowl of still, clear water, raised on bricks, makes a lovely focal point in a garden.

I particularly like the emphasis on seats and arbors in medieval gardens, and the climbing plants that twine around them make the best use of a little space. I would not

recommend the constant use of climbing roses behind seats. They are generally too prickly, and so are best planted at the sides of the seat or arbor and trained across well above head height. Other sweet-smelling climbers, such as honeysuckle or jasmine, are more comfortable to lean against.

If the garden is regularly used by children, there is no point in attempting to grow small flowers in a lawn in the medieval way, apart from really tough ones like daisies and the most decorative piantain, *Plantago media.* A central area of pavement or brick is usually best in a small urban children's garden, with sturdy flowerpots set around the edge or on the embanked bench. But where there are no children there can be a small area of flower-studded turf. The grass can be sown, or laid as turfs with selected low-growing, flowering herbs planted in drifts or at regular intervals. Have strong plants ready to put among the seed or the grass, so they can become well established before the grass has settled and becomes competitive. If you are sowing grass seed, set out clumps of flowering plants such as daisies, violets, primroses, wild strawberries or plantain, and sow the seed around them, leaving a 7cm/3in circle of bare earth around each clump. If you wish to plant the herbs in a regular pattern (as some contemporary paintings show), lay square turves and cut a small triangular piece off each corner with a knife to leave small squares of bare earth in the lawn for planting with flowers. The grass is best clipped with shears to a height of about 6cm/2½in, but this is not a great labor in a small area.

An alternative method is to buy one of the mixtures of grass and wildflower seed that are on the market and sow the lawn as a small meadow. In this case, let the grass flower and seed before clipping down to 6cm/2½in in the late summer, when most of the flowers will be over.

Opposite far left Honeysuckle is ideal for growing around an arbor.

Opposite left The scented petals of the apothecary's rose were an important medicine in medieval Europe. They were taken for their astringent, antiseptic, binding and strengthening action, and were often prepared as a syrup or simmered in honey as an electuary. Roses also had symbolic value, first representing Venus, the Roman goddess of love, and then becoming a medieval symbol of the modesty of the love of the Virgin. The periwinkle growing through this rose was also a medieval favorite, and was woven into garlands.

Right Honeysuckle, on the trellis behind the seat, entwined with red and white rambling roses.

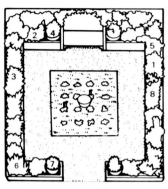

PLANT LIST
1 *Adonis annua*, pheasant's eye
2 *Aquilegia vulgaris*, columbine
3 *Convallaria majalis*, lily of the valley
4 *Dianthus caryophyllus*, clove carnation
5 *Fragaria vesca*, wild strawberry
6 *Iris spp.*, iris
7 *Lavandula stoechas*, French lavender
8 *Lilium candidum*, madonna lily
The central lawn contains the following:
Bellis perennis, daisy
Plantago media, hoary plantain
Primula veris, primrose
Viola spp., violets

MEDIEVAL HERB GARDEN PLAN

This small garden can either be enclosed by a fence or wall, fitting an existing space, or it could be set within a larger garden and left freestanding with the raised perimeter bed acting as a boundary. Some, or even all, of the flowers in the raised bed could be left out, and the space turfed for extra sitting places; flat stones could also be laid among the flowers for this purpose. The raised bed or bench should be higher than the arbor seat (which will be more convenient for tending the plants or clipping the grass). The path shown is gravel. Pots of tender and scented herbs flank the arbor and the entrance. The small central lawn could be planted instead with a mixture of grass and wildflower seed.

Renaissance Gardens

The Italian influence on garden design began to spread through northern Europe toward the end of the fifteenth century. In France, Charles VIII became enraptured with Italian gardens after his invasion of Italy. The firm lines, the symmetry, the use of water, sculptured foliage and statues in French and Italian gardens were described by one English traveler as 'mere cities of verdure' with garden walks like streets, and hedges like walls 'cut into colonnades, arcades and porticoes', and all 'well manned with statues of marble and lead, ranged in regular lines, like soldiers at a procession'.

In France these developed eventually into enormous, formal 'vista' gardens – gardening in the grand manner. Box was used as low, tightly trimmed hedging for elaborate beds that might contain flowers and herbs, but which were equally likely to contain patterns of brightly colored brick dust, spar, pink marble, crushed coal, cockle shells and sand. The designs of these *parterres à compartiments de broderie* were often reminiscent of the recently introduced and fashionable embroidered silks which came from India.

In Holland the Italian influence became apparent in hedged parterres or knots, but here the emphasis was on the flowers themselves, as might be expected from a nation which developed such a strong horticultural tradition. The Dutch also developed a passion for topiary work which William III brought with him to England during the seventeenth century. Topiary was a feature of gardens in classical Italy; fourteen hundred years earlier Pliny described part of the garden of his Tuscan villa as having 'box trees cut into a thousand shapes – sometimes in the form of a small pyramid, or letters to indicate the name or initials of the owner'.

In England it was Cardinal Wolsey who influenced both Henry VII and Henry VIII with his taste for the Italian style. The garden at Hampton Court, begun by Wolsey and taken over by Henry VIII, is well documented and gives an interesting picture of the mingling of the haphazard medieval style and the elaborate Renaissance garden.

This colorful Dutch garden of the early seventeenth century is planted mainly with bulbs but shows the features of a Renaissance garden. The beds are no longer simple squares or rectangles, but are laid in curving patterns and are surrounded by low, clipped borders, and the long tunnel arbor is supported by rows of statues.

Left This tightly clipped knot is bedded in gravel, and was one of the first knot gardens to be reconstructed in recent years. The designs are planted in box and wall germander and are copied both from a French gardening manual published in 1583, and from an English design for a true lovers' knot published in 1664.

Right The best view of this patterned knot garden is from an upper window, as here, which shows clearly the low-clipped hedges, mounds and cones and the central spiral of box. The small beds are filled with a mass of spring-flowering herbs and cottage garden plants. Among them are roses, daisies, dianthus, campanulas, lavender and savory.

There were still embanked benches against the high walls, and the arbors, alleys and raised beds typical of the medieval garden, but there were also quantities of statues of kings and queens, dragons and heraldic animals. There were hundreds of yards of wooden rails painted green, white and vermilion, bronze sundials and carved 'beasts' on tall poles. A mount was built by piling earth upon a great heap of over a quarter of a million bricks, with a path spiraling to the summit, like 'the turnings of cockle shells', to arrive at a large, lead-roofed summerhouse from which to survey the view.

The English gardens of this period adopted the firm structure and the more architectural layout of the continental Renaissance gardens, but instead of creating 'cities of verdure' their scale was smaller and they were more like richly ornamented rooms.

THE ENGLISH KNOT GARDEN

The English version of the French parterre (or *ricami* as it was called in Italy) was the knot garden, which is one of the most successful of traditional herb garden designs. The knot garden always had an essentially domestic quality and a special feeling for the color and character of the individual plants, and is far removed from the stiff formality of the Continental gardens.

English knot gardens were first recorded in the fifteenth century, when decorative and aromatic hedges of lavender and rosemary were used to support and scent drying linen, and the hedge clippings used for strewing and distillation. During the sixteenth and the early seventeenth centuries, designs for knots were illustrated in every English gardening manual.

Each knot was generally contained within a square or rectangle, and these were grouped together below a window or terrace or other vantage point. The knot pattern was traced in low-clipped hedges of scented evergreen herbs such as germander, lavender, santolina, box, thrift, hyssop, savory, marjoram and thyme. The patterns were often reminiscent of the carved wooden detailing or molded plasterwork in houses of the period, or they might be

formed from the entwined initials of the lord and lady of the house, or from heraldic emblems or family mottoes. Often the pattern was punctuated with small clipped trees or topiary work in juniper, bay or box. Tightly interlaced patterns were called closed knots; open knots had a looser design with more space for herbs and flowers or, occasionally, colored stones, earths and sand, between the aromatic hedges.

Clipped and scented hedges were also used to make mazes, either of the penitential variety (symbolic of the pilgrimage through life and to be followed on the knees) or for dalliance and amusing puzzle games.

DESIGNING A KNOT GARDEN

The containing lines and evergreen patterning of a knot garden is an ideal way to show off herbs, for it divides and distinguishes these subtle plants, and restrains any untidiness, while bright colors can be set off against a green or silver hedge background. Whether the design is simple and geometric, or more elaborate with interlaced scrollwork, much of its character comes from the types of hedging herbs used and the way in which they are clipped. They might be grown 60cm/24in high and either cut smooth and flat on top and squared off down the sides, or given a more rounded, even billowing shape. Or the pattern might be picked out in ribbonlike hedges of dwarf herbs clipped low to the ground. (See also pages 102–106.)

A modern knot garden can take inspiration from the graceful and traditional designs illustrated in early gardening books, or a very simple motif can be taken from household objects – fabric, wallpaper or patterned china, clothes or a favorite brooch or ring, or from an abstract design that is related in some way to surrounding buildings or countryside.

A closed knot design, with thick, broad, tightly interlaced hedges, has little space for herbs in between. There might be just an upright rosemary in the center, or an apothecary's rose or artemisia. A closed knot with low, narrow hedges might contain bright flowering herbaceous herbs such as pot marigold, dyer's chamomile or red bergamot.

There is more space for plants between the less complex hedges of an open knot, and herbs can be planted in variety. Although a knot garden is generally planted for

Above A newly planted knot in late seventeenth-century style has hedges of box set in diamond patterns around Irish yew trees. A decorative border of serrated wood surrounds brightly colored gravels.

Opposite An open knot adapted from a rather severe design published by Leonard Meager in 1660. He was influenced by the French parterres being laid out at Versailles. The hedges are close-clipped box with different colored gravels between them. Meager recommended box as 'the most durable, and cheapest to keep to sette knottes'.

decoration, some of the culinary herbs such as parsley, fennel and dill look pretty among the brighter plants. The height and habit of the contained herbs need to be in proportion to the hedges, and they should be neat or easily controllable. Avoid invasive herbs such as the mints, comfreys and soapwort which would soon escape their compartments and overrun the garden.

A knot hedge of dwarf silver santolina or low-clipped germander could enclose violets and primroses in the spring and then, in the summer, blue-flowered flax, green and purple basils or the curious rose plantain. Feverfew has daisy flowers through the summer, and the saffron crocus or the taller and poisonous meadow saffron produce their pink flowers in the autumn. Upright, shrubby, silver or gold variegated thymes keep their decorative leaves throughout the year, and corn salad produces lush leaves during winter.

A bold and handsome design can be made by planting

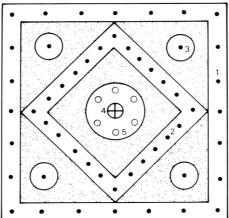

Far left A simple knot design, together with its planting plan, **left**, using two species of hedging herbs. On prepared ground, mark out a 2m/6ft square; divide into smaller squares using pegs and string. Press a plywood ring into the centre up to its rim. Plant up, putting in corner herbs first. Maximum spacing of plants is shown. Clip hyssop and savory flat along top and outer edges; trim marjoram to neaten.

Below left A curving hedge has been added in this design for a complex knot.

Opposite Four knot designs from a seventeenth-century gardening book.

SIMPLE KNOT: PLANT LIST
1 *Hyssopus officinalis*, hyssop or *Satureja montana*, winter savory
2 *Origanum vulgare* 'Aureum', golden marjoram
3 *Santolina chamaecyparissus*, cotton lavender
4 *Laurus nobilis*, bay
5 *Bellis perennis*, daisy

COMPLEX KNOT: PLANT LIST
1 *Hyssopus officinalis*, hyssop
2 *Satureja montana*, winter savory
3 *Origanum vulgare* 'Aureum', golden marjoram
4 *Juniperus communis*, juniper
5 *Viola sp.*, violets

one species of herb *en masse* within each compartment. In this case, the leaves are more important than the flowers as they must look good throughout the growing season. Red sage, curled-leaf tansy (whose creeping roots need containing), broad-leaved sorrel or clary sage, with its great wrinkled, scented leaves, look well grouped in this way.

Planting out the knot garden

If the soil is heavy, lighten it with compost and gritty sand, then rake and level it as for a lawn, treading it repeatedly.

Work out the design carefully on squared paper, then mark it out on the ground using sticks and string. Plant the perennial shrubby herbs that form the structure of the knot, remembering to plant the corner herbs first to ensure even spacing. Clip the top and outer sides of each plant lightly to neaten them up.

Ideally it is best to take cuttings for the knot garden in late spring (see page 102), and then to grow them in a row, keeping them lightly trimmed, until planting them out in their final positions the following spring. If you are using container plants, buy each species at the same time from the

A knot garden in a London churchyard planted in memory of the Tradescants, father and son, who are buried here. They were gardeners, travelers and plant collectors in the seventeenth century and introduced some of our best-known garden plants. The hedges are of box and the silver dwarf *Santolina incana*. Each of the large beds holds a shrubby apothecary's rose or its form *Rosa gallica* 'Versicolor' which is striped pink and white. Around them grow hyssop, lilies, savory, dianthus, daphne, violets, irises and thymes. In the foreground of the picture are pot marigolds and in the center a shrub of southernwood.

Spread across a wide area in front of the Old Palace at Hatfield, England, this large knot garden was planted only three years before the photograph was taken. It is encouraging to see how quickly herbs spread and fill the small beds between the clipped hedges of a knot. The herbs and flowers here were all cultivated in the sixteenth and seventeenth centuries in England. They include many varieties of dianthus, lupins, roses, astrantia, foxgloves, golden sage and irises.

same place to make sure they have reached the same stage of development and have the same form.

The hedges should be clipped back hard in late spring each year to encourage strong, new, bushy growth, and then trimmed as needed during the summer. The last trimming should be done in late summer, leaving the plants time to develop new, protective growth for the winter months.

Hedging herbs for the knot garden

Box, particularly dwarf box, is a common hedging plant for knot gardens. It is slow-growing and has a strange, dry scent which is not to everybody's taste, but it is hardy and reliable and can be clipped almost to the ground. There are gold and silver variegated varieties.

Of the other common hedging herbs, the glossy-leaved aromatic germander and the santolinas and dwarf lavenders are among the most hardy. Winter savory, hyssop, southernwood and garden thyme may lose some leaves in a cold winter, but usually reclothe their bare branches the following spring. Rosemary makes a wonderful scented hedge but needs a sheltered site. The pungent-leaved curry plant is hardy and makes an excellent hedge (although it was introduced to northern Europe after the vogue for knot gardens was past).

The whole knot can be designed using a single species of hedging plant, but one of the pleasures of designing a knot is to use the contrasting colors and textures of several species. The silver-leaved *Santolina chamaecyparissus* and green-leaved *S. virens*, for example, can be used in an interlacing pattern or simply crisscrossed. Or use the contrasting foliage of long-leaved hyssop and darker leaved germander.

For a low-growing knot design use box, germander,

dwarf hyssop or *Santolina incana*, all of which are most amenable to being clipped close to the ground. If possible, make the knot where it can be seen from a window or terrace as the pattern of varying greens, grays and silvers looks particularly attractive from above.

A MINIATURE KNOT GARDEN

A miniature knot garden can be designed like a piece of delicate, subtly colored needlework, and looks best when it is planted in very dark earth.

The most suitable herbs for this small scale pattern-making are those that take very easily from cuttings, such as the common red and green sages, the artemisias in shades of green and silver, dark germander, the rosemaries, silver curry plant, the lavenders, dwarf box, the santolinas and the rue, 'Jackman's Blue'. Little plants that spread from the low-growing *Chamaemelum nobile* 'Treneague' chamomile or small clumps of chives can be used in between. The choice depends upon the mature herbs available for use as stock plants for the cuttings.

For a miniature knot approximately one yard square, add half a bucketful of coarse sand and mix it with good clean soil. Mark out the design using white string or tracks of pale sand. Take softwood or semihardwood cuttings from the herbs (see pages 112–113) and press them firmly into the soil, directly into their places along the design. For the next few weeks, until the roots develop, the cuttings will need to be kept damp (sprinkled, not drenched, with water) and protected from hot sun, either with a canopy of network or by pushing some twiggy branches into the earth around the knot at an angle to provide shade.

The ideal season for settling the cuttings well is late spring, but with extra care early summer or early autumn will do. Once the little threadlike hedges are established, keep them snipped low otherwise they will lose their compact shape and become leggy.

This is not a long-lived garden, but a pretty one. It needs very little space and could even be grown in a big wooden box by those with no garden. It is what a sixteenth-century gardener might have called 'a conceit'.

As a complete contrast, this miniature knot garden is only 1.5 m/5 ft long and is made with cuttings of small herbs pressed directly into the soil where they are to grow. A border of rosemary surrounds patterns picked out in purple sage, curry plant, wall germander and rue. A miniature herb garden needs very little space and could even be grown in a large wooden box. Although it is not a long-lived garden, it is a pretty one.

Physic Gardens to Herb Gardens Today

The plants in sixteenth-century European gardens were beginning to undergo a dramatic change. There had been only a limited number of them; they had been simple and familiar, each with its uses and significance. Now they were added to, almost daily, by navigators and explorers. Holinshead, the sixteenth-century historian, describes his amazement:

'It is a wonder also to see how many strange herbs, plants, and annual fruits are daily brought unto us from the Indies, Americas, Taprobane, Canary Isles and all parts of the world. I have seen in some one garden to the number of three or four hundred of them, if not more, the half of those names within forty years past we had no manner of knowledge.'

Among those concerned with medicine there was a feeling of high optimism. They believed (and many still believe today) that a merciful God could not have created man and then allowed him to suffer from sickness and disease without providing cures – a plant for every ill. The European flora had not proved sufficient, but now at last the flora of the world was to be amassed and studied and all would be finally revealed. There would be 'herbs fit to heale all sores, and cure all paines'.

The first botanic gardens were founded for comprehensive collections of plants at Padua in 1545, at Leyden in 1587 and at Oxford in 1621, and doctors were appointed to lecture on their healing properties. The *Jardin du Roi*, founded in Paris in 1626, was supervised by the physician to the King.

Private gardens were flourishing and new foreign plants were eagerly collected and cultivated. Although many writers still expressed the feeling that a garden of non-medicinal plants must be a self-indulgence, there was now an increasing emphasis on the ornamental garden. This was encouraged by the fact that familiar garden herbs were being changed and distanced from their origins following new advances in plant breeding. Gardeners in northern France and the Low Countries had always been particularly skilful plant breeders, and many left their homes as refugees from religious persecution during the midsixteenth century, settling in southern Europe and Britain. They were able to double, enlarge and change the colors and habits of flowers and plants.

The herbals of the early botanists

A great number of herbals were published throughout the seventeenth century. Generally their authors were doctors of medicine, but there was increasing emphasis on botanical characteristics. Hieronymus Bock's *Nene Kreütter Buch* ran into many editions and attempts some classification of plants. In Italy Pierandrea Mattioli, known as Matthiolus, published his vast commentaries on the *De Materia Medica* of Dioscorides, written fourteen hundred years earlier. Portuguese and Spanish doctors wrote on the medicinal and useful herbs from the East and West Indies, and Nicolas Monardes, from Seville, wrote his herbal on medicinal plants from America, published in English in 1577 as 'Joyfull Newes out of the Newe Founde Worlde'.

In London, England, John Gerard cataloged 1030 plants in his London garden in 1596, and in 1597 he published his herbal. There is some scepticism over his catalog, and certainly much of the contents of his herbal were lifted from the Belgian botanist Dodoens, but his vigorous style and vivid descriptions have given much pleasure for nearly four hundred years.

In 1629 and 1640 two of the greatest English books on herbs and plants were published. These were John Parkinson's *Paradisi i Sole Paradisus Terrestris*, and his *Theatrum Botanicum: the Theater of Plants*, a 'Manlike Worke of Herbes and Plants', which is an enormous herbal describing over 3000 plants. They are among the last books to bring every aspect of plants together: botany, pharmacy, horticulture and history. There is some botanical classification (plants are divided into 'classes and tribes') and an indication of the tremendous developments being made in horticulture (fifty kinds of carnation are named, for instance).

Nicholas Culpeper's herbal, *The English Physitian*, is a contrast. He published it in 1652, partly as a protest against 'proud, insulting, domineering Doctors' and to extol 'Dr Reason' and 'Dr Experience'. 'I could wish from my soul', he cries, 'that blasphemy, ignorance, and tyranny were ceased among physicians, that they might be happy and I joyful'. His often sensible advice, although mixed with fairly wild astrological observations, is written in such spirited style that his herbal has never been out of print.

Nel primo lib. di Dioscoride.   79

con una non eccessiva caldezza, sono concottiue, come habbiamo dimostrato. Et al secondo delle compositioni de medicamenti secondo i luoghi, disse egli che il croco ferma col suo odor il capo, & perturbana l'intelletto, così come il peucedano, & i frutti del lentisco. Chiamano i Greci il Croco Krokos: i Latini Crocus: gli Arabi Zahafaran, ouero Zafaran: i Tedeschi Saffran: gli spagnuoli Azafran: i Francesi Saffran.   Nomi.

Dell'Helenio.   Cap. XXVII.

LO Helenio fa le foglie simili al uerbasco, che produce le foglie piu strette, ma piu aspre & lunghissime. In alcuni luoghi non fa fusto. La sua radice biancheggia, & qualche uolta rosseggia, è odorata, grossa, & alquanto acuta: dalla quale si spiccano le propagini, & piantansi nel modo, che s'usa di fare con i gigli, & con l'aro. Nasce ne i monti, in luoghi ombrosi, & secchi. Cauasi la radice la state, & tagliata in pezzetti si secca. La decottione sua beuuta, prouoca l'ori-

ELENIO.

Above A woodcut of elecampane showing its large aromatic root. This is from the first illustrated commentaries on the works of Dioscorides, published in 1554 and written by Mattioli.

Herbs from the new world

Seeds and roots of medicinal and culinary herbs and vegetables, together with the herbals of Parkinson and Gerard, were an important part of the cargoes in the colonists' ships that crossed the Atlantic. Returning ships brought native North American plants to be cultivated and studied in the European botanic gardens.

The settlers learnt the properties of these native plants from the American Indians, and in 1672 John Josselyn published his *New England's Rarities Discovered* which includes 'The Physical and Chyrurgical Remedies wherewith the Natives constantly use to Cure their Distempers, Wounds and Sores'.

Many of these herbs were half familiar to the settlers, being related to European plants. The European species of golden rod, for instance, has a long tradition as an astringent wound herb and dye plant. The North American species, with its yellow flowers (which is also now familiar in English gardens), was used by the Indians in the same way. European veratrums were described by Dioscorides in the first century AD as emetics and to provoke abortion; the North American *Veratrum viride* is described by John Josselyn: 'The Indians cure their Wounds with it . . . The Root sliced thin and boyled in Vinegar, is very good against Herpes Milliaris'. Hemp agrimony was familiar as a laxative and emetic in Europe; in North America an Indian medicine man named Joe Pye showed settlers how to cure typhus fever by using the root of the closely related giant herb *Eupatorium purpureum*, which was thereafter named Joe Pye weed.

The first botanic garden in North America was founded in 1728 near Philadelphia by John Bartram, a Quaker and an amateur doctor and botanist. He sent collections of native plants to London, England (many of which were sent on to the botanist Carl Linnaeus in Sweden for classification). In 1765 Bartram was appointed by the King as 'Botanizer Royal for America', and commissioned to travel and collect plants, accompanied by his artist son.

By the early nineteenth century a herb industry had begun to develop in North America, supported by the fashion for patent medicines and a general lack of confidence in physicians. This is hardly surprising as the medical profession at this time tended to rely on blood letting and the prescription of toxic substances such as mercury, arsenic and antimony.

Religious groups, and especially the Church of the United Society of Believers, the Shakers, preferred to rely on diet, faith and herbal remedies. There was soon a commercial demand for the Shakers' medicines and their first medicinal herb garden was established in New York in 1820. Their catalog listed over 300 simple and 300 compound medicines, and their herb business lasted for over a hundred years.

Herb gardens to the present day

By the early seventeenth century, gardening books were published at a great rate and were immensely popular. William Lawson's *The Country Housewife's Garden* gives a vivid picture of the garden of a modest estate in Britain in 1617. The herbs are listed first according to height and then as to cultivation and purpose. He suggests planting two gardens, one for 'comely and durable' herbs and flowers to be set in squares and knots, the other a 'Kitchingarden' to be separated from the former as it must 'yield daily Roots, or other herbs, and suffer deformity'.

The English knot was giving way before French garden fashions. Sir Thomas Hanmer describes this clearly in his *Garden Book* of 1659:

'In these days the borders are not hedged about with privet, rosemary or other such herbs which hide the view and prospect, and nourish hurtful worms and insects . . . but all is now commonly near the house laid open and exposed to the sight of the rooms and chambers, and the knots and borders are upheld only with very low coloured boards or stone or tile . . . *parterres*, as the French call them, are often of fine turf, but as low as any green to bowl on . . . with but few flowers in such knots, and those only such as grow very low, lest they spoil the beauty of the embroidery.'

Left An eighteenth-century garden scene showing the influence of the French landscape architect, André Le Nôtre. A small but elaborate parterre is cut in turf against a red-colored ground (probably brick dust). The narrow beds, symmetrical arrangement of pots, the rectangles of grass and high-clipped hedges are typical of the period.

Opposite Part of the ornamental garden at Château de Villandry, France, which is made up of nine squares, each with its own geometric pattern of box hedging. The garden was reconstructed this century using sixteenth-century plans as a main source (the château was begun in 1533).

Eventually herbs were removed altogether to walled vegetable gardens behind the house, making way for 'Exoticks' grown in glasshouses.

In North America the colonists were unconcerned with fashion but profoundly concerned with self-sufficiency. By the end of the eighteenth century the *Gardener's Kalender* was still lamenting that 'America has not yet made that rapid progress in gardening, ornamental planting, and fanciful rural designs, which might naturally be expected from an intelligent, happy, and independent people'.

In nineteenth-century Europe the industrial revolution sent labor costs soaring, and suburbs began to spread around towns and cities. The gardens of the new middle classes were comparatively small, too small to be 'land-scaped' in the fashion that prevailed on large estates. The urban population were provided with basic culinary herbs and vegetables from the enormous market gardens that flourished around the cities, and their gardens were stocked with many types of plants from nurserymen and seedsmen. Botanic gardens were established in most large cities. Gardening magazines became popular, and in England John Claudius Loudon published *The Suburban Gardener and Villa Companion* (1838) which describes the garden styles of the time as the geometric and the natural. Loudon did not approve of the 'geometric' style. Although it was in some ways a revival of the parterre, with beds cut in symmetric or ribbon shapes, instead of being filled with the subtle colors of old-fashioned plants, the beds were

Herbs ready for harvesting at a herb farm. Goat's rue in the background and chamomile in the foreground will be dried and supplied to medical herbalists; the seed of the parsley that has flowered will be collected and packaged.

packed with half-hardy bedding-out plants of the most dazzling colors: pelargoniums, lobelias and verbenas.

A reaction against this 'pastry work gardening' toward the end of the century led to the return of herbs to the ornamental garden, together with old-fashioned cottage garden plants and other recently introduced hardy species. One of the most passionate advocates for natural and harmonious garden design was the Irishman William Robinson. His love for wild flowers and cottage gardens, his designs for curving lawns, creeper-covered walls and generous beds of hardy plants and roses, and his plantsmanship influenced Gertrude Jekyll, a professional artist with a great talent for gardening. Working first with Robinson, and later with the architect Edwin Lutyens, Jekyll used her eye for color and form, her love and knowledge of plants, and her feeling for high standards of craftsmanship to create many outstanding gardens. She was particularly fond of the subtle grays and mauves of lavender, santolina, catmint and rosemary, and of the creeping silver donkey's ears (*Stachys lanata*) among the brighter roses, bergamots, hollyhocks, poppies and anchusa, evening primrose and mulleins. Her warmly practical books are still read widely and have played a part in bringing herbs back into decorative gardening.

Productive herb gardening became suddenly important again during the First World War. Whereas in France and Italy a strong tradition of self-sufficiency continued, which included the use of herbal medicines and the cultivation of herbs, industrial Britain had almost lost this knowledge. As supplies of medicinal herbs from abroad were no longer available, a new generation had to be taught how to cultivate and prepare quantities of these plants for chemists. Among their instructors was Mrs Maude Grieve. Her influential *A Modern Herbal* (1931) did much to revive the herb industry in English-speaking countries and educated and inspired many to grow and use herbs. It gives both scientific and traditional information on the medicinal uses of over a thousand European and North American herbs, with details of their cultivation and habitats. (The editor of the book was Mrs Leyel, who, in England, founded the Society of Herbalists, now incorporated in The Herb Society, and opened Culpeper House in 1927. Here, culinary, medicinal and cosmetic herbs and products were sold.)

Since Mrs Grieve's herbal was published, the growing interest in herbal medicine and popularity of herbal cosmetics and shampoos has meant that large scale commercial herb farms have become established in Europe and the USA. Herb nurseries and garden centers supply private gardens with plants and seeds for domestic remedies, and physic gardens are being opened to the public, where healing plants are grouped according to family, to habitat, or to the relevant healing properties.

A very different writer was working in England at the same time as Mrs Grieve. This was Eleanour Sinclair Rohde, who played an important part in the movement to restore herbs to their rightful places in both contemporary gardens and reconstructed historic gardens. Her books on herbs are filled with enthusiasm and lively anecdote. Her research was based less on the scientific aspects of herbs and more on their historical background, and her wide-ranging knowledge was firmly based on practical work, for she ran a herb and vegetable nursery with a comprehensive list which included many reintroductions. She designed herb gardens which reflected her passion for the medieval pleasaunce and for cottage gardens, and she became particularly popular in the USA where she lectured after the Second World War.

PLANNING
THE
HERB GARDEN

The early part of this book looked at historic designs for herb gardens; this section considers different styles of herb garden and the decorative use of herbs. Herb gardens are then discussed according to their specific uses, whether for cooking, for remedies, for scent or for home-dyeing, or for a garden to encourage bees and butterflies, with plans and plant suggestions for each one. In this way I hope the choice of design and planting will be made easier and clearer, and that the suggestions will help to fuel the imagination.

Most people's gardens are quite small, especially in cities or towns, and even larger suburban or rural gardens are often designed as a series of small linked areas, partly enclosed by hedges, fences or low walls. Herbs grow especially well in enclosed spaces where they are sheltered from cold winds and where their subtle, aromatic scents can be contained within the enclosure. It is these smaller gardens that I have had in mind while writing this chapter.

The garden can be planned along formal lines or to an irregular plan, following intuition rather than methodical patterns. It can be planned with few plants and with easy upkeep in mind, or it can contain as many plants as can be packed into the beds.

Formal gardens are often designed as if they were an extension of the house, with beds and boundaries clearly defined. Pavements will often play an important part in formal design, as in a patio garden, a terrace or an area for barbecues. Stone or brick make a steady base for pots of scented herbs, and small regular beds can be left between stone or concrete flags to hold an evergreen shrub, such as myrtle or bay, or a mound of woodruff, or perhaps a single handsomely shaped herb like rue or angelica.

Shrubby aromatic herbs in a formal garden will need to be kept neat by regular clipping; some can be shaped into standards or simple topiary. Choose compact forms of herbs if possible: the upright rosemary, Dutch lavender and the more restrained mints. Honeysuckle can be pruned and trained up a pole and over a wire frame as a 'lollypop' (see page 118).

Traditional designs can be used as inspiration for a small, formal herb garden. Use the idea of a medieval courtyard garden, for instance (see page 26), with its emphasis on a sitting place, a central fountain or sundial, its potted herbs and regular plantings; or plant low herb hedges in a simple knot design punctuated with clipped knobs of juniper, bay or box (see pages 30–34).

An informal garden tends to obscure boundaries and draw nature around the house. Use ramblers and climbers to grow up house or garden walls, fences, trellises and trees. Jasmines, honeysuckles, rambling roses, the wild bryonies, old man's beard and hops are all suitable plants. Contrary

Above Large shrubs of *Santolina neapolitana* lean across a narrow brick path. To the left grow tall motherwort and fennel and in the background a colony of giant chives are flowering.

Right Pot marigolds, foxgloves and mulleins have self-seeded among the gravel in this brightly colored herb garden. To the left, Welsh onion is flowering against a shrub of blue-green wormwood.

to expectations, such a garden needs a sound plan. By the careful placing of small trees, shrubs or a trellis, the eye can be led up winding, partly obscured paths, which suggest new mysteries beyond.

Pennyroyal, thymes and chamomiles can spread out from the beds. Changes in level, or low banks or small sunken areas, help give a natural look to the garden. Plant herbs with a graceful, falling habit such as pink- or white-flowered musk mallow, catmint, lady's bedstraw or wild marjoram. The planting should be close so that no bare earth will be left to be seen once the plants are established. By planting a few of those herbs that self-seed most prolifically – foxglove, mullein, evening primrose, opium poppy, borage – there will soon be a mass of seedlings to be thinned through, with the remainder left to grow on in random fashion.

SMALL TOWN GARDEN PLAN AND PLANT LIST

In this design for a small, sloping town garden, sunny brick terraces of herbs lead from the house down to a lawn and covered pergola. Ground cover plants edging the path are bistort, lungwort, and white-flowering comfrey. The terraces contain (top to bottom, left to right):

Origanum sp., marjoram
Sanguisorba minor, salad burnet
Mentha suaveolens 'Variegata', pineapple mint
Salvia officinalis, common sage

Thymus vulgaris, common thyme
Coriandrum sativum, coriander
Artemisia dracunculus, tarragon
Santolina sp.

Origanum vulgare 'Aureum', golden marjoram
Pimpinella anisum, anise
Mentha sp., garden mint
Petroselinum sp., parsley
Rosmarinus officinalis, rosemary

Hyssopus officinalis, hyssop
Allium sativum, garlic
Anthriscus cerefolium, chervil
Balsamita vulgaris tanacetoides, costmary
Levisticum officinale, lovage

Allium schoenoprasum, chives
Ocimum basilicum, basil
Satureja hortensis, summer savory
Melissa officinalis, lemon balm
Foeniculum vulgare, fennel
Inula helenium, elecampane

Alchemilla vulgaris, lady's mantle
Ocimum basilicum, basil
Achillea millefolium, yarrow
Monarda didyma, bergamot
Mentha × piperita, peppermint
Teucrium chamaedrys, wall germander
Angelica archangelica, angelica
Laurus nobilis, bay

The Hardy Herb Border

One of the simplest plans for growing herbs is as a border, running along one side of the garden and backed, if possible, by a fence or hedge. The principles for planning such a border, using the height and depth of plants, and making the most of their statuesque qualities and the colors of flowers and foliage, can also be applied to island beds in a larger garden.

The border can be any length from about 4m/13ft. A depth of not more than 2m/6ft 6in is practical as you can then reach to the back of the bed without taking more than one step onto the cultivated ground. As so many herbs lean or spread from the front of the bed, make sure that a path running alongside the border is sufficiently wide: 1m/3ft would be ideal, though not always possible in a small garden. If the border is cut into a lawn, edge the bed with a strip 20cm/8in wide of brick, stone or concrete pavement, set flush into the grass, to prevent the lawn mower damaging leaning herb plants.

Make sketch plans of the border and write lists of the herbs you like best, taking into account the soil and aspect

This long border of pale, silvery herbs ends at the foot of a silver birch tree. *Santolina neapolitana* is in the foreground.

On the left is *Artemisia absinthium* 'Lambrook Silver', developed here by author and gardener, Margery Fish.

of the bed. (Lists of herbs for bright and shady, dry and damp positions are on pages 129–131.) If the border is long, approach the planting boldly and plan the herbs in groups and drifts rather than as single specimens, and include small trees or large shrubs at intervals. My favorite small deciduous shrub for a large herb border is the guelder rose. In the spring its flowers look like large cream-colored plates, the outer petals of the outer flowers much larger than those within. In the autumn there are shiny red berries and the leaves turn purple and red.

Toward the front of the bed grow the lower herbs, again in groups if possible; catmint, orris, hyssop, feverfew and bergamot. Low and creeping herbs can spread from the bed onto the path or lawn: golden marjoram, white and purple violets, chamomiles, bugle, dianthus and thymes.

The colors of flowers and foliage are as important as the habits and textures of the herbs. Gertrude Jekyll, who is considered the originator of the herbaceous border (though she called it the 'hardy flower border') tended toward 'broader and simpler effects, both of grouping and of color'. She planted in long drifts rather than in blocks so that color and form could merge without obvious boundaries, and she used color harmoniously rather than for dramatic contrasting effects. Her borders were often designed with cool colors at either end (silvers, blues, pale pinks and mauves) which became warmer toward the middle of the bed, with rich yellows, oranges and scarlets.

Feelings about color are so personal that I can only suggest combinations that please me. I find little but curiosity value in beds that are confined solely to white, blue, red or yellow flowers and foliage, unless there is some special inspiration in arrangements of shade and form. Restricting color in this way can often enhance the different colors and textures of foliage. On page 131 I have listed herbs according to color to help in planning a border or garden of mixed or single-colored herbs.

An evergreen background

In a larger bed, small evergreen trees or shrubs, which are easily controlled by clipping, such as bay and myrtle, juniper and bayberry, will provide a dense dark background for finer pale and silvery herbs. Young bay and myrtle trees may need some special care to protect them

during winter in cold northern climates. Grow them in a sheltered position and protect their roots from frosts by laying straw, bracken or matting around the base. In a small border the dwarf juniper, *Juniperus communis* 'Compressa', is ideal as it grows as a narrow column, taking up little space and casting only slight shade. Bayberry is glossy-leaved and handsome but will only tolerate an acid soil.

Shrubby evergreen herbs will give substance to the bed and provide interest during the winter. Broom and dyer's greenweed are a good dark green. The common rosemary has spreading curving branches, but the upright variety, *Rosmarinus officinalis* 'Miss Jessup's Upright', grows more tightly as a narrow column and takes up less space. The lower silver or gray-leaved evergreen shrubs may become overwhelmed by the lush growth of tall herbaceous or annual herbs during the summer, so plant them toward the middle or front of the bed. Among them are the santolinas and the rich-scented curry plant, the handsome lavenders and the garden and Jerusalem sages.

Statuesque border herbs

Among the most spectacular of the herbaceous perennial herbs is the massive poke root from North America with its succulent stems and long blunt heads of pink flowers followed by poisonous black berries. It will outgrow a small border after a few years, before it reaches its full size. Elecampane is another herb that reaches 2m/6ft 6in in height, with long leaves and yellow daisy flowers that open with a twisting motion.

Left A herb garden filled with color and movement. Grass paths lead between the beds which are edged with young curry plants. Red bergamot is blossoming in the foreground with tall alliums and mulleins behind it. Against a dark background of foliage the yellow flowers of elecampane and pale spikes of clary sage show vividly.

Right Statuesque herbs and cottage garden flowers grow around an old chimney pot that holds a bowl of sedums. In the foreground is the cultivar of clary sage, *Salvia sclarea* 'Turkestanica', with its large scented leaves. To the left grow wild meadow geranium, variegated figwort and ornamental alliums. In the far beds there are tall foxgloves, hollyhocks and mulleins.

Angelica generally dies after flowering in its second year but it is statuesque and pungently scented with cartwheels of flowers that become ornamental seed-heads. Clary sage, *Salvia sclarea*, is another large, beautiful and strongly scented biennial, with long wrinkled leaves and spires of flowers with papery bracts. Two other biennials, burdock and teazel, are often seen growing wild on embankments, especially along railroad tracks and motorways; burdock especially is a very useful medicinal herb and worth bringing into the garden. Both need plenty of space and are at their best in early summer.

During their first year these biennials can grow from seedlings into strong young plants in a separate bed or as space-fillers among young perennial herbs, being moved to their final positions in the border in the autumn or spring before flowering.

All these herbs have large, sculptural leaves. As a contrast, grow tall herbs with feathery or finer leaves among them: green and purple fennels, for instance, the large bushy goat's rue with lush pinnate leaves and pink or mauve-tinged flowers, and licorice. Marsh mallow, too, gives a light effect with its many stems, pale downy leaves and soft pink flowers. Sow a patch of dill seed directly into the ground where it is to grow so that this annual will develop into a strong, tall plant with finely divided leaves before producing its big yellow head of flowers.

Pink- or white-flowered foxgloves and the annual purple-leaved orach have tall, spirelike shapes that counter the curving, bushier herbs. Grow them in small groups.

HARDY HERB BORDER PLAN

A plan for an aromatic border to run beneath the windows of a house. Included are many evergreen herbs that will keep their scent throughout the year, together with an iris, roses, clematis, campanula and peony.

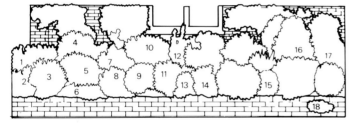

PLANT LIST

1 *Saponaria sp.*, soapwort
2 *Malva moschata*, musk mallow
3 *Lavandula spp.*, lavender
4 *Althaea officinalis*, marsh mallow
5 *Salvia sp.*, sage
6 *Thymus spp.*, thyme
7 *Aquilegia sp.*, aquilegia
8 *Helichrysum angustifolium*, curry plant
9 *Hyssopus officinalis*, hyssop
10 *Artemisia sp.*
11 *Monarda didyma*, bergamot
12 *Lilium candidum*, madonna lily
13 *Origanum sp.*, marjoram
14 *Melissa officinalis* 'All Gold', golden lemon balm
15 *Santolina sp.*, cotton lavender
16 *Foeniculum vulgare*, bronze fennel
17 *Lavatera arborea*, tree mallow
18 *Chamaemelum nobile* 'Treneague', chamomile

A Wild Herb Garden

Many of the more unusual wild and naturalized herbs only survive now in open ground, in industrial wasteland or on roadsides. Others are threatened by the destruction of their habitat and by pollution.

By growing wild herbs in the garden you will be contributing to their survival and also encourage bees and butterflies by providing food and breeding sites. You will learn far more about the characters and habits of wild plants if you are able to watch them day by day in the garden.

In comfortable, well-fed conditions, the habits of some wild herbs become exaggerated. Salad herbs are likely to be sweeter and improved by cultivation, but medicinal herbs may lose some of their potency, and flavoring herbs their pungency.

One of the most satisfactory ways of growing wild herbs is by creating their wild habitat as closely as possible in the garden. Note how they grow in the wild and watch the way they have adapted to drought, shade, or heavy competition in grassland. Build a rough rockery for a collection of creeping thymes, dianthus and calamint. Use the shady woodland herbs, bugle, woodruff, violet and self-heal, to make a thick ground cover beneath trees. Bank up soil in the garden, or use an existing bank, to grow ground ivy, wood avens, musk mallow, greater celandine, wood sage, figwort and ploughman's spikenard.

A wild herb meadow

Be prepared to spend some time establishing a herb meadow and you will be rewarded, as this is one of the loveliest ways of growing wild herbs. Even a small area of meadow herbs can be beautiful, just a 'wild corner' or a circle of rough grass under a deciduous tree. In a larger area you will need to mow paths among the tall grasses in order to see and tend to the herbs.

Remember that in some countries it is now unlawful to pick or dig up in the wild certain plant species that have become endangered or rare. For the best start, sow wild herb seed in seed flats, prick on into pots and only plant them out when they are sturdy. Clear existing grasses or lift a good sized piece of turf for each, set each in a pocket of fine-textured good loam to encourage growth and water well. Keep checking to make sure that they are not suffering from drought or encroaching grasses and weeds. By autumn the following tough perennial herbs should be able to cope with competition: comfrey, tansy, meadowsweet, hemp agrimony, marjoram, lady's bedstraw, sweet cicely and bistort. Betony, meadow clary and cowslips, which all have bright flowers, may continue to need some care as they are less aggressive growers. Annual poppies, melilot and biennial foxglove, mullein and evening primrose should self-seed.

Another method is to sow the seed of meadow herbs direct and already mixed with suitable grass seed. Packets of these seeds are available commercially, but choose the mixture carefully and check to make sure it will suit your situation. Clear the area as you would for a lawn by thoroughly weeding it and rolling it level, and sow seed broadcast. The area must not be allowed to dry out before the seedlings are well established. Don't expect all your seedlings or plants to flourish. Some wild herbs are surprisingly fussy and you will have to discover by trial and error those that will grow happily in your garden.

A wild herb meadow will be at its best during early summer. By high summer flowering will be over and most plants will have seeded. By late summer the area should be scythed to a height of about 25cm/10in.

Betony, with its bright flowerheads and scalloped leaves, grows wild in grassy meadows. Young plants should be kept clear of weeds and grass roots for a year or two in the garden until they are well established and can compete successfully. The flowers bloom from midsummer and the leaves used to be infused as a remedy for headaches – this is no longer recommended. Growing with it here is wild basil or cushion calamint, *Clinopodium vulgare.*

A Low Maintenance Herb Garden

With thoughtful planning it is easy to design a herb garden that needs little maintenance. Use hardy perennial herbs, especially those with brightly colored or well-shaped foliage, that will look good during much of the year. Once established, these will need little attention and will make a varied and handsome display. All are highly scented and most are useful in the kitchen. Clipping to shape in late spring and possibly again in late summer, and a light feed of compost every year or two is all that is necessary to maintain them.

As usual, make a plan of the planting, considering the color and texture of the leaves and the heights and habits of the herbs. Take care in the placing of the shrubby evergreen and herbaceous species to preserve a balanced design during winter months. Plant red, green and gold sages, golden marjoram, variegated lemon balm, rue (*Ruta*

graveolens 'Jackman's Blue'), bronze and green fennels, sword-leaved orris, lavender and hyssop, silver-leaved santolinas and curry plant. These species are all relatively long-lived, easy to propagate and virtually disease-free, though the leaves of golden marjoram may brown or scorch slightly during a hot summer.

Herbs for ground cover
Single species of fast-spreading herbs can be grown to cover large areas, or in small beds if their invasive roots are con-

Below An easily maintained garden of perennial herbs with the bright foliage of golden sage in the foreground. *Santolina chamaecyparissus* and lady's mantle are coming into flower.

Right Against a background of rugosa roses, herbs are growing through a thick layer of gravel. Foxgloves and fennel have self-seeded here among purple sage and lavender.

tained and cannot smother neighboring plants. They will soon fill the bed with a dense ground cover that will crowd out weeds.

There are many low, spreading herbs that will soon fill a small bed. Woodruff makes a thick cover with its whorls of hay-scented leaves and white starry flowers. In the shade, grow bugle, ground ivy (at its best in late spring when its leaves are downy and its flowers most profuse) and penny-royal. Creeping thymes and chamomiles prefer a sunny position.

Grow tall herbs with good foliage such as the rampant comfrey, meadowsweet with plain or variegated leaves and creamy, scented flowers, tansy, either plain- or curly-

leaved varieties, and valerian with graceful pinnate leaves and pink-tinged flowers.

In shady beds include three spring-flowering herbs of medium height: pink-flowered bistort, white-flowered ramsons and pink-and-blue-flowered lungwort. Grow a selection of mints in partial shade and in sunny beds grow lady's bedstraw, plain-leaved or variegated lemon balm.

A PAVED OR GRAVEL GARDEN

Laying stone or gravel will help to cut down work in the garden and will also provide the sharp drainage and warm surface that many herbs prefer. Leave spaces between stone slabs or bricks for herb plants, planting one species to a space. See pages 95–97 for construction of paved areas and paths. If your garden is very small, consider spreading gravel right across it and planting herbs among the stones. Gravel acts as a protective mulch, holding in warmth and protecting tender roots from frost.

For a more formal effect, borrow an idea from Japanese gardens and rake sweeping, curving patterns into the gravel. If the area is not walked over, the patterns should stay for several weeks. Place one or two large rocks to set off the herbs, or separate the gravel areas with paths or lines of brick or pavements, which, apart from containing the gravel, will prevent it from being trodden in so quickly, and will add variety. Use cobbles or areas of larger stones to vary textures.

Gravel colors vary tremendously, so choose a shade that suits the walls of the house or garden, or perhaps a pale color to lighten a shady area. It is worth setting a few stone or concrete slabs among the gravel to use as stepping stones during wet weather when gravel tends to stick to the soles of shoes. Advice on laying gravel and planting herbs is on page 98.

Give shape to the garden with plantings of shrubby Mediterranean herbs: lavender, sage, Jerusalem sage and curry plant, rosemary and hyssop. A trough, sink or other large container, raised on bricks, gives height, and can be planted with herbs with graceful sprawling foliage such as catmint, musk mallow and alpine ladies' mantle. Plant groups of some of the larger herbs that self-seed most freely and that will spring up each year in colonies to be thinned out as necessary.

A Cottage Garden of Herbs

In old-fashioned cottage gardens, vegetables, flowers and aromatic herbs were interplanted, giving an appearance of cheerful profusion and informality. But this mingling of different plants was not done haphazardly, for it was known that certain species, when grown together, would actually increase their vigor and vitality. This lore and legend of companion planting is often found to be soundly based on common sense.

The traditional cottage garden provided for all the needs of the family from one small, intensively cultivated piece of ground. There would be a large bed, which was dug over every autumn, weeded and manured and planted with rows of vegetables, salads, annual herbs, and flowers for picking and for decorating: annual sunflowers, sweet peas and sweet williams. Surrounding the bed would be a border of perennial herbs, culinary, medicinal and sweet-scented: bushes of sage and thyme, southernwood, santolina and wormwood. Against the house a narrow bed might hold roses and lilies, columbines and old-fashioned red peonies. The path to the front door, edged with cat-mint and feverfew, and with hardy dianthus and purple- and white-flowering thymes among the stones, might lead to a gate flanked by woody lavender bushes and arched over with honeysuckle.

A cottage garden that is thickly planted and self-sown with herbs and old-fashioned flowers. Troughs and old sinks hold low-growing dianthus and alpine lady's mantle that would otherwise be lost among the mass of larger plants.

Companion planting with herbs

Mixed planting in the cottage garden is similar to a community of wild plants where the many different species are adapted to each other and one can see the natural plant associations at work. The first colonizing weeds on open ground, with their brief life cycle, provide further humus and sustenance for those needing a longer period of development; tall, sun-loving plants with deep roots provide shelter for lower, shade-tolerant, shallow-rooting species; this is natural intercropping.

Study the structure of the plants and you will soon find their natural defenses. Leaves armed with stings, or thickly felted with hairs, or spiked and prickled, or with pungent essential oils that are excreted as waste products of the plant and also act as protection against browsing animals and excessive heat.

There is also an invisible process at work below the surface among the enormous and complex root systems, as root excretions play an important part in the defense and development of plants. These will affect the roots of those around them and also attract or repel other organisms in the soil.

Cultivated plants, on the other hand, are often grown in unmixed communities and many have had their natural defenses bred out of them. Thousands of years of breeding have sweetened the leaves of the bitter wild lettuce and plumped out the tap root of the carrot, have produced double flowers and enlarged fruits, and this has often left them far more susceptible to disease and pests. Growing vegetable crops for years on the same plot of ground will often increase the likelihood of disease too. So the natural defenses of wild plants, and especially of herbs, whose potent properties are so valuable to us as medicines and food, can be used to a certain extent as protection for more vulnerable garden plants, and to increase their vigor and health.

The relationships between plants are infinitely complex and are little understood. They are minutely adjusted to climate and soil, and conditions of growth. However, there are examples of companion planting in the garden that are worth bearing in mind and that have proved valuable for many generations.

Many members of the daisy family (*Compositae*) have pest-repellent properties. Fleabane, tansy, elecampane and feverfew, for instance, were traditional fumigants and insect repellents in the house. They have the same use in the garden, in varying degrees. Some varieties of marigold, *Tagetes*, excrete a powerful pesticide from their roots which destroys many soil pests, especially the tiny nematodes such as the eel worms, which can be so destructive in a crop of potatoes or tomatoes. These were planted among crops in Peru in pre-Inca days as a protection. Pot marigolds have a similar, though much weaker, effect.

The pyrethrum (chrysanthemum) family from Africa is the source of another important pesticide. Familiar members of the *Compositae* family, which contribute to the health of nearby plants in the garden, are chamomile and yarrow. Both appear to strengthen their neighbors, improve the flavor of vegetables and increase the essential oils in other herbs.

The onion family acts as pest repellents with varying strengths. As in the kitchen, garlic has the most powerful effect in the garden. Its strong excretions of sulfur strengthen and improve the scent of roses and appear to protect them to some extent from black spot. (Try using onion waste as a mulch for roses.) All members of the family seem to benefit fruit trees and bushes and improve the health of most vegetables apart from legumes. The strong smell of their leaves helps to mask the scent of carrot foliage, foiling the carrot root fly. The aromatic labiate herbs – thyme, savory, hyssop, marjoram, sage and rosemary, for instance – produce rich nectar for bees and butterflies, but deter fly and beetle pests and contribute generally to the health of the garden. They seem to be especially beneficial to members of the cabbage family, and will attract pollinating bees to rows of beans and peas.

Mint is another herb that helps protect and invigorate the cabbage family. Pennyroyal is especially pungent (and has a long history as an insect repellent among stored food), and is less threateningly invasive than the larger varieties.

Other herbs that have proved helpful are the annual, fast-growing nasturtium, and borage, and the biennial foxglove, all of which improve the strength of nearby plants and thus encourage resistance to pests and disease.

Wormwood and rue, with their profoundly bitter-tasting leaves, are strong pest repellents and will also discourage

moles and cats, but may have an inhibiting effect on nearby plants that are young or ailing.

So bear the traditional cottage garden in mind when planting herbs. Make a border of perennial herbs around the vegetable garden, where they will be out of the way during digging and harvesting operations, or plant them among the herbaceous garden plants in the ordinary flowerbed.

Annuals such as summer savory or Mexican marigold can be grown in rows or half rows in between rows of veget-

Vegetables and fruit have been interplanted, cottage-garden style, with aromatic and culinary herbs in this beautiful kitchen garden. Chives encircle the trunks of young apple trees, and lavender and parsley make an attractive edge to the beds.

ables. Pot marigold and borage will self-seed year after year.

Low hedges of thyme or hyssop, borders of chamomile, chives or everlasting onion, patches of creeping non-flowering chamomile, yarrow, thyme and pennyroyal along the paths will all contribute to the balance and health of the garden.

The Kitchen Herb Garden

Herbs as flavorings, as aromatics to cut the fattiness of meat, as pungent digestives for heavy meals, for spicing and transforming everyday food, for sharpening and refreshing the palate; these are the most familiar roles for the enormous variety of culinary herbs.

Herbs are essential ingredients for many of the finest dishes: basil for *soupe au pistou*, tarragon for Béarnaise sauce, garlic for the potent aioli mayonnaise; beef roasted on a bed of thyme, lamb rubbed with cumin seed, fennel with fish, tarragon chicken, parsley sauce with gammon, sorrel with lentils, and chervil with carrots.

Apart from the few herbs that dry really well – thyme, marjoram, rosemary, mint and savory with their tough, aromatic leaves – culinary herbs are infinitely more delicious when eaten fresh. As they wilt after only a few hours in shops, and as most of the interesting varieties never appear in shops at all, they must be grown in your garden or windowbox, and there is no reason why they shouldn't make a beautiful display.

It is also a pleasure to be able to grow a variety of herbs for different cuisines and types of food. For instance, dill is an essential in Scandinavian cooking where it is constantly used with fish and with the pickles, and with the smoked foods that were traditionally eaten during long winters. Basil is a vital ingredient in Italian pastas and soups. Fresh coriander leaves with curries, or fenugreek leaves in Persian food, or coriander root crushed with garlic in Thai food all give a powerful individual character to national dishes. For vegetarians, herbs with a strong earthy or yeasty flavor, such as lovage, wild celery and the savories, are especially useful to spice bland dishes. (A table of herb flavorings follows on page 61.)

The traditional partnerships of herbs with meat, fish or vegetables are often based on principles of nutrition and a balanced diet, and some go back to classical times. Greek physicians in the fourth century BC wrote recipe books for their patients. Herbs were used on the one hand to counterbalance the effects of otherwise indigestible food. On the other hand, the food itself would often be used as a vehicle for curative herbs so there might be no dividing line between a recipe and a medicine. Thus a chicken stock strongly flavored with garlic was a common Roman laxative; thin barley soup flavored with licorice was given to feverish patients in the sixth century; buttered gruels of oatmeal mixed with appropriate herbs for various ailments, such as wild celery gruel to purify the blood, were still common two hundred years ago in Europe, and a seventeenth-century French recipe for *potage de santé* includes sorrel, purslane, chervil, borage and bugloss.

Popular candies in seventeenth-century Europe were 'sucket candies', which were the candied roots of medicinal

An illustration showing the harvesting of dill from a medieval Manual of Health, or *Tacuinum Sanitatis*. These illuminated manuscripts listed the nature, uses, dangers and effects of various herbs, food and clothing as well as some activities and emotions. Dill is described as being moderately nourishing, bringing relief to a windy stomach.

herbs. Those of borage and bugloss were taken to 'engender good blood', those of elecampane to aid digestion, and sea holly root, or eryngo, as an aphrodisiac.

The Greek theory that the four humors (hot, cold, dry and damp, corresponding to fire, earth, air and water) must exist in harmony within the body in order to preserve health was still commonly held in Europe in the late seventeenth century and was, of course, closely related to the idea of a balanced diet. Thus salads were commonly mixed to suit the health and temperament of the eater. Watercress, rocket, nasturtium and mustard leaves enlivened the lethargic; purslane, borage, and salad burnet were thought to cool a fiery nature.

An enormous number of wild and cultivated herbs were eaten in the past compared to the limited number considered edible today. They were used to flavor the basic peasant pottage of oatmeal or beans; or, the leaves of mallows, borage, orach, dandelions, red nettles, daisies, and parsley and fennel roots were simmered in broth, thickened with oatmeal and seasoned with parsley leaves, sage, thyme, and mint as a green pottage. A medieval uncooked green sauce for fish or boiled roots consisted of a mixture of pounded parsley, mint, garlic, sage and thyme, mixed with vinegar, thickened with bread and liberally spiced – a potent version of today's mint sauce. A flower pottage for the gentry might be made from pounded rose petals, primroses, violets and elderflowers, mixed with ground almonds and sugar syrup, and garnished with whole flowers.

Some of these flavors and textures might seem coarse and strange to us but they add variety and often color to a dish, and many have a special nutritional value.

PLANNING THE KITCHEN GARDEN

Most culinary herbs need well-drained soil and plenty of sun, so ideally a kitchen herb garden should face south with some protection from the prevailing wind. They are also best grown near the house as they are so often needed in a hurry or in the rain or dark. If possible, a hard path should lead to the kitchen herb garden, and around it, to avoid having to put on rubber boots to fetch a bunch of thyme.

In contrast with medicinal herbs and those grown especially for their scent, there are few culinary flavoring

herbs with really showy or bright-colored flowers. Most rely for their beauty on their leaves (purples, yellows, grays and greens), their aromatic scents and their lushness.

If left to their own devices, many culinary herbs become untidy and tangled or spread wildly. By grouping them in blocks, or by emphasizing divisions between the plants with stones, bricks, wooden planks or low herb borders, they can be more easily controlled. The simplest way of doing so is by planning the garden as a series of narrow strip beds rather like the early monastic gardens (see page 22). The most complex and ornamental way is by designing a formal garden, like the classic French *potager*. Here, the herb planting is planned in the same way as you would a flower garden, arranging both colors and forms of herbs in an imaginative way, and with low borders of herbs around each bed.

The size and the design of the kitchen garden is governed

Opposite A long, narrow border outside a kitchen door is divided into diamond-shaped compartments with box hedging. Each part contains a different herb: Welsh onion, chives, silver thyme, lovage, purple sage and tarragon among them.

Above Bright herbs are planted among the vegetables in a small yard kitchen garden. Pot marigolds and opium poppies are to the right, and there are thymes, tarragon, dianthus and marjoram.

Right This ornamental red variety of *Atriplex hortensis*, the garden orach, can be eaten when young as a pot- or salad herb.

by the type and quantity of herbs that are to be grown. Most households need only one or two plants of large perennial herbs, such as sage, lovage and fennel, but need to grow the annuals, such as basil, chervil and coriander and the biennial parsley and caraway, in bulk.

The perennials and annuals can be arranged in various ways to preserve a pleasing design in the garden all year round. If there are to be small beds, perennials can be planted in the center of each bed, with annuals around them, or the beds can be edged with low perennials, such as chives, thyme or compact marjoram, with a block of annuals in the center. Large beds can be planted with regular groups of perennials with spaces left between them where young annuals can be planted or sown each spring, or, alternatively, the bed can be planted like a vegetable garden, the annuals in rows or blocks, the perennials grouped around the edge.

KITCHEN HERB GARDEN PLAN AND PLANT LIST

The herbs, vegetables and fruit included in this kitchen garden plan are beautiful as well as useful and their leaves and colors look pleasing together. There are several unusual varieties.

The northfacing fence has a morello cherry, *Prunus cerasus*, and a fruiting quince, *Cydonia oblonga*. The bed at their feet contains herbs which thrive in a relatively cool, damp soil:

Mentha suaveolens, apple mint
M. × piperita, peppermint
M. spicata, spearmint
M. suaveolens 'Variegata', pineapple mint
Beta vulgaris 'Cicla', spinach
Rumex acetosa, sorrel
Allium schoenoprasum, chives

The southfacing fence holds dog rose, *Rosa canina* (both petals and hips can be used for jelly and syrup), runner beans and sweet peas. At their feet sun-loving herbs grow in clumps:

Angelica archangelica, angelica
Borago officinalis, borage
Cynara scolymus, globe artichoke
Artemisia dracunculus, French tarragon
Rosmarinus officinalis, rosemary
Ruta graveolens, rue
Salvia sp., sage
Origanum sp., marjoram
Thymus sp., thyme
Calendula officinalis, marigold

The four central beds are intensively cultivated and their dimensions are worked out to give access without treading on the soil. They are planned for a typical four-part rotation – usually potatoes, legumes, brassicas and roots, but substituting annual and biennial herbs for the potato

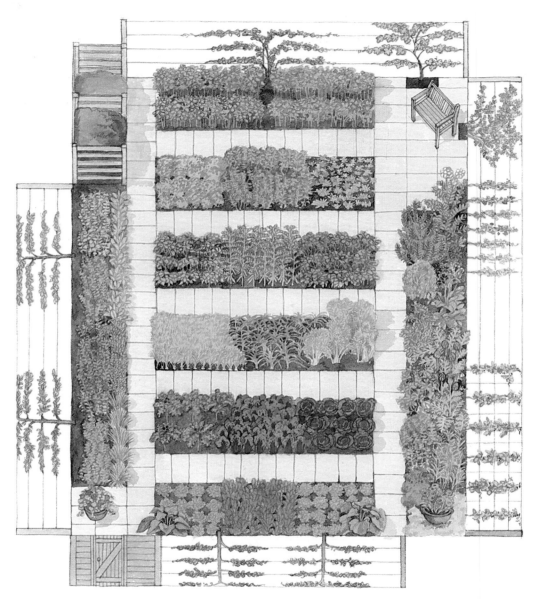

bed. From top to bottom they contain:

Petroselinum sp., parsley
Ocimum basilicum, sweet basil
Valerianella locusta, corn salad

Broad beans
Green beans
Carrots
Leeks
Florence fennel
Red cabbage

Along the back fence, near the compost boxes, is a loganberry, with early and late-fruiting raspberries. The near bed contains lettuce, spinach and rhubarb.

Another simple method is to grow annuals and perennials quite separately. This has the advantage that seed can be sown early in rows or blocks, under the protection of plastic or glass cloches, to hasten the annuals' development. (See page 115, for cultivating herbs using cloches.) The annuals can then be heavily cropped without spoiling the appearance of the more permanent garden of perennial herbs.

The garden will keep shape and interest during the winter if the structure is marked out with some of the larger evergreen herbs. Bay and myrtle can be clipped to shape or left to grow large. There are many forms of the common juniper, from shrubby trees to upright or dwarf forms. Sage, rosemary, winter savory and curry plant make shrubby bushes or can be planted close together as protective hedges.

Thyme, everlasting onion and salad burnet make evergreen borders. Other members of the onion family – chives and giant chives with their papery pink flowers, and garlic chives with white starry flowers – make good border plants,

and will keep neat if regularly cropped with scissors. Well-trimmed golden marjoram makes a bright border.

Grow mint in a part of the garden that is lightly shaded, together with the small group of annuals that grow best in partial shade. These are the umbelliferous chervil, coriander, anise and cumin which have powerfully flavored leaves. In full sun and dry soil they will shoot too quickly into flower and make feeble, spindly growth, though too heavy a shade will prevent their valuable seed from ripening well. They also need well-composted, rather damp earth. Anise and cumin are usually rather frail little plants and need care, but once chervil and coriander are in a position that suits them they will continue to self-seed vigorously for many years.

For information on cultivating culinary herbs in pots, indoors or out, see pages 127–128.

A CHOICE OF CULINARY HERBS

For a small garden a choice of basic perennial flavoring herbs might include one plant each of tarragon, mint,

Above Flowering chives and Welsh onion with sorrel behind.

Right A beautifully laid out kitchen garden. Thymes and lavenders flower next to green beans; curly kale stands beside an ornamental but edible cabbage.

garden thyme, tall fennel and a clump of chives, together with six plants of biennial curled parsley, six of annual sweet basil and one plant of annual sweet marjoram, for example.

Listing my own essentials, I find there are nineteen. The annuals basil, chervil, coriander, dill, summer savory and sweet marjoram; the biennials parsley, caraway and garlic (which is treated as an annual); and ten perennials: chives, fennel, lovage, rosemary, sage, tarragon, garden thyme, lemon thyme, winter savory and mint.

Singly or blended, these give a tremendous range of flavors, and by growing several species of mint, basil, thyme and marjoram the range can easily be extended even further.

The mint family
The mints in particular vary widely in looks and flavors. The tall, vigorous Bowles' mint has a fine flavor and is one

A bed of culinary herbs growing in profusion near a kitchen door includes marjoram, sage and lemon balm.

of the best all-around mints. Cook it with potatoes and peas and in lettuce soup, or chop it into salads (especially those with yogurt and cucumber), or mix it with vinegar for mint sauce, or infuse it with green tea to make refreshing Moroccan mint tea. Its flavor is similar to that of spearmint but the plant is more resistant to rust, a fungus that can attack members of the mint family.

Black peppermint, tall with dark purple stems and mauve flowers, is best for tisanes and for mixing in potpourris. Eau de cologne mint has shiny, dark-edged leaves and a sweet scent; add a few leaves to fresh fruit salads or summer drinks.

Mint flowers are generally in small spikes of pale or dark purple but you may feel it is worth cutting down flowering mints to encourage the growth of the leaves and to prevent the plants becoming too rampant. However, the buddleia mint has decorative long mauve flowers, and the North American mint (also known as anise hyssop), *Agastache anethiodora*, which is closely related to the *Mentha* family, has especially long spikes of purple flowers which are beautiful in late summer.

The two mints with the most decorative leaves have a shorter and less sprawling habit than the others. Pineapple mint has slightly downy, rounded, variegated cream and apple green leaves, and has the most refreshing fruity scent. Ginger mint has more pointed bright yellow and green variegated plants the contrasting colors in the leaves vary Both make lovely garnishes for salads. As with many variegated plants the contrasting colours in the leaves vary in strength according to the season and climate and they usually become most vivid by midsummer, especially if they are grown in a position where they get some direct sunlight each day.

Most mints will tolerate some shade, and all grow well in slightly moist soil. A shady border beneath a fence or wall will suit them well. They will also all need containing as they spread fast with creeping stems, rooting as they go. Generally the stems travel just below the surface of the soil so that the container – a buried bottomless bucket or plastic box, an old sink, or a barrier of slates or stones – need not go deeper than about 35cm/14in.

If you have a large patch of mint, then it is worth spreading dry straw over the bed in the autumn when the foliage has died down, and setting fire to it, letting it smolder for an hour or so. This will kill off any spores of rust fungus on old stems or on the surface of the mint bed.

Basils

The most useful all-around culinary basil is sweet basil with its rich succulent leaves. In temperate climates this is best grown under a cloche, in a greenhouse or on a sunny windowsill. It will survive outdoors but will only thrive during a really hot summer. Pounded with garlic and salt, mixed with Parmesan cheese and sometimes with pine kernels, basil makes the delicious *pesto* or *pistou* sauce which is mixed into soups or into freshly cooked pasta or rice. Roughly chopped leaves mixed with salads, especially tomato salads, give an unmistakable flavor – warm and pungent, rich and redolent of summer.

The flavor of the smaller leaves of bush basil is similar, and this neat plant is especially suitable for growing in a pot. Purple basil leaves have a different flavor, more spicy, but the plant is very ornamental. Add the leaves as a garnish to soups – pale celery soup or dark borscht, or mix them in salads or rice dishes. Lemon basil has graceful pointed, lemon-scented leaves which are more suitable for light chicken, fish or egg dishes. Sacred basil leaves have a rough downy texture; use their spice-scented leaves fresh in curries or with strong-flavored oily fish such as mackerel or herring.

Thymes and marjorams

The flavors of thyme and marjoram vary in strength according to climate and soil. The tough, narrow leaves of plants of *Thymus vulgaris* and *Origanum vulgare* found growing among the stones on a Mediterranean hillside have a more powerful flavor than those of similar plants growing among lush grasses or in a herb bed in a northern climate. For dishes where the characteristic flavor of these herbs is especially important, such as in daube of beef with olives, or on a pizza or onion tart, it is worth buying a few packets or branches of good-quality dried thyme and oregano grown in a sunnier climate.

Garden or wild thyme (*Thymus vulgaris*) is the most useful culinary thyme and, given a light well-drained soil and sunny position, it is strong and hardy, amenable to

CULINARY HERBS
(Use leaves unless otherwise stated)

Stews, hearty soups	bay, coriander *seeds*, garlic *bulb*, juniper *berries*, lovage *seeds and leaves*, onion *greens and bulbs*, parsley *stems*, rosemary, wild celery, savories, thyme
Egg dishes, summer soups	basil, chervil, chives, dill, fennel, sweet marjoram, mint, parsley, sorrel, tarragon, lemon thyme
Poultry	fennel, sweet marjoram, tarragon, summer savory
Tomato dishes	basil, garlic *bulb*, marjoram, mint, summer and winter savories, tarragon
Curries	aniseed, bay, coriander *seed*, cumin *seed*, fennel *seed*, fenugreek *seed*, garlic *bulb*, mint, mustard *seed*
Salad flavourings	anise, caraway, chervil, all chives, coriander, dill, ramsons
Salad herbs	bistort, borage, chicory, corn salad, dandelion, mustard *seedlings*, purslane, rocket, salad burnet, sorrel, watercress
Stuffings and pâtés	lovage *seed and leaves*, marjoram, onion, parsley, sage, thyme
Fish	alexanders, caraway, dill, fennel, lemon thyme, parsley
Sweet dishes	angelica, aniseed, bergamot, elderflower, lemon balm, pelargonium, pineapple sage, rosemary, saffron, sweet cicely
Breads	caraway *seed*, lovage *seed*, poppy *seed*, sunflower *seed*
Roasting meats	bay, fennel *stems*, rosemary, savories, thyme
Marinades	bay, coriander *seed and leaves*, cumin *seed*, dill, garlic *bulb*, juniper berries, onion *greens and bulbs*, parsley *stems*,
Potherbs	celery, chicory, fat hen, good King Henry *leaves and young flowers*, hop *shoots*
In drinks	borage *flowers*, elderflowers, mint, woodruff
Fines herbes mix	chervil, chives, parsley, tarragon
Bouquet garni	bay, marjoram, parsley *stems*, thyme

clipping, and makes a good low hedge or border. It is one of the best winter herbs with its strong, warm, aromatic flavor; ideal in soups and stews, in dumplings and stuffings, and able to keep its flavor during long slow cooking with pot roasts. The hybrid lemon thyme has a lighter flavor and combines well with fish, chicken and sauces. *T. herba-barona*, the traditional flavoring used to give a baron of beef a slightly spicy, caraway flavor, grows prostrate with long, arching, red stems. (For more information on thyme species, see page 99.)

The flavor of the wild and pot marjorams is also warming and aromatic but with a slightly bitter edge to it. Again it combines well with robust dishes and will stand long cooking. The annual sweet or knotted marjoram has a distinctive, pungent flavor and a sweet and subtle aroma. It is good with light dishes, in a creamy chicken sauce, or as a garnish and flavoring for baked eggs and omelets.

SALAD HERBS

Fresh, often spicy flavoring herbs, used in small quantities, enhance and enliven salads; the blander salad herbs can be used in larger quantities as the basis of single or mixed salad dishes.

Today we are extremely conservative in our choice of salad greens, and it is salutary to look at the hundreds of herbs that were eaten raw in the past, especially those hardy wild herbs that were among the first to appear in the spring. Included in these salads and saladings (salads of small-leaved herbs) were buds of primroses and alexanders and the flowers of violets and borage, with leaves of wild cresses, purslane, calamints, daisies, rocket, dandelion and fennel. Most of these less usual herbs should be eaten while their leaves are young and tender and before their flavor becomes too coarse and pronounced.

A garden of salad herbs will need to be regularly cropped and can look most ornamental when planned as blocks or patterns, with perennials grown as borders or in rows to mark the divisions between each mass of annuals.

Among the most useful cultivated salad herbs are the annuals. Rocket has hot, spicy leaves that coarsen with age, and purslane, either the golden or green variety, has rounded, fleshy, cooling leaves.

Corn salad has a slight, delicate flavor and good texture

Above The pale cream petals of flowering rocket.

Left Young salad herbs ready for picking: rocket in the foreground, red lettuce and alfalfa behind.

and lives through the winter, self-seeding prolifically after the tiny, forget-me-not flowers are over.

Borage is a handsome plant and another self-seeder; once sown, it will appear again every year. The leaves are cooling and succulent but need to be eaten while they are young and tender as they soon become quite painfully bristly. It takes up a lot of space and in a small garden it is best to leave one plant to grow to maturity and to self-seed, picking the others, roots and all, while they are still young.

Salad burnet is a useful herb with slightly bitter-tasting leaflets and a curious knob-head of flowers. In the wild it may grow only a few inches high; in the garden it can reach 1m/3ft and makes a decorative, slightly untidy border which responds well to regular cutting.

Sharp-tasting sorrel leaves make excellent soups and sauces and will liven up a bland salad. Grow this large-leaved perennial as a border or in a group of two or three plants and cut down any flower stalks.

Closely related chicory and dandelion need special treatment to lessen the fierce bitterness of their nutritious leaves. Tie the leaves of the young plants loosely together to blanch and sweeten the inner leaves, or blanch for two weeks beneath an upturned flowerpot (with its drainage hole covered). Cultivated varieties make more tender leaf especially when grown in good enriched soil. The largest roots can be brought indoors during winter and buried in a bucket of sand in a dark basement or cabinet to sprout a pale, sweeter head of leaves.

The Medicinal Herb Garden

In contrast to the fairly limited number of culinary herbs, there are many hundreds that can be described as medicinal, although some are no longer considered safe to use. However, the extracted properties of others are prescribed daily by the medical profession while many are still used as traditional herbal remedies. Thousands of species wait to have their properties examined scientifically. Among medicinal herbs are found the loveliest and most curious forms in the plant world. Some of the most beautiful are familiar garden flowers: the single-flowered, dark red peony, the madonna lily, early-flowering daphne, yellow gentian and clary sage. Often the most potent have bizarre flowers or seed pods: thornapple with its drooping, sinister flowers and prickled pods, the helmeted monkshood, and mandrake with its large, poisonous 'apples'. Among the more curious are the glamorous white dittany which has an inflammable oil secreted in its stem, the rose plantain with its large, blowsy flowers of green, the fierce and bristling viper's bugloss, and houndstongue, a lush biennial with little ruddy flowers and large leaves that smell of mouse.

The smaller, less obvious herbs are often complex and interesting, wild wood sage and agrimony, for instance, the tiny eyebright, creeping ground ivy and birthwort, a potent little plant with pale funnel-shaped flowers and swollen womb-shaped berries.

There are also many culinary herbs that are effective medicines such as sage, rosemary, dill and garlic, and umbelliferous herbs such as fennel and caraway with their strong digestive properties.

These are the plants that have been relied upon for many thousands of years to provide cures or alleviations for even the most desperate illnesses and wounds and whose special properties have been singled out by observation and experiment, by trial and error, since prehistoric times.

TRADITIONAL HERBAL MEDICINE

Many herbs have associations with magic and were considered to be strongly protective against 'afflictions of the devil' and 'elf sickness'. They are often mentioned in ancient European manuscripts and pre-Christian poems and charms.

The pagan-inspired ceremonies of midsummer came to be celebrated as St John's Day, when many herbs were traditionally collected, among them St John's wort, yarrow and vervain. St John's wort is one of the most effective of the mid-summer healing herbs, its small leaves· producing a bright red oil. Yarrow is both a vulnerary and a herb of divination (it is also used for divination in China). Betony was another herb thought to have strong protective powers over a man's soul, and the *Herbarium* of Apuleius Platonicus recommends it against forty-seven ailments. Houseleek was used by the Romans as a magical protection against fire and also as a remedy for burns. Vervain, the *sacra herba*, was a purifying herb, an ingredient in the Holy Salve. It is described in a fifteenth-century translation of the Stockholm Medical Manuscript as 'comely be weye and gate . . . with heye stalkys, many smale brawnchys, smale bloysh flouris owt of hym lawnchys'. In cultivated ground it will grow tall and bushy, the leaves gathered round the base and the stiff symmetrical stems covered with little spikes of flowers that flash in the sun like Christmas lights.

Some legendary herbs are extremely powerful and often fatally poisonous – the hellebores and veratrums, hemlock, monkshood and opium poppy, for instance – and many do

An apothecary's garden in Germany during the Renaissance. It shows the cultivation of herbs in raised beds, the preparation of herbal remedies, consultations and the examination of the patient's urine.

Left Medicinal herbs growing in raised beds. Those in the foreground belong to the daisy family. To the right grow fleabane and large-leaved elecampane, to the left are tansy, chamomile and feverfew. Far beds hold members of the thyme family: hyssop and bergamot on the left, marjoram and motherwort on the right. In the background grow goat's rue and melilot, members of the pea family.

Opposite left Motherwort's specific Latin name, *cardiaca*, refers to its soothing and cheering effect upon the heart.

Opposite right Poke root can grow 3m/10ft high. The pink flowers will develop into shining black poisonous berries.

in fact play an important part in orthodox medicine. It is not so easy to understand the importance of others, such as betony, vervain, agrimony and motherwort, until one remembers that even mildly tonic herbs would have a beneficial effect upon a badly undernourished body, particularly after a hard winter or during pregnancy, whereas the effect on a well-nourished body might pass almost unnoticed.

Herbs with an astringent and healing action, such as yarrow, lady's mantle, sage and bistort, were used externally to wash wounds and internally to cure diarrhea and restore the womb after childbirth. Antiseptic healing herbs, such as elder, St John's wort and houseleek, were used to clear running sores and poisoned wounds. Emollient herbs, the mallows, marigold and the seeds of clary, were used to soothe sore throats, cure constipation and alleviate aches and pains. The tremendous number of emetic herbs listed in old herbals shows the importance placed on the clearing of the system and the flushing out of impurities and toxic substances.

There are many effective domestic remedies for simple ailments that can be made from herbs that are easy to grow and use today. A table indicating these is shown on page 67, but it does not attempt to give specific prescriptions. Even such simple remedies must be approached with an attitude of sound common sense, and if there is any serious problem or any element of doubt over the species of herb or the nature of the ailment, then a professional practitioner must be consulted immediately.

HERBAL REMEDIES TODAY

Interest in herbal cures is growing today following concern over the use of modern medicines, which use purified extracts of herbs, or manufacture the therapeutic substance in a plant synthetically. One of the main problems is that side effects produced by these drugs are often so uncomfortable or even dangerous that further strong medicines are necessary to counteract them, often creating a chain effect. No one can deny the profound benefits that modern medicines have brought to mankind, but many feel that powerful artificial drugs are prescribed far too liberally and are often used to suppress isolated symptoms rather than as part of a whole and balanced treatment.

Herbal medicine uses whole plants or unadulterated parts of them – leaf, flower, root or seed – fresh or dried, or as a liquid extract or tincture. Thus 'impurities' are in-

cluded and it would appear that they have a value of their own, acting on the body alongside the active principles of the plant in a way that makes for a balanced remedy with few side effects.

Herbal treatments prescribed by a herbal practitioner take the diet and general lifestyle of the patient into account, and attempt to treat the whole person rather than just a symptom of disease. Herbal prescriptions tend to be mild and often work more steadily and slowly to achieve a cure. They are less easily standardized as active principles vary widely in herbs, their production being influenced by the season, the time of day, the weather, and the site where the plant is growing. We still know so little about the complex chemical interaction between plants and their habitats. The old herbalists were struggling with these problems when they wrote of different methods and times for herb gathering – with wooden or iron implements, at the waxing or waning of the moon, or on saint's days.

PLANNING A MEDICINAL HERB GARDEN

A good proportion of medicinal herbs are native to woodland and grow best in lightly shaded, moist rich ground, so a partly shaded site will suit a medicinal herb garden. Ideally a quarter could be shaded, a quarter semishaded and half in full sun. Access to the beds should be easy, and I think it is especially important to allow enough space between medicinal herbs, whose shapes are often fine and sculptural when given plenty of room to develop.

One of the first considerations when choosing species is whether to grow poisonous herbs, and if so how to show clearly that they are dangerous, and also to keep them well out of the reach of children. It is surprising how many people think that all herbs are benign and will nibble any leaf as they pass through a herb garden. Monkshood, thornapple and henbane leaves, and the berries of deadly nightshade, mandrake, pokeroot and daphne are poisonous. It is easy to confuse poisonous meadow saffron flowers with the culinary saffron crocus, or the long wrinkled leaves of poisonous foxglove with the rough-textured leaves of comfrey. I would not grow deadly hemlock with its lacy leaves and blotched stems in the garden; it is far too easily confused with the many good umbelliferous herbs.

So grow poisonous herbs separately and indicate their nature with clear labels and possibly fence them in or surround them with some other form of barrier. If young children play regularly in the garden, it would be wiser not to grow deadly nightshade or mandrake at all, as their fruits may prove tempting.

The purpose of the garden will help give shape to the design. A herbalist would need to grow large numbers of certain medicines that will be cropped throughout the season, and which should perhaps be grown in rows or blocks. For those interested in the history of medicine, the herbs could be grouped according to the parts of the body they are traditionally associated with, although such uses are not necessarily recommended today. Lavender, rosemary, betony and feverfew are for headaches; eyebright, clary sage and greater celandine for the eyes; yarrow, lemon balm, meadowsweet and marigold for fevers; eryngo, licorice and wintergreen for sore throats; white horehound, angelica, ground ivy and mullein for coughs; and so on, right down to houseleek for corns.

Comparing medicinal herbs of the same family is interesting and they can be grouped in that way, as in a botanic garden. Sometimes these groupings will highlight the uses of certain families of herbs. A bed of *Solanaceae* (potato family), for instance, includes some of the most potent and often poisonous plants, such as deadly nightshade and henbane, that are used in orthodox medicine today. Foxglove, hedge hyssop and figwort belong to the *Scrophulariaceae* family and all affect the action of the heart. Many of the *Compositae* family, such as burdock, elecampane and coneflower, will clear skin complaints.

Several small trees with medicinal uses can be used to mark the design of the garden. The barks of the related guelder rose and the black haw from North America have been used as sedatives in the past. The guelder rose grows most gracefully with beautiful creamy flowers, translucent berries and leaves that turn purple in the autumn. The spindle tree is ornamental, with pink autumn berries splitting to display orange seeds, and witch hazel (the North American species *Hamamelis virginiana*, not the Chinese species *Hamamelis mollis*) has narrow ribbons of yellow flowers in late autumn. Bay and juniper, though used in small quantities in the kitchen, have berries that provoke abortion when used in number, and leaves that are burned as fumigants, so they qualify equally for a place in a medicinal garden. Daphne makes a lovely central shrub for a small garden, although it should be kept away from children who may be tempted by its berries. Elder, whose leaves, flowers and berries are valuable medicines, should be given a space to itself, as it tends to retard the growth of any plants beneath it.

The garden could be enclosed within a hedge of apothecary's rose with its scented (and strongly antiseptic) flowers, or within shrubby hedges of rosemary, hyssop or lavender. In a sunny, well-drained position shrubs of the golden-flowered common broom make a good windbreak, especially if they are kept compact and well pruned. (This is an ancient mystical herb which contains dangerous narcotic principles and should not be used as a remedy by amateurs.)

Lungwort, with its spotted leaves and early spring flowers, or the little wild lady's mantle with pleated leaves and tiny yellow-green flowers, make good edging plants for slightly shaded beds. Single- or double-flowered chamomiles or golden feverfew make bright borders for sunny beds.

Size can be a problem. There are so many spectacular medicinal herbs that become very tall and quickly outgrow a small garden. If you have only little space, then choose two or three large herbs and plant creeping, shade tolerant species close around them, such as scented woodruff, the old wound herb bugle, ground ivy and wood avens.

Large herbs that cast a heavy shade include burdock (a

Left A physic garden where the herbs are divided according to their uses. The near bed contains plants that are in use today, the large medicinal rhubarb in flower, broom, licorice and ginseng; in the right hand bed there is a border of golden marjoram around plants used in drugs, perfumes and flavorings.

Below Milk thistle, a striking biennial.

MEDICINAL HERBS (Use leaves unless otherwise stated)

To reduce fevers	angelica, basil, boneset, catmint, chervil, elder*flowers*, lemon balm, lime *flowers*, marigold *petals*, marjoram, meadowsweet, peppermint, safflower *petals*, saffron, sage, thyme, yarrow	**To relieve indigestion**	angelica, coriander *seed*, cumin *seed*, dill *seed*, elecampane *root*, fennel *seed*, lovage *seed*, melilot, peppermint
To soothe sore throats and coughs	borage, elderberry, elder*flower*, hyssop, liquorice *root*, lungwort, marsh mallow *root*, rose *petals*, sage, St John's wort, sea holly *root*, thyme, viper's bugloss	**To relieve constipation**	elderflower, licorice, marsh mallow *root*, pellitory of the wall, sweet cicely *seed*, violet *flowers*
Antiseptic gargle	bayberry, elecampane *root*, lavender, lovage, marjoram, rosemary, rose *petals*, sage, thyme, vervain, wintergreen	**To relieve diarrhoea**	bilberry *berries*, bistort *root*, meadow-sweet *leaves*, mullein *leaves and flowers*, plantain, wood avens *root*
For bladder complaints	angelica, dandelion, ground ivy, horse-radish, lady's bedstraw, parsley piert, pellitory of the wall	**Tonic herbs**	agrimony, costmary, fenugreek, ginseng, ground ivy, lady's mantle, motherwort, parsley, rosemary, sage, salad burnet, . watercress, yarrow
To induce sleep	chamomile *flowers*, hop *flowers*, lemon balm, lemon verbena, lime *flowers*, mullein *flowers*, violet *flowers*	**Externally to: help heal wounds**	agrimony, betony, bistort *root*, elder *leaves*, garlic *bulb*, golden rod, house-leek, hyssop, lady's mantle, woad, yarrow
Against headaches	anise, eyebright, feverfew, ground ivy, lavender *flowers (in small quantities)*, lemon balm, rosemary, woodruff	**soothe bruises and sprains**	arnica *root and flowers*, bogbean, burdock, comfrey, ground ivy, marigold, plantain, wintergreen, witch hazel
Appetizers	bogbean, dandelion, fenugreek *seed*, gentian *root*, wood sage	**reduce inflammation**	comfrey, marsh mallow *root*, violet
To calm upset stomach	basil, lemon verbena, marjoram, peppermint	**soothe stings**	basil, betony, costmary, lemon balm, mints, onion juice, plantain
		soothe skin complaints	burdock, chamomile, comfrey, elecampane, mullein, rosemary, sorrel

useful plant medicinally but one that becomes rough and ragged after flowering), the handsome elecampane, angelica and teazel.

To cast lighter shade, plant the downy marshmallow with its pink-white flowers, and goat's rue and licorice, which have delicate leaflets, as well as evening primrose and mullein. American poke root grows up to 3m/10ft high and wide, with bright red stems and black berries in the autumn. The graceful white-flowered valerian needs containing as its aromatic roots (which have a sedative effect) spread so fast.

A CHOICE OF MEDICINAL HERBS

My own garden is a mixture of the practical and ornamental, of plants for remedies that I have found to be most useful together with other historical medicinal plants that are particularly interesting or beautiful.

A number of medicinal herbs should not be used by the lay person, but there are many simple (as opposed to compound) medicines which are basic domestic remedies and have a mild effect unless taken in excessive quantities. Even a small herb garden will have enough space to grow some of the most pleasant and beneficial herbs for tisanes (herbal infusions), for instance. To begin with I would choose five: peppermint, lemon verbena, rosemary, sage and chamomile.

Peppermint makes a delicious tisane for reducing fevers, for clearing the head during a cold (when it can also be used in a strong infusion as an inhalant) and for preventing or reducing morning sickness. Lemon verbena makes a

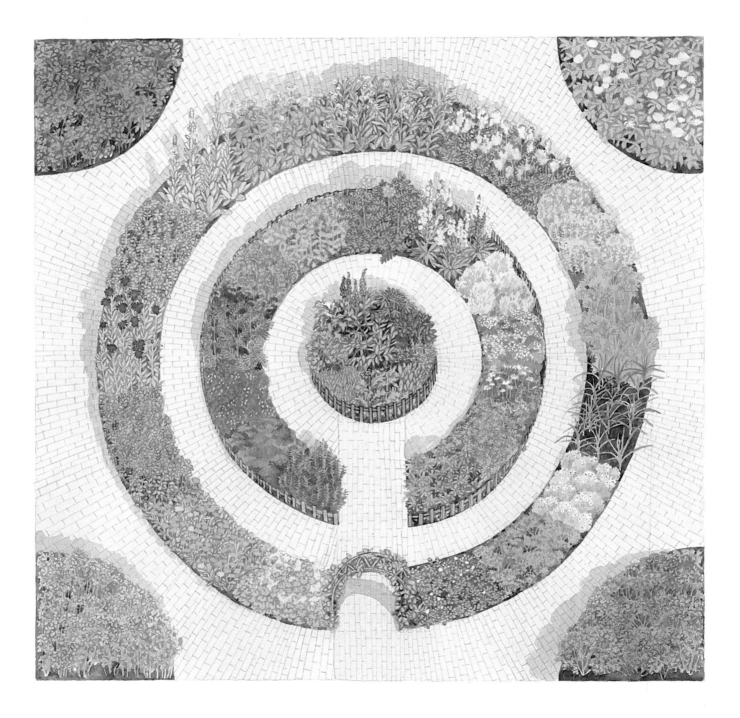

MEDICINAL HERB GARDEN PLAN

This is a plan for a large garden, 8m/27ft square, but it can easily be adapted for a smaller area. The central bed holds powerful medicinal herbs that are poisonous, and which can be enclosed by a fence if necessary. (The poke root may need cutting back occasionally to limit its size.) Herbs in the second bed have a fairly strong action, too.

The outer bed holds many domestic remedies. The berry bushes have medicinal uses.

The taller herbs are mainly grown at the northern end of each circle, both as a protection for the smaller plants and to give an uninterrupted view of the garden.

PLANT LIST

Inner circle:
Hyoscyamus niger, henbane
Chelidonium majus, greater celandine
Colchicum autumnale, meadow saffron
Convallaria majalis, lily of the valley
Aconitum napellus, monkshood
Digitalis purpurea, foxglove
Atropa belladonna, deadly nightshade
Helleborus niger, black hellebore
Datura stramonium, thornapple

Centre:
Phytolacca americana, poke root

Second circle:
Salvia sp., sage
Rosmarinus officinalis, rosemary
Thymus sp., thyme
Galium odoratum, woodruff
Achillea millefolium, yarrow
Viola tricolor, heartsease
Valeriana officinalis, valerian
Tanacetum parthenium, feverfew
Artemisia sp., wormwood
Tanacetum vulgare, tansy
Oenothera biennis, evening primrose
Angelica archangelica, angelica

Outer circle:
Humulus lupulus, hops
Alchemilla vulgaris, lady's mantle
Sanguisorba minor, salad burnet
Petroselinum sp., parsley
Calendula officinalis, marigold
Chamaemelum nobile, chamomile
Melissa officinalis, lemon balm
Allium sativum, garlic
Monarda didyma, bergamot
Mentha × piperita, peppermint
Anethum graveolens, dill
Marrubium vulgare, white horehound
Verbascum thapsus, mullein
Inula helenium, elecampane
Filipendula ulmaria, meadowsweet
Symphytum officinale, comfrey

Corners:
Rubus idaeus, raspberry
Rubus sp., blackberry
Sambucus nigra, elder
Ribes nigrum, blackcurrant

refreshing lemon tisane that is gently sedative and helps to settle the stomach. Rosemary is used in small quantities (a small sprig combined with lemon verbena or lemon balm is good) against headaches and colds, and to invigorate and liven the spirits. In a stronger infusion use it as an antiseptic gargle for sore throats and as a hairwash against dandruff. Sage is another excellent antiseptic and one of the best all-around medicinal herbs. Make an infusion to help clear colds and reduce 'flu and fevers, to encourage menstruation and, in a stronger infusion, as a gargle and mouth-wash for sore throats. Also rub fresh leaves over teeth and gums each day as an antiseptic mouth freshener. Chamomile flowers make a pleasant, soothing tisane for calming the nerves and encouraging sleep.

For first-aid herbs, grow a good patch of comfrey, the leaves of which (blanched for a few seconds in boiling water to soften their bristly surface) are extremely effective in reducing inflammation and also have a healing action or can be infused and used as a healing wash. They contain allantoin, a valuable healing substance included in many medical treatments. Crushed, fresh houseleek leaves are soothing and healing and make one of the best herbal treatments for minor burns. A wash made from a strong infusion of burdock leaves or a decoction of its root is a good remedy for skin complaints and dandruff. The leaves of the elder tree can be used externally as a healing wash or to make an ointment; the flowers as an expectorant, a gentle laxative and to reduce fevers; and the juice from the stewed berries, flavored to taste with ginger and cloves, against colds, 'flu and bronchitis.

If possible, add the annual prince's feather to the list of herbs to grow. The erect, red flower racemes bloom in late summer, and the whole plant is astringent and is used externally as a wash against ulcers. Even if you never have an ulcer, grow it for its irresistible Latin name, *Amaranthus hypochondriacus*.

A HERBAL INFUSION

A standard herbal infusion is made like tea, by pouring 450ml/1 pint of boiling water on to 12g/½oz dried or 25g/1oz fresh herbs, and leaving it to infuse for a good 10 minutes before straining. A standard dose is a small teacupful, taken warm or cold, flavored if you like with honey or lemon, three times a day. An infusion is generally made using leaves, stems, flowers or occasionally seeds of a herb.

A HERBAL DECOCTION

The roots or woody stems of a herb need to be simmered for at least 10 minutes to extract their properties and produce a standard herbal decoction. Put 12g/½oz dried root or stem into a nonaluminum saucepan, and add 450ml/1 pint of cold water. Cover with a lid, bring slowly to the boil and simmer gently. Strain, and take as for infusion.

The Scented Herb Garden

The first impression of any herb garden is likely to be of mingled scents: aromatic, sharp, sweet and richly pungent. It is a great pleasure to walk among herbs on a warm summer's evening, brushing against and pinching leaves and smelling the newly opened flowers of honeysuckle and evening primrose.

The herbs may be used as flavorings or medicines but many highly scented herbs can be dried for potpourris and for scenting linen, or used as ingredients for homemade cosmetics, soaps, bath bags, candles, and for stuffing pillows and sachets. Fresh or dried, their scents are evocative and stirring. They have been used for thousands of years to arouse our emotions – as scents for the body and as an important part of religious ceremonies. Traditionally, the scents of various herbs have their special effects: rosemary and marjoram to cheer and invigorate; mint to refresh the senses; southernwood to increase awareness; hops and lavender to calm the nerves.

The scent of most herbs is contained in their leaves, where tiny cells of essential oils can often be seen as pinprick dots when the leaf is held against the light. Since the scent is released by bruising or brushing the leaf, these herbs need to be within easy reach of the path, or should be allowed to overhang or creep over the path itself.

Some scents – myrtle for instance – are released only by crushing the leaves, as the oil-containing cells are buried deep. When these cells are close to the surface, as in thyme leaves, the scent is released simply by the heat of the sun. In fact, the oils and the tough surfaces of the leaves of rosemary, thyme, savory and other Mediterranean herbs act as barriers, giving protection against the heat of the hot summer sun.

The scents of herb leaves are likely to be more aromatic and pungent than those of flowers, and their essential oils are often simple chemical substances. The scents of flowers are usually much sweeter, with their essential oils, or 'attars', made up of a more complex mixture of chemical compounds.

Individual reactions to these scents vary widely. While one person may find the scent of the madonna lily deliciously sweet, another may detect a faint and unpleasant

The flowers growing around the Virgin in the garden symbolize her virtues. Her bench is a raised bed of wild strawberries, symbolic of the fruits of righteousness. The violets at her feet represent humility, and the rose divine love. The garden with its raised bench, trellis and herb carpet is a setting seen often in medieval paintings.

odor of decay. Reactions to scents are also governed by their strengths. The scents of the inflated sheaths around the base of angelica stems, or the flowers of clary sage, are rich and pungent as you pass by, but may become almost sickening if much time is spent weeding around the plants. Aromatic leaves, on the other hand, can be gathered by the armful and it is almost impossible to tire of their strong scents.

PLANNING A SCENTED HERB GARDEN

A garden of herbs grown particularly for their scent will need many paths and small or narrow beds, a place to sit and, near the seat if possible, some raised beds or pots for low-growing or delicate plants. Most important of all, this garden will need to be enclosed or at least protected from the prevailing wind which would drive the scent away. By planting creeping scented herbs in the paths and using the enclosure or windbreak as a support for climbing honeysuckles, jasmines, hops and the virgin's bower clematis, and by growing the most highly scented hedges such as sweetbriar, old roses, lavender, rosemary and santolina, every part of the garden can be sweet-smelling.

The design of the garden will probably be based around the soft grays and greens of the most aromatic shrubby herbs, with the more showy flowering herbs among them: the scarlet bergamot, purple-blue spikes of hyssop with their scented leaves, white orris and yellow elecampane with scented roots, and the fragrant flowers of evening primrose and meadowsweet. While a rather ordered design may suit culinary or medicinal herbs, sweet-scented herbs could be grown in a more informal cottage garden style, in pleasing disorder. Hedges can be given the minimum trimming needed to prevent legginess; borders of violets, double-flowered chamomile and variegated wild strawberries can escape onto the paths; woodruff and the most fragrant and least invasive mints, such as the variegated pineapple mint, can grow in the shade of daphne and myrtle bushes, or scramble through shrubby artemisias or catmints. Creeping thymes, pale and downy, bright or dark-leaved, fruit-scented creeping chamomile or prostrate mints can grow between stones or among the gravel of paths, or be used to make a scented mat at the entrance to the garden.

Creeping thymes spread fast along cracks and crevices in pavements and paths, forming thick, scented mats. There are many varieties to choose from: flowers may be white, through pink or mauve, to dark purple, and leaves may be pale and downy, golden, variegated or deep green. Common varieties have the familiar aromatic scent, while others smell of lemon or spices.

Left An old chimney pot holding a red pelargonium provides height amongst low-growing, highly scented herbs.

Below left In another view of the garden, a shallow sink set on bricks is filled with lady's mantle and surrounded by a mass of self-sown white-flowered violets.

SCENTED HERB GARDEN PLAN AND PLANT LIST
Opposite The plan shown here, adapted from the same garden, has gravel paths crossing at a central point marked by a container planted with pineapple sage. In the four beds, scented herbs are planted in drifts.

1 *Satureja montana*, winter savory
2 *Rosmarinus officinalis*, rosemary
3 *Myrtus communis tarentina*, myrtle
4 *Lavandula spp.*, lavender
5 *Fragaria vesca semperflorens*, alpine strawberry

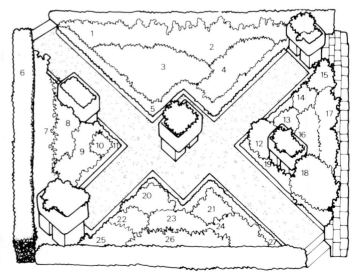

6 *Taxus sp.*, yew
7 *Monarda didyma*, bergamot
8 *Santolina neapolitana*
9 *Mentha spp.*, mint
10 *Allium schoenoprasum*, chives
11 *Viola cornuta* 'Alba'
12 *Calamintha grandiflora*, calamint

13 *Hyssopus officinalis*, hyssop
14 *Sanguisorba minor*, salad burnet
15 *Balsamita vulgaris tanacetoides*, costmary
16 *Nepeta cataria*, catnep
17 *Levisticum officinale*, lovage
18 *Melissa officinalis*, lemon balm

19 *Thymus drucei*, creeping thyme
20 *Helichrysum angustifolium*, curry plant
21 *Geranium macrorrhizum* 'Roseum'
22 *Artemisia pontica*, Roman wormwood

23 *A. abrotanum*, southernwood
24 *Tanacetum vulgare*, tansy
25 *Origanum vulgare*, wild marjoram
26 *Oenothera biennis*, evening primrose
27 *Thymus × citriodorus* 'Aureus', golden thyme

Such an informal garden needs a sound basic design to hold the rather unrestrained planting together, and also the judicious pruning and weeding out of unwanted seedlings to prevent the most rampant herbs from taking over. Low hedges or well-placed groups of old English lavender, the largest rosemaries or southernwood will help create a structure. Changes in the level of the garden will help too. The garden could be partly sunken, with a bank thrown up against the prevailing wind (even a bank or barrier 50cm/ 20in high will act as an effective windbreak). Terracing will also divide the garden up into smaller areas, and in this way the disorder is more easily managed and the plants unobtrusively contained.

A CHOICE OF SCENTED HERBS

For a scented herb garden in a limited space bergamot would be one of my essential plants, together with lavender, clove carnation, violets, honeysuckle, pineapple sage, cowslip and evening primrose, with an apothecary's rose and a shrubby daphne.

Daphne grows best in a sheltered position in a limy soil and may need protecting with straw during very cold winters, but it is well worth the trouble to see and smell the deliciously scented flowers – white, pink or red – blooming on the leafless twigs early in the spring. All varieties of bergamot or bee balm have scented leaves, but the one with the sweetest and least camphor-scented leaves, and the best for making a light tisane, is the red-flowered *Monarda didyma*. This spreading perennial, with its curious and beautiful flowers that often seem to grow through the cushion centers of each other, is shown off well among fine-leaved pale artemisias or the feathery *Santolina neapolitana*.

A scented garden of potpourri herbs would be dominated by the rose, with bushes of lavender and lemon thyme, a shrub of lemon verbena in a pot, a bay tree perhaps, bergamot, sweet marjoram, an assortment of tender pelargoniums, especially those with small leaves, such as the *Pelargonium crispum* varieties that dry especially well, and the modest spring-flowering woodruff with its brilliant white blossoms. Both woodruff and the large annual melilot have leaves which smell of newly mown hay and whose scent develops as they dry (due to the presence of the chemical coumarin).

Those who go out to work during the day will want to include herbs that are most scented during long summer evenings. White dittany, woodruff and the close relation to weld, the smaller mignonette, would be good choices. The flowers of the tall evening primrose hang sadly during hot days, but watch them slowly lift and open out into pale, scented bowls every evening, from early summer to the first frosts. Grow the goat-leaf honeysuckle, *Lonicera caprifolium*, in an evening herb garden, as this is when its scent reaches its full richness. (This is related to the fact that the flowers have an especially long tube, which means that the nectar can only be reached by moths with a proboscis at least 3cm/1¼in long.) At dusk a garden of pale-flowered herbs will be haunted by many species of moths.

Opposite Low, brightly colored aromatic herbs edge a path of old bricks.

Above In this stone-flagged garden are the cultivar of clary sage, *Salvia sclarea* 'Turkestanica', wild strawberries and wood avens.

Right An enclosed, scented garden in early summer with *Santolina virens* beginning to flower and a bed of gray-green Roman wormwood.

Silver-leaved artemisias, eryngos and santolinas become almost luminous in the half-light.

Several species of salvia have their place in a scented garden, apart from the usual culinary sages. Here the dividing line between herb and nonherb becomes rather indistinct. I include clary sage, *Salvia sclarea*, and its paler-leaved cultivar 'Turkestanica' with its silver-mauve bracts; both have a powerfully rich scent. Jupiter's distaff has a similar habit with pale yellow flowers and an oozing resinous gum in the autumn. Bog sage has pungent leaves and a looser, finer habit with flowers of a startling light blue. The more distantly related Jerusalem sage, *Phlomis fruticosa*, is a large handsome scented shrub with evergreen woolly silver leaves and whorls of yellow flowers.

There are comparatively few scented herb flowers, and it is worth planning to keep a succession blooming through the summer.

First in the year are primroses, cowslips, and violets. The wild varieties of primrose and cowslip have the strongest scent: the primrose a delicate and mossy fragrance, the cowslip rich and powerful. Plant them with sweet violet, *Viola odorata*, among creeping herbs in wild corners, or beneath herbaceous herbs whose later growth will shade their leaves during the summer. The mauve-blue *V. cornuta* flowers from midspring through most of the summer and makes a charming low border to a herb garden, among pinks and chamomile. The white *V. cornuta* 'Alba' and the tiny *V.c.* 'Minor' are sweetly scented too.

Spring-flowering, strongly scented wallflowers are not usually associated with herb gardens, but they do have a long medicinal history ('cheirinum' oil being used to treat ulcers, aches and palsy) and the little wild *Cheiranthus cheiri* or the taller old-fashioned double yellow *C.c.* 'Harpur Crewe' with its extra strong scent, have a place among the herbs. Their sixteenth-century names were 'chevisaunce' and 'stock gilliflower'.

In the early summer the dianthus family begins to flower. The hardy border pinks and the compact dwarf species grow well in troughs or pots or as edging plants, but the clove-scented *Dianthus caryophyllus*, the clove carnation, which is a rich maroon and is the source of our hardy border carnations, is the one specially suited to a herb garden. Try growing it in a pot through a framework of looped flexible twigs. This supports the long stems and the gray-bloomed leaves can spread out freely. (For other scented herbs to grow in containers, see page 128).

Then there are the roses. Descended from the original Provins rose is *Rosa gallica* 'Officinalis', the apothecary's rose, which is the most obvious choice for the scented herb garden. It is a lovely shrub rose, its semidouble flowers richly scented and a clear, deep crimson pink, showing yellow stamens as it opens. The thick-textured petals hold their scent well when dried. *Rosa gallica* 'Versicolor' or 'Rosa Mundi' is streaked deep pink and white. Both may need thinning in spring or late summer and can be trained to make a hedge around the garden or to cover an arbor, for example.

The tall *Rosa alba*, and the white rose of York *R. alba semi-plena*, the cabbage rose *R. centifolia*, the damask rose and the climbing musk rose are all old roses well suited to the soft grays and greens of aromatic herbs.

Scented climbers

The wild sweetbriar *Rosa eglanteria* is the natural choice for a twining plant to climb through a hedge or along a trellis enclosing a scented garden. Parkinson in his *Paradisus* suggests entwining it with whitethorn with 'roses of one, two or three sorts, placed here and there amongst them'. The scent of the delicate leaves is so refreshing it almost quenches one's thirst to smell them, especially after a rain storm. The pale pink single flowers have only a faint

Left All parts of the monumental angelica are powerfully scented.

Opposite Tall yew hedges enclose a large scented herb garden with turf paths that are edged with low hedges of santolina. Honeysuckles are trained up poles as standards and sweet peas climb a wigwam of brushwood. To the right are the ferny, sugary, aniseed-scented leaves of sweet cicely.

scent. There are many hybrid varieties with the same scented foliage.

The obvious partner for the sweetbriar is the honeysuckle with its sweet-scented flowers. This herb is no longer used medicinally; the preserve made by pounding its flowers with sugar, to treat asthma and hasten childbirth, is not recommended today, nor should the berries be eaten. By planting several species it should be possible to have honeysuckle in flower from midspring to late summer. First choice would be the early- and late-flowering Dutch varieties *Lonicera periclymenum* 'Belgica' and 'Serotina' which are bred from the vigorous and strongly scented wild honeysuckle. *L. caprifolium* has its upper leaves united at the base and pale flowers that are most scented at night. *L. americana*, a hybrid from North America, has purple-tinted, very richly scented flowers.

Other hardy climbers to suit a scented herb garden are the strong white-flowered jasmines, *Jasminum officinale* or *J. x stephanense* (which doesn't grow so high and has slightly larger, pink flowers) and *Clematis flammula*, the virgin's bower, with sweet-scented small white flowers in the early autumn. Green- or golden-leaved hops make prodigious growth each year from a root that lies dormant all winter. They are most successful when grown along horizontal poles or trained against a fence, so that the curious, papery conelike flowers hang down from among the leaves and are clearly seen.

A Garden for Bees and Butterflies

All herb gardens make wonderful feeding grounds for bees and butterflies as herbs are usually highly scented, rich in nectar and closer to their wild forms than many scentless and hybridized garden plants. To make an especially attractive herb garden for bees and butterflies, choose the sunniest and most protected corner of the garden. Plant a sheltering hedge of the largest old English lavender or rosemary, and train honeysuckle (early- and late-flowering varieties) up an enclosing fence or trellis.

Bees will forage for up to half a mile from their hive, but various herbs have traditionally been grown around the hive itself. Virgil suggested savory, while whole plants of sweet cicely and lemon balm used to be rubbed over the hives to attract bees. However, bees are more attracted by color, and especially by blues, purples and yellows. Bees with short tongues will feed from rue, achillea and chamomile flowers, but hive bees with their longer tongues gather nectar from long-tubed flowers such as those of the labiate family which bloom from early summer. First there is thyme blossom, then marjoram and sage; lavender and catmint are blooming by midsummer, with hyssop and finally winter savory in the early autumn. The annual borage is rich in nectar, so are other members of the family such as viper's bugloss and the anchusas and alkanet. Melilot, another annual, produces quantities of nectar and derives its name from honey (Latin, *mel*).

Butterflies are more attracted by scent and prefer rather faded colors. They are more likely to visit the pale mauve flowers of old English lavender than the darker 'Hidcote' varieties, and the pink dianthus rather than the more richly colored clove carnation.

It is worth making sure that there are early- and late-flowering herbs in the garden to provide continuous nectar throughout the season. In the autumn the pink- or white-flowered (not the double) forms of meadow saffron are valuable. Provide the bee garden with hellebores in the early spring, then primroses and cowslips, and in late spring the herbaceous monkshood.

Among the best spring bee herbs is the wallflower, which used to be called 'bee flower'. In the early seventeenth century Gervase Markham wrote 'The Husbandman preserves it most in his Bee-garden, for it is wondrous sweet and affordeth much honey'. The small, wild, yellow-flowered wallflower blooms for several months.

Left Hyssop, much loved by bees, blooms from high summer.

Right Eleanour Sinclair Rohde's design for a bee garden was included in her nursery catalog of 1943. Surrounded by hedges of sweetbriar and rosemary, the herbs are planned to provide nectar throughout the season, from daphne in early spring to marigolds and bergamot in autumn.

The Dyer's Herb Garden

Two of the most decorative of the traditional dye herbs, woad **left** and weld **right**. They are both biennial and self-seed well, often in the small cracks between stone flags. Woad flowers in early summer with a mass of yellow flowers. Weld flowers later, with long spikes of a paler green-yellow which often curve elegantly as they seed.

The best traditional dyeing herbs are mainly herbaceous perennials whose richly colored flowers and beautiful shapes will make a fine border or central bed in a herb garden. The serious dyer will need to grow these herbs in masses for cutting regularly, as large quantities of foliage, roots or flowers will be needed. For those who dye only a few skeins of wool at a time and who would enjoy experimenting with the infinitely subtle color variations from herbs, then the most effective dyeing herbs can be grown in smaller groups.

As a rough guide, plant material must at least equal the weight of material to be dyed, but the amount of dye in each plant varies tremendously. For fast colors you will need a mordant of some sort, such as alum, chrome, iron or tin, or natural fixing agents such as wood ash, vinegar or soda. However, it is interesting to experiment with dye plants on their own, though the colors may fade fast or wash out eventually.

Most plants will give a dye of some sort, if only faint fawns and ochers, but the old-established dye plants, whose second Latin name is often *tinctoria* or *tinctorum*, can be relied upon to give strong colors. These plants need to grow in full sun, so plan a dye garden facing south if possible and enrich the earth, in the same way that you would a herbaceous border, with compost every two years.

As so many dye herbs die down in winter, the dyer's broom or dyer's greenweed is especially valuable as a central focus for the garden, or as a boundary marker. This handsome shrub has small glossy dark leaves and yellow pealike flowers that bloom for two or three months in the summer and make a good yellow dye. Common broom yields a similar yellow.

Dyer's woodruff makes a good border; it has narrower leaves than the woodland species, and graceful creeping stems; hops (whose flowers and leaves give a good brown dye) can be used to climb a trellis or scramble round the entrance to the garden.

Three traditional dyeing herbs are the biennials weld and woad, and the perennial madder. Weld has long spires of green-yellow flowers that often curve gracefully when seeding; the yellow cruciferous flowers of woad are followed by black seeds that hang like earrings, and its long leaves have a blue tone that hints at its use as a blue dye. Both self-seed well and are worth growing for their beauty alone. In medieval times they were used together to yield the famous Lincoln green color. Madder is interesting rather than beautiful, rather like a giant, coarsened woodruff, with a scrambling habit and whorls of leaves that rasp like abrasive paper. Its thick root gives a strong red dye. The related lady's bedstraw gives a fainter, more rusty color.

The flowers of the annual safflower have been used for many thousands of years to make a red or yellow dye. Sow some seed each spring among the perennials; the thistle-like flowers are a deep rich yellow.

Yellow is a color that will keep recurring among dye herbs. There are marigolds, spires of golden rod, the yellow button flowers and handsome dark foliage of tansy and the yellow daisies of dyer's chamomile, and the medley of rusts, terracottas and dark golds of *Coreopsis*

The dark gleaming seed pods of woad hang heavily and were described by Gerard as being 'like little black tongues'. The leaves, which have a blue bloom, are astringent, 'cold and dry' as Culpeper says, and good for drying up ulcers and other 'corroding and fretting humours', and for cooling the terrible skin inflammations of erysipelas or St Anthony's fire, which was a common disease in Culpeper's day. The leaves are better known as the source of a good dark blue dye. The extraction of the dye can be a complicated process, involving grinding and repeated fermentation of the leaves, which produces a noxious smell. A simpler method uses ammonia as an alkaline agent. (Blanch 12 large woad leaves in $\frac{3}{4}$ liter/$1\frac{1}{3}$ pints of boiling water, adding one capful of ammonia. When the water has cooled to lukewarm, take a small skein of wool and dip and aerate it several times until it becomes dark blue. Rinse several times in cold water.

tinctoria. Distribute among them the purple sawwort and alkanet or dyer's bugloss whose blue flowers appear in the spring. The white-flowered low-growing bloodroot also blooms early, and will tolerate shade. It thrives on leaf-mold and its fleshy roots give a red dye.

The real indigo cannot be grown successfully out of doors in northern climates, so replace it with the splendid *Baptisia tinctoria*, the indigo broom, a tall perennial with large, lush pea flowers of a rich mauve blue.

Most of these herbs have also been used medicinally, mainly as slightly astringent or antiseptic wound herbs; none are edible.

Berries often yield good dyes. Juniper berries give fawn or khaki colors; elder and poke root berries, lavender or gray; and bilberry, a range from pink to purple. Collect berries for dyeing as they ripen. Flowers are best gathered just as they are opening, and leaves when they are approaching maturity. Roots of dye herbs are at their best in the autumn, and bark in the spring.

A simple nonfast dyeing method
Fill a cheesecloth bag or old stocking with 100g/4oz of dye herb – flowering tops, leaves, roots, bark, berries – and cover with 5 liters/9pts of cold soft water. Add 60g/2oz of wool or cotton (do not use synthetic materials). Bring slowly to the boil and simmer gently until the wool or cotton has a strong color. Rinse several times, reducing the temperature of the rinsing water each time until the wool or cotton is cool. Spread out to dry. Be prepared for the dye to fade or to wash out.

CONSTRUCTING
A
HERB GARDEN

This section covers as many as possible of the practical aspects of designing and building a herb garden, including boundaries and paths, arbors and seats, banks and hedgings, paved areas and lawns.

The plants themselves can be used as windbreaks, as scented paths or as edgings to contain and give shape to beds and borders. Fences or trellises can support climbing herbs, and herbs that flourish in cracks and crevices can be planted in walls and rocky banks and among the stones or gravel of paths and courtyards. A small garden may only have room for a low chamomile seat and an arch of honeysuckle by the herb bed. A large garden could be divided into smaller areas by a pattern of aromatic hedges and sheltered from the wind by a bank of creeping herbs. A paved yard could hold pots of tender herbs with hardy annuals among the stones and a trellis of sweetbriar.

An interesting range of possibilities for garden constructions are to be found in medieval paintings and manuscript illuminations. The Madonna and Child are often shown, with attendant patrons and saints, either sitting on a turf bench in a garden or perhaps in a room with a clear view of an enclosed garden through a window or archway. The garden might be a simple flowery mead, but is likely to be elaborate, with stone walls, a fountain, wrought iron railings, paths of checkered flagstones, and raised beds. Bench seats are built of planks or brick, and topped with herbs. Fences are close-boarded, post and rail, or crisscrossed lattice, and there are often beautifully arched arbors, or tunnel arbors covered with vines and roses. Medieval manuscript calendars sometimes include scenes showing gardening through the year. The gardens may be enclosed with hurdles, or with fences of brushwood held in place with split hazel branches, and gardeners dig, plant and harvest in beds that are surrounded and contained within rough boarding or strips of low, woven wattle.

Even though some of these early structures may be impracticable today, they do provide a wonderful source of ideas for modern herb gardens.

A late fifteenth–century miniature displaying a rather formal garden design, but showing many features that might be adapted for a herb garden today. The couple lean against, rather than sit on, the brick-built turf bench, and a flowery mead surrounds them. The trellised post and rail supports flowering plants at right. One of the elaborate pots on the bench shows off red carnations, newly introduced and at the height of their popularity in northern Europe; the other contains a shrub clipped into circular tiers, a style which was called 'estrade'.

Boundary and Retaining Walls

The most permanent boundary for a garden is, of course, a wall. To build a high wall needs time and skill and can be a great expense, but it is surprising how a low wall, even one only 60cm/24in high, will transform a piece of ground into an enclosed garden. It is recommended that none of the walls discussed here should be higher than 1m/3ft unless you have skilled help.

A double dry-stone wall is ideal for herbs, especially in a small garden, for it can be planted up both sides and along the top with the more tender species sheltered and warmed at its base.

A wall of mellow old bricks can be built either double or single thickness with unmortared gaps left for planting some hardy herbs.

Low walls of hollow concrete blocks are the easiest to build, with the blocks placed either in a single or double row, and either one or two blocks deep. Pack earth into the hollows, and plant herbs, preferably with a falling habit, to cover the concrete. (Its raw surface could be toned down with a slurry of manure thinned to a creamy consistency with milk for instant weathering.) Even a single row of blocks as a low protective wall will provide shelter for a nursery bed.

Low retaining walls in a sunken or terraced garden, or to contain a bank, are suitable for herbs that are quite large and less tolerant of drought, since their roots can grow deep into the earth behind the wall. By terracing a bank or a steeply sloping garden, or by artificially creating several changes of level on a flat site, you will add interest and substance to the garden design and make an ideal habitat for special herbs that need well-drained conditions. Even a retaining wall just two or three stones high will provide extra protection and drainage.

If any major digging out is needed, keep all precious topsoil in a separate heap, to spread over the bank or terrace when the wall-building is finished.

Using the dry-stone wall method (see page 85), dig out the soil to make a steeply sloping bank. Position the stones in rows against this, setting the herbs in between the stones as you build, and tucking their roots in deeply. If the soil is crumbly, hold the plants in place with a plug of clay.

Creeping thyme is well adapted to growing over a low stone wall. The button flowers of *Santolina neapolitana* are coming into bloom behind it. The leaves of this santolina have a looser habit and more feathery shape than those of the more common *S. chamaecyparissus*. *Lychnis coronaria*, an old-fashioned cottage garden plant, can be seen on the left.

It is important that the design and materials of any wall should be compatible with those of the house, the surrounding garden paths, or other paved areas.

HERBS FOR WALLS

Among the hardiest herbs for growing along the top of a wall are the little wild yellow wallflower, creeping thymes and the toughest dianthus varieties with their mats of gray-green foliage. The big rosettes of houseleek are very resistant to drought, and dwarf forms of the common juniper are the most wind-resistant. Pellitory of the wall will survive almost anywhere, and it will soon spread by fibrous creeping root or by seeding into crevices down the sides of the wall. Although the leaves are pretty and fresh in the spring, they become dull by midsummer.

The shrubby herbs that grow among the stony hillsides of the Mediterranean are well adapted to loose, dry-stone walls. Grow the dwarf varieties as the woody branches of larger shrubs might be damaged by wind. Hyssop is one of my favorites, with its thick, bushy foliage and rich blue-purple flower spikes. It flourishes along walls and will often self-seed into crevices. The most easily obtainable dwarf lavenders suitable for walls are usually *Lavandula spica* 'Hidcote' with dark purple flowers and *L. spica* 'Munstead' with paler mauve flowers.

These curving terraces fronted with stone flags make well-drained beds for herbs. Lavender is flowering in the foreground and behind it grows sorrel and creeping donkey's ears (*Stachys lanata*) with its downy silver leaves. Lower beds hold decorative alliums.

A low dry-stone wall runs beside a path of crazy paving. It is built simply, with no foundation and with plenty of cracks and crevices for drought-resistant herbs like lavender, dianthus and creeping thymes. At its foot, upright thymes self-seed among the stones.

Wall germander is dark and glossy with bright pink flowers. For silver foliage grow *Santolina chamaecyparissus*, which will need to be kept low by regular clipping, or its dwarf form 'Corsica'. *Artemisia canescens* makes a loose, curly mound of leaves, and the less hardy *Artemisia nitida* or *A. pedemontana* form soft, silky cushions.

Add some herbs that have a graceful, curving habit, such as musk mallow and the little alpine lady's mantle. Since rainwater will drain freely to the foot of the terrace wall, plant moisture-loving herbs there, such as primroses and violets, and the taller sweet cicely and meadowsweet.

BUILDING A DRY-STONE WALL

With patience, most people can manage to build a low wall. The one described here is a low, sloping dry-stone wall, ideal for clothing with plants.

The stones for the wall should be more or less of equal size, and the task will be easier if they are flatter rather than rounded. Select the largest stones for the bottom of the wall and lay them with their grain running horizontally in a double course. As you lay each parallel course of stones, fill the space between with earth. Make sure the earth is packed between the ends of the stones along each course,

A FREESTANDING DRY-STONE WALL

This wall (a cross section is shown below) is 1m/3ft high, with double walls of roughly equal-sized stones, packed and filled with earth. The top is capped with earth and herbs are planted along the top and down the sides. At the base the wall

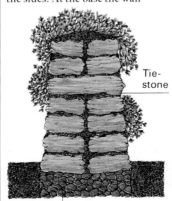

Tie-stone

Hardcore

measures 60cm/24in wide, and at the top 45cm/18in wide.

Begin by digging a shallow trench 20cm/8in deep and 60cm/24in wide, to run the length of the wall. Fill this with rubble to a depth of 6cm/2½in. Above this, position the largest stones which will form the base of the wall, laying them end-to-end in a double course hard against the sides of the trench. Pack earth firmly between the stones.

The grain of the stones should be horizontal and the smoothest side of each stone should face outward: use a level to maintain a roughly even height for each course. Tilt the outside edges of the stones upward slightly so that rainwater runs into the wall. Use an extra long tie-stone at 60cm/2ft intervals across the width of the wall to strengthen it.

into every space, leaving no air pockets. Remember to slope the wall gradually inward toward the top.

The usual rule for building dry-stone walls is to tilt the outer edges of the stones slightly downward to drain off rainwater. In this case, reverse the rule and tilt them slightly upward to catch and conserve rainwater and tip it toward the roots of the plants.

Cap the wall with a tightly packed bed of earth, curved slightly to help drainage. The wall is then ready for planting up. Alternatively, if your herbs are ready for planting, set them into the crevices of the wall as you build, remembering to put the more tender species on the sunniest side of the wall and where they are protected from the prevailing wind.

According to your district, there will soon be other wild seedling plants growing in the wall: foxgloves, feverfew, wall pennywort, stonecrops, parsley piert and hart's tongue ferns, for example. With the extra height of shrubby lavender or juniper along the top, the total screen will be 1.5m/5ft high, giving solid and lasting protection to the garden, and even some privacy.

Left A brick wall makes an ideal support for white bryony, which holds tightly to it with corkscrew tendrils. Bryony grows each spring from a large perennial root, then turns yellow and dies down in the autumn as the poisonous berries ripen.

Below A sturdily built low stone wall with thickly mortared joints and space left along the top for a narrow bed of thyme plants. There are creeping and upright thymes here, and plenty of space to sit on the wall and enjoy their scent.

Fences and Arbors

Fences are cheaper and quicker to build than walls, and they give privacy, as well as being useful as partitions to divide the garden, as windbreaks, as screens to hide garbage cans or an ugly view, or as supports for plants. Low fences can act as a barrier around a garden bed to contain tall, leaning plants, and even a low fence of board or bamboo 45cm/18in high will give some protection from wind, and will hold the scent of the plants and shelter tender species. A stout fence can be useful as a barrier surrounding poisonous herbs to discourage children from picking the berries.

Fencing materials can be softwoods or hardwoods, wooden or bamboo poles, demolition lumber, such as old floorboards, rafters or even doors, wattle made from split branches of hazel or chestnut woven together, rushes or brushwood bound together with hazel strips, or the ready-to-erect sections of fencing sold in lumberyards and garden centers. They can be simple post-and-rail or picket fences to mark boundaries, or they can be close-boarded for privacy. For climbing plants which need light and circulating air, fences with a fairly open structure are best.

A permanent fence must have sturdy and absolutely vertical posts to support the horizontal boarding or rails. Treat the posts with preservative, having selected a brand that will not be toxic for plants. Dig good deep holes for the posts, at least 60cm/24in deep for a fence 2m/6ft 6in high, and embed them in concrete if you can. This is the most time-consuming part of fence building and is well worth any extra trouble. But don't forget that even the strongest fence will need some maintenance, and be prepared to paint wooden fences with preservative every two years to make them last longer.

Simple, less permanent fences can be very quick to build, but don't use an insubstantial fence to hold woody climbing herbs. It is extremely difficult to untangle sweetbriar or jasmine from a rotting wattle fence and to fasten them, undamaged, to a new one. For growing on insubstantial wattle or bamboo fences, or temporary archways or wigwams of bamboo poles, plant herbaceous climbers that die down in the autumn and grow from a perennial root each spring, such as hops or white bryony.

In this late fifteenth-century French miniature, St Elizabeth sits at the entrance to a tunnel arbor, teaching John the Baptist to read. A path leads from the arbor covered in red and white roses toward the garden gate, past symmetrical rectangular beds, to the open country beyond the garden.

The most instant herb garden fence or windbreak that I can devise would be a row of bamboo or hazel poles, 1.5–2m/5–6ft 6in high, stuck firmly into the ground about 15cm/6in apart and anchored to each other with wire or tarred string. Several white bryony roots planted in rich soil in the autumn or early spring will soon cover the poles with twining stems, making a delicate screen that should last a season or two.

Arches and arbors

A small wooden pergola in a paved town garden, or a simple archway of stout poles and willow covered with scented creepers, or an arbor with a bench or turf seat can all be built quite simply and on a scale to suit even small herb gardens. Prepare the wooden poles or planks as for a fence and sink the supporting posts deeply and firmly.

Take a chair to the garden and spend some time sitting in different places to plan the position of the arch or arbor. Do you want to face the morning or evening sun, with shade at midday? Would you like to sit hidden from the

Left Vigorous golden hops cover a latticed arbor, giving a heavy shade. The stems wither and die each winter but spring up again early in the year and climb fast. Only the female flowers develop into valuable, conelike fruit.

Below A simple wire arch is the foundation for an arbor over a garden bench and is covered with a mass of scented honeysuckle.

SIMPLE WINDBREAK AND ARCH

A simple windbreak made in a few minutes by pushing stout bamboo or hazel poles into the earth about 15cm/6in apart and linking them together with tarred string or wire. This temporary structure will last for a season or two and will protect the garden while a young hedge is growing or until a permanent fence can be built.

A garden arch or arbor can be similarly made using stout poles as uprights, with flexible branches bound in an arch between them with wire.

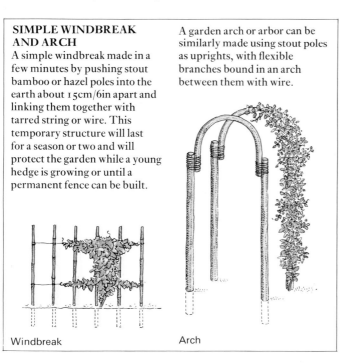

Windbreak   Arch

A stout post-and-rail fence supports an apothecary's rose and honeysuckle. The woodruff at the foot of the fence has just finished flowering and the tree onions (*Allium cepa* 'Proliferum') to the right are beginning to develop their strange heads of bulbils.

house or from neighbors? Which view of the garden do you most enjoy looking at?

Make a mock archway using two pairs of long bamboo sticks tied together at the top to form a V, with a shorter bamboo as the crosspiece. Look at it from the windows of the house. The eye should be led through the archway and to the view beyond. Make sure that no favorite part of the garden will be obscured from the house when the arch is well covered with creepers and flowers.

Climbing herbs for screens and windbreaks

Evergreen and deciduous honeysuckles (see page 77), climbing roses, the sweetbriar rose with its scented leaves, and green- or golden-leaved hops are all good climbers for the herb garden. Although hops die down each winter, they grow up to 7m/23ft during one season to provide a thick screen, and their vinelike leaves and long tendrils are very graceful. Buy only the female plant as the male doesn't bear the scented flower cones.

Several clematis species are flourishing climbers and

TYPES OF FENCING

An openwork wood trellis makes a good support for a twining climber like honeysuckle

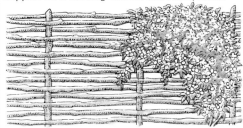

Substantial wattle fencing makes a good support for a twining climber like clematis

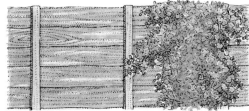

Close board fencing provides a support for a sweetbriar rose, which needs tying in

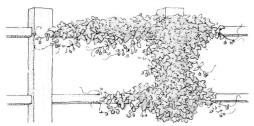

Post-and-rail fencing can be used as a support for a scrambling climber, such as hops

Far left Openwork trellis fencing is ideal for climbing plants, giving the best support and providing plenty of light and air. It doesn't act as a substantial barrier so use it within the garden as a dividing partition, or along the top of a firmer, closer fence or wall.
Left Close board fencing or lap-fencing gives maximum privacy and will last for many years if it is well built and maintained.
Below, far left Made from split and woven branches of hazel or chestnut, wattle is the most sympathetic and pleasing of fencing materials and blends in naturally among the plants. If well constructed, it will support most climbers.
Below, left Stout post-and-rail fencing should last for many years.

were once used medicinally, mainly as powerful irritants (though this use is no longer recommended). The wild traveller's joy, *Clematis vitalba*, is a rampant grower with looping stems that become fibrous and woody with age. The sweet-scented virgin's bower, *C. flammula*, and the herbaceous upright virgin's bower, *C. recta* (a low scrambler rather than climber), are more delicate growers. Both have rather fine, tangly foliage and small, white, sweet-scented flowers that bloom in midsummer (*C. recta*) and late summer (*C. flammula*).

Species of climbing jasmine have medicinal properties, including the hardy and vigorous *Jasminum officinale* with its neat leaflets and sweet-smelling pure white flowers.

A relative of the spindle tree, *Celastrus orbiculatus*, is a twining climber which is at its best in the autumn, with

Old lumber was used to build this short fence which acts as a windbreak, protecting the author's herb garden. Early- and late-flowering Dutch honeysuckle and sweetbriar rose climb through the slats and variegated pineapple mint grows beneath the seat. Woad and houndstongue flower in the righthand bed and the path is flanked by violets and dianthus.

yellowing leaves and brilliant spindletype seeds (formerly used as an emetic and treatment for skin cancers).

The root of the wild white bryony, *Bryonia dioica*, is a powerful irritant and purgative. Culpeper called it and the black bryony, *Tamus communis*, 'furious martial plants'. The white is a very pretty, hardy climber, 'twining with its small claspers' (Culpeper again), with pale green flowers and red berries. Like the hop, it dies down to the thick perennial rootstock each winter.

Seats and Benches

A seat, for me, is the most important structure in the herb garden. Ideally I would have two: one large and comfortable, protected from the wind, and with a good view of the garden; the other a low bench, hidden and private, surrounded by scented plants.

There are many possibilities. Good seats and benches of wood or stone can be bought or made and herbs grown around them, with a scented hedge or trellis behind. Position raised beds or pots to either side containing choice, tender herbs. Shade-tolerant mints can grow beneath the bench. Box can be clipped to make a comfortable sofa shape around a wooden bench, or a recess can be cut in an existing hedge to protect the sitter from the prevailing wind.

The sweetest scented herbs should be close to the seat. As it is likely to be in a sheltered, sunny spot, try growing the tender scented salvias: *S. rutilans*, pineapple sage, and *S. grahamii*. A bush of lemon verbena with its sharp citrus scent might stand the winter here, and also the curious stoechas and woolly lavenders.

A bench of turf or creeping herbs and flowers was a common feature in medieval gardens, according to contemporary paintings. The Virgin and Child are often shown sitting on a flowery embanked bench backed by a trellis of roses. Elsewhere, earth benches, like high raised beds, are shown in enclosed castle gardens, running the length of the wall inside the battlements. Here the inhabitants play games such as chess or on musical instruments or stand on the bench looking out over the countryside.

Herbs to grow on the bench

An earth bench suits a herb garden very well, and is ideal as a base for growing thick mats of creeping thymes and chamomiles. There should be one or two large flat stones or pavements set among them, for sitting on during damp weather or for setting down hot teapots. Take into account that chamomile holds moisture longer than quick-draining thyme, but that thyme can be positively dangerous to sit on during its flowering season as it will probably be covered with feeding bees. The beauty of the plants, the fruity apple-camphor scent of chamomile and the warm aroma of thyme far outweigh these disadvantages.

A section of the bench could also be used as a raised bed for flowering herbs – orris and bergamot, lily and columbine – or for containing invasive herbs such as the more decorative mints or tansy.

Such a bench can be short, with room for two to sit, or can run the length of a herb garden, backed by a wall, fence or hedge. If it is open on both sides, the bench can be used to form a boundary and the sitter can either face into, or away from, the herb garden. A long bench could accommodate some shrubby scented herbs (for example those described for growing along a wall on page 84), with creeping herbs and turf, and the occasional flat stone or couple of bricks laid flat in between.

A lady sits on a turf bench making a garland of red and white roses in this illustration from a fifteenth-century French manuscript. The tiny garden, surrounded by castle battlements, has many medieval features: a trellis, a tunnel arbor and low fences and railings around the herbs. In the foreground grow dianthus, lavender and rosemary, columbines and stocks.

A CHAMOMILE BENCH

Build a chamomile bench like a broad double wall, deciding first on the height and width that would suit you best – 50cm/20in would be a minimum width and 40–45cm/16–18in would be an average and comfortable height. It can be of any length and either freestanding or built against an existing wall. Plant thickly with Roman chamomile.

large stones

bricks (or concrete blocks or planks)

7.5cm/3in concrete platform

15cm/6in layer of rubble

BUILDING AN EMBANKED BENCH

Apply the same rules for building an earth bench as for a double wall (pages 85–86) although the containing walls for a bench need to be straightsided, which makes dry stone difficult for an unskilled builder to use. Brick or concrete blocks set in cement are easier to use, or planks of treated wood can be used instead but will not last as long. They can be quite easily replaced, and blend well with the plants. Stout stakes must be driven into the ground at intervals to support and reinforce the planks. Remember to consider the height of the bench and make sure it is comfortable.

When the walls of the bench are built, two-thirds fill the space inside with rubble and coarse gravel, then top with a mixture of equal parts of gravel, coarse sand and peaty compost. If mints or other larger herbs are to be grown, give them a pocket of richer soil. If you are growing creeping thymes, add a number of larger stones at the top of the bench to encourage them to spread.

A thyme bench built against a bank in the author's garden is fronted with bricks and railroad ties to contain the earth. Stone chippings and slabs of stone along the seat improve drainage and encourage creeping thymes to spread until they interweave to form a thick mat. Upright thymes, mixed with catnep, calamint and self-sown foxgloves, grow along the bank.

Above A sheltered seat is surrounded by scented herbs. Honeysuckle, mixed with ivy, climbs the wall behind it and pale hedges of santolina edge the path that leads to it.

Right A stone bench and stone trellis blend with the silver and gray-green leaves of lavender. Gaps have been left in the brick path where creeping herbs can be planted, and rambling roses give a rich scent.

Paved Areas and Paths

Many herbs grow particularly happily among stones and will self-seed or creep between pavements, concrete slabs or bricks. With such a large choice of color, foliage and scented plants to choose from, herbs can become an important element in the design of a courtyard, patio, terrace or path.

For an ordered or formal garden, herbs with a creeping or compact habit such as pennyroyal, the thymes and calamints are most suitable. For a more casual design, try planting a few of the larger species that self-seed or spread most freely such as feverfew and poppies.

Consider the color and texture of the paving material used. The feathery leaves of chamomile will soften the bland surface of concrete. The pink, long-throated flowers of calamint go well with russet-colored brick. The large, ribbed leaves of purple plantain make a bold edging for dark slate slabs.

Herbs that tolerate treading

The natural habitat of the herbs gives a clue to the most suitable species for growing among stones or concrete slabs. Those that survive drought well like the creeping thymes and the dianthus family grow in stony, sunny places; the chamomiles like dry sandy soil; and those that grow on open banks like the calamints will do well in gravel or among flagstones. These are all strongly scented and will survive a certain amount of crushing underfoot, especially the creeping lawn chamomile, *Chamaemelum nobile* 'Treneague', which spreads without flowering.

The creeping thymes are ideal herbs for growing in pavements, and usually survive the coldest winters. They are likely to be defeated by constant wet weather and stagnant damp, so it is important to make sure that the earth around their roots is well drained, with plenty of gritty sand and stones mixed in with the compost. There is an enormous choice of cultivated and botanical varieties, and plenty of choice in the color of leaves and flowers, and in scent. Select those which will suit best the color of stone used, remembering that the more subtly scented thymes need a windfree position and that those with powerful scents can be planted in more exposed places.

Other adaptable paving or path herbs are the wild yarrow with its faintly scented, downy leaves, the broad-leaved plantain and several garden forms of bugle, with leaves splashed with pink, cream or purple, or with dark or pale blue flowers.

In shady corners, creeping mints like the hardy pennyroyal or the tiny, less hardy, Corsican mint spread fast and have a refreshing scent. Wood avens with its small yellow flowers and shaggy seed heads will self-seed among stones.

Above An illustration from a fifteenth-century Book of Hours showing King René d'Anjou writing in his garden house. He is well protected, almost fortified, in his garden, with high walls, gates and a bridge across the encircling river. Steps lead past an embanked turf bench to a picket gate.

Opposite Around the old stone font in this courtyard garden scented herbs have self-seeded among marguerite daisies. Among the stone cobbles and flagstones grow clary sage (*Salvia sclarea* 'Turkestanica'), wood avens and wild strawberries.

The little wild lady's mantle, *Alchemilla vulgaris*, with its pretty pleated leaves, will bear some treading, but don't confuse it with the large garden variety, *A. mollis*, whose seedlings soon dominate any paved area.

Cultivating herbs among pavements

When planting herbs in existing paths or yards, it is important first to get rid of all weeds. This is the only time when I would use a weedkiller as it is almost impossible to pull out the roots of tenacious bindweeds, nettles and ground elder from under stones. Depending on the weed-

killer used, you may have to let the area lie fallow for a while, according to the instructions for the particular brand you are using.

When they are thoroughly cleared, fill the cracks or gaps with a mixture of coarse sand and light compost, scatter the herb seed and keep watering regularly until the seedlings have established a good root system.

To plant young herbs, ease their roots gently into cracks with a knife blade, then fill the cracks with compost and sand. Again, water regularly until the plants are properly established.

If a path or paved yard is to be specially built to accommodate herbs, it is a simple matter to leave out a brick or stone at intervals, or to leave gaps between pavement slabs. The herb-filled spaces can be irregular, or form part of a design, which takes into account the color, texture and habit of the plants.

LAYING A PATH OR PAVED AREA

It is always difficult to remember to make a path wide enough. In the words of an early eighteenth-century book on the theory and practice of gardening, 'In the business of design, a mean and pitiful manner ought to be studiously avoided'. Unless the path is to be a perch from which to do the weeding, or unless it is a series of stepping stones, make its width as generous as you can. Well-proportioned paths influence the character of the garden and give plants room to spread or allow for them to lean from their beds and soften hard lines of brick or concrete.

Concrete slabs or concrete laid *in situ* can look bland and toneless. Alternating areas of concrete with cobbles or

Left Regular spaces for creeping chamomile and thyme have been left at intervals in this broad brick terrace which runs alongside a large herb garden.

Below A stepping stone path leads across a bed of brightly colored and scented herbs. Creeping thymes grow among the stones and golden marjoram and purple sage are on the right.

FOUNDATIONS FOR THREE TYPES OF PATH

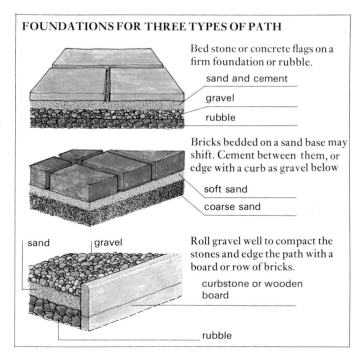

Bed stone or concrete flags on a firm foundation or rubble.

sand and cement

gravel

rubble

Bricks bedded on a sand base may shift. Cement between them, or edge with a curb as gravel below

soft sand

coarse sand

Roll gravel well to compact the stones and edge the path with a board or row of bricks.

curbstone or wooden board

sand   gravel

rubble

PLANTING HERBS IN PAVEMENTS
Bricks set in a herringbone pattern with creeping thyme planted between them (right); stone flags bedded in gravel with dianthus planted between the stones (center); the smooth surface of concrete contrasts well with the surrounding flints (far right). Bugle has been planted between the stones.

flints bedded in mortar, or with areas of brick or granite setts, will help break up the surface. The smoothness of new-laid concrete can be given a rougher texture by brushing it while it is drying with a stiff broom, or by giving it a very brief, light watering to wash the concrete from the surface and reveal the aggregate.

If you are building a path or area of bricks, keep them in place with an edging of some sort: with a line of bricks bedded in mortar, or curbstones, or with planks of durable, treated wood. Bricks are lighter than pavement slabs and tend to shift more easily.

All the time and thought spent on the construction of paths or paved areas is always worthwhile. Without a firm foundation, gravel will soon be absorbed back into the earth, and bricks and pavement slabs will tip and work their way into the herb beds.

A checkerboard herb garden
Use bricks and pavements in the herb garden to act as barriers between the more invasive herbs, which can present a problem in the herb garden. Contain the large mint family, and also tansy, soapwort, alecost and the big, medicinal

Right Single species of herbs grow in regular beds between a checkerboard of concrete pavement slabs. Divided thus, each plant is seen clearly and is easily accessible, and invasive herbs can be contained easily. Everlasting onions are growing in the center foreground with giant chives to the right and common chives behind them. On the left can be seen the potherb, good King Henry, and the large wrinkled leaves of clary sage.

valerian. Left to roam free in a mixed bed, they need constant attention to prevent them from suffocating their neighbors. A checkerboard pattern of concrete slabs with herbs between, and with slates pushed deep down around each plant, will contain them. It is also a useful arrangement because it gives easy access to individual plants. Or, as several of the invasive herbs can bear some shade, they can be planted in a narrow bed against a wall or fence, divided from one another with slates, stone flags or concrete slabs.

GROWING HERBS IN GRAVEL

Dig out all the weeds from the area to be graveled, rake it level and tread it firmly, then spread with a good layer of gravel mixed with compost, in the proportions of three parts gravel to one part compost, to a depth of about 5cm/2in.

Tread or roll the gravel to compact it as much as possible. As there is no proper foundation for the stones, they will eventually sink into the earth below and you may need to add a new layer of gravel from time to time. The gravel will need containing with an edge of concrete, bricks, or wood if it is not to escape onto neighboring lawns or beds.

Plant groups of some of the larger herbs that self-seed most freely and that will soon spread to make a dramatic display. Among them you could include perennials such as the decorative purple-leaved plantain, vervain, Jacob's ladder, fennel, perhaps the shorter-lived golden feverfew, biennials like foxgloves, woad and mullein, and annuals such as the opium poppy and borage. Creeping thymes and dark-leaved bugle are ideal carpeting herbs among the gravel stones.

Plant each herb in a little pocket of earth and make sure that the gravel stones do not crush any delicate stems.

These paths have been edged with pottery borders which prevent gravel from spreading onto nearby beds. Herbs and other scented plants – cultivated lady's mantle, corn cockle and foxgloves – have self-seeded abundantly across the path, and sinks and pots have been set about the garden to hold low-growing herbs.

Herb Lawns and Banks

MAKING HERB LAWNS

Grouped plantings of either of the two most hard-wearing herbs, thyme and chamomile, will knit together to make a lawn that is both scented and beautiful. Begin by planting a small area, around a seat perhaps, where you can sit and enjoy the scent from their trodden leaves. Don't attempt a large herb lawn unless you have plenty of spare time or a dedicated work force, as even a well-established thyme or chamomile lawn will need regular weeding.

Chamomile is the more hardwearing of the two; its apple-scented, feathery leaves grow thick and lush even when regularly trodden. A chamomile lawn is an unvaried green, but a thyme lawn of mixed, creeping species in bloom becomes as patterned as a Persian carpet.

The ground for such a lawn needs to be well prepared, and it is most important to get rid of every scrap of perennial weed, especially couch grass and bindweed. Mix the soil with coarse sand and light compost, then level it and tread or roll it firm.

If part of the lawn dies or becomes thin, or the plants grow too straggly, take small pieces of rooted thyme or chamomile from the thickest part of the lawn and plant as replacements.

A thyme lawn

For a thyme lawn, sow seed broadcast, water with a fine spray and keep moist until the seedlings are established, usually in about three weeks. When these have produced at least two sets of leaves, thin them to about 7cm/3in apart. If you are sowing several species for a patterned effect, then sow seed of each species or variety in groups to make bold shapes. There should be at least five plants in each group – any fewer and the patterned effect may be lost and the plants probably overrun by more vigorous neighbouring species.

Thymus drucei, with rich purple-red flowers, is a wild creeping species from which many of the cultivated varieties have been bred. *T. drucei coccineus* also has good red flowers and a strong habit, and both tend to come into bloom before those with paler flowers. The majority of thymes have mauve, lavender or purple-pink flowers. These include Corsican thyme, *T. herba-barona*, which has a slight caraway scent and strong, dark, spreading stems and *T. praecox* with long, yellow-green leaves and a loose, elegant habit.

The pink-flowered thymes may bloom slightly later. Among these *T. drucei* 'Pink Chintz' has soft hairy leaves and *T. d.* 'Annie Hall' is neat, with small bright leaves. The white flowers of *T. d.* 'Albus' barely rise above the yellow-green leaves; it is one of the hardiest cultivars and is especially pretty when it is planted among cobbles and pale flints.

Several creeping thymes have decorative leaves. *T. drucei* 'Lanuginosus' is a fast spreader and grows close, with small, pale gray, woolly leaves. It looks good mixed with brighter-leaved varieties, or against honey-colored stone. *T. d.* 'Doone Valley' has dark, rounded leaves, strongly marked with gold, and a delicious lemon scent. It will make low hummocks among stones. Among those with small leaves, *T. d.* 'Minus', *T. d.* 'Minimus' and *T. d.* 'Elfin' are all compact little plants with minute mauve flowers.

Before planting mixed species, make a rough plan of the lawn and use thymes with leaves of contrasting color and texture next to each other. One of the most useful is again *T. drucei* 'Lanuginosus' with its pale gray leaves which will set off dark-leaved *T. d. coccineus* or light-leaved *T. d.* 'Albus' beautifully. As with so many other woolly-leaved herbs, however, *T. d.* 'Lanuginosus' needs especially sharp drainage to prevent it from rotting during a damp winter.

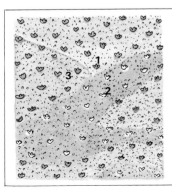

THYME CARPET
Use thyme varieties with flowers of different colors and leaves of different colors and textures to make a diffused pattern. The three used here are *Thymus drucei* 'Lanuginosus' which seldom flowers but has pale, downy leaves (1), *T.d.* 'Albus' with yellow-green leaves and white flowers (2) and *T.d. coccineus* with darker leaves and purple flowers (3).

A thyme lawn will need no clipping unless there has been profuse flowering, when dead flowerheads and stalks may become unsightly and should be snipped off with garden shears.

Chamomile lawns
The cultivar *Chamaemelum nobile* 'Treneague' is best for lawns since it doesn't produce flowers, thus conserving its energy for fast growth, and it has a prostrate habit so it seldom needs to be cut. Roman chamomile (*C. nobile*) needs regular clipping during the summer to prevent flowers forming. A lawn of Roman chamomile (*C. nobile*) can be sown with seed broadcast and the seedlings thinned in the same way as the thyme lawn (see page 99). However, the plants will need cutting down hard from early summer to prevent them from blooming. It is well worth

Left A small, lush chamomile lawn, thickly planted and edged with brick. In the foreground pelargoniums flower in a terracotta pot.

Right A bank in the author's garden, recently cleared and set at intervals with flat stones and planted with creeping thymes and, **below**, the same bank the following year. The thymes have become a carpet and the bank is clothed with upright thymes, foxgloves and viper's bugloss.

spending more money to buy young plantlets of *C. n.* 'Treneague' (which cannot be propagated from seed as it doesn't flower). Space the plantlets 10–15cm/4–6in apart.

GROWING HERBS ON BANKS

A series of gently sloping banks can be made down a steep garden, or low banks can be created on a level site as windbreaks and suntraps, enclosing and protecting tender herbs. Herbs growing on a bank are not only decorative, but are easily accessible for weeding and harvesting. A bank is also a good place for herbs if space in the garden is limited.

The bank will have a small microclimate of its own. Herbs that grow on a slope will have to be those species that withstand some drought, while those at the bottom will have plenty of moisture. Erosion is the main problem, and can be prevented to some extent by knocking blocks of natural stone into the bank at intervals to support earth and plants. These 'ledges' will give protection to small species that can shelter beneath the overhang, and their roots will be able to find a firm grip. A low stone retaining wall at the base of a steep bank will also help prevent erosion. See pages 83–86 for construction of walls.

A hedge of lavender or santolina along the top of the bank will help give some stability, though it will draw some of the already limited moisture from the bank.

Wait until the earth is wet from rain or from prolonged watering before planting or weeding the bank, as it is then less crumbly and less likely to slip. Use a narrow trowel, twisting it gently round like an apple-corer in the earth, to make holes for planting or for easing out the roots of weeds.

As plants become established their roots will begin to bind the earth and the bank will become far more stable.

Watch the way wild herbs grow to find those most suitable for growing on banks. The meadow clary, *Salvia pratensis*, and viper's bugloss, *Echium vulgare*, have rich purple-blue flowers and grow wild on dry banks. St John's wort, ground ivy, wild strawberries and violets grow wild on shady woodland banks. Foxglove, primrose and cowslip plants will self-seed freely. Large and creeping thymes are ideal, as are calamints and marjoram, and compact varieties of savory and hyssop. White and black horehound both withstand harsh conditions and drought very well.

Herb Hedgings and Edgings

Even the most informal herb garden needs a basic shape – a backbone – and this applies just as much to a small as to a large garden. It is easy to become so distracted by the plants themselves that planning is forgotten and the garden becomes a shapeless tangle.

Herb hedges can help shape even the simplest garden design. Since many of the shrubby, aromatic herbs are evergreen, they make good hedges and most are particularly amenable to cutting and clipping. Most are easily propagated and there is always a use for their clippings in potpourri or scented sachets or bags.

The long tradition of herb hedges is most clearly seen in the knot gardens that were popular in the sixteenth and seventeenth centuries (see pages 28–34), and the cool grays and soft greens of lavender, santolina and artemisia hedges make a peaceful background for the more dramatic flowering and seeding herbs.

Decide whether the hedge is to be formal (tight-clipped, squared-off, following a geometric pattern) or informal (freegrowing, rather blowsy, and only lightly clipped). For any pattern-making there must be some formality and control; for simple boundary-marking a hedge can be neat and formal or loosely informal.

Herb hedges may last for only four or five years before they become excessively woody, fall apart at the heart and need replacing, but they do grow fast.

CULTIVATING A HERB HEDGE

Cuttings taken in late spring should form a continuous low hedge within two years, and little container-grown plants put in 30cm/12in apart in the spring should become a low but bushy hedge by the following autumn. For an almost instant hedge, the plants can be spaced closer, 20cm/8in apart, and if by the following season they have become too close together, alternating plants can be transplanted to form a new hedge.

If a hedging plant dies during winter frosts, it can be replaced with a plant dug from one end of the hedge the following spring.

Cuttings can be set directly into their final position in late summer, using a line and spacing them regularly. If the soil is heavy, bed each cutting in a trowelful of sand mixed with a little compost to encourage rooting. Put some extra cuttings in a little bed or flowerpot to fill in any gaps later. Remember to keep them well watered and lightly shaded until they are established.

When buying container-grown herbs for hedging, try to get them all at the same time and from the same place, to be quite certain they will match each other. There are many variations of color and form, even within the same varieties, and it is irritating to find one piece of hedge growing differently from the rest. If you cannot buy enough of one type at a time then you could try making a pattern using different types.

As the plants will be unnaturally close together, they will need some feeding each year. Spread well-matured

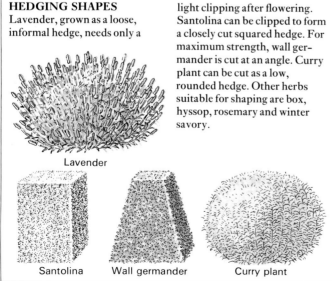

HEDGING SHAPES
Lavender, grown as a loose, informal hedge, needs only a light clipping after flowering. Santolina can be clipped to form a closely cut squared hedge. For maximum strength, wall germander is cut at an angle. Curry plant can be cut as a low, rounded hedge. Other herbs suitable for shaping are box, hyssop, rosemary and winter savory.

Lavender

Santolina

Wall germander

Curry plant

Opposite A large formal herb garden seen through a narrow doorway cut into a high yew hedge. Eight beds – four large and four small – are filled with highly scented plants and are clearly defined by low, well-clipped hedges of santolina. Grass paths meet in the center of the garden where eight standard honeysuckles are set in a circle.

compost around the stems in the spring. Remember, too, that other spreading plants should not be put too close to the hedge, as this can make clipping very awkward.

Keep clipping the hedge plants as they grow, especially along the top, to encourage bushy side growth. This business, which makes for a good dense hedge, has one disadvantage: it prevents light and air from reaching the lower branches, which may cause them eventually to lose their leaves and rot. By clipping the hedge at a slight slope, narrowing toward the top, and by keeping other plants at a little distance from the hedge, the problem will be lessened. This shaping will also strengthen the hedge, which will be better able to cope with excessive rain and snow.

Lay a piece of cloth or plastic alongside the hedge to catch the clippings, particularly if the hedge overhangs a gravel path.

A choice of hedging herbs

Lavenders make good, hardy hedges. Although they respond well to hard clipping in late spring, this prevents them from summer flowering, which would be a pity as they bloom for several months, attracting bees and butterflies, and scenting the garden. Let them grow freely through the summer, then clip well after harvesting the flowers in late summer, cutting well back to prevent the branches from flopping over and perhaps even splitting.

I would grow the pale mauve and deep purple-flowered varieties of lavender for hedging, leaving the pink- and white-flowered varieties to grow singly, since they tend to look unsightly as the flowers die. There are neat dwarf forms that make a low hedge, and the big, pale old English lavender makes a good-sized, billowing hedge, 1m/3ft high; Dutch lavender is slightly lower and has a more compact habit. Lavender hedges of mixed varieties can be very pretty but each will grow at a different rate and make an irregular outline.

If you have the space, particularly on a gentle slope or bank, try growing double or even triple rows of lavender bushes using dwarf varieties spaced 20cm/8in apart at the front and old English at the back, set 35cm/14in apart.

Rosemary makes a wonderful hedge, but it is not always completely hardy in cold climates. The upright varieties, planted in a sheltered spot, can grow 2m/6ft 6in high. *Rosmarinus officinalis* 'Miss Jessup's Upright' is a particularly vigorous grower with midblue flowers. Plant out 35cm/14in apart and trim during late spring and summer, leaving time for new protective growth to develop before frosts begin.

Santolina, or cotton lavender, is a most tolerant hedging shrub, particularly *Santolina chamaecyparissus* with its

---

HEDGING HERBS
These shrubby herbs are all richly scented and respond well to clipping, becoming thick and bushy. They are shown here in order of height, ranging from 30cm/12in to 2.5m/8ft. For a hedge 60cm/24in high,

you could use instead of *Helichrysum angustifolium*, either *Santolina virens* or *Lavandula vera*, for example. For a smaller hedge, 45cm/18in high, you could use a dwarf form of santolina, *Santolina chamaecyparissus* 'Corsica'.

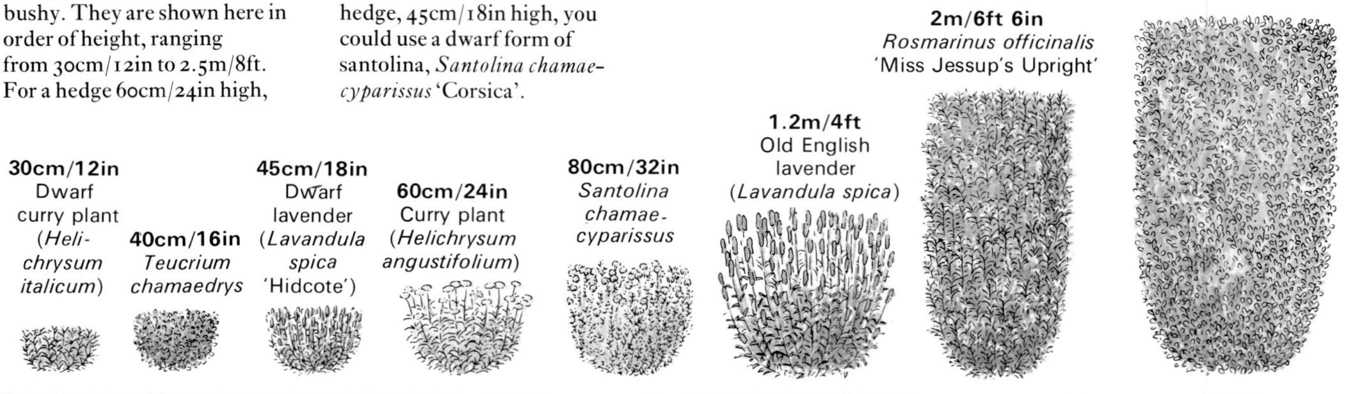

30cm/12in
Dwarf curry plant (*Helichrysum italicum*)

40cm/16in
Teucrium chamaedrys

45cm/18in
Dwarf lavender (*Lavandula spica* 'Hidcote')

60cm/24in
Curry plant (*Helichrysum angustifolium*)

80cm/32in
Santolina chamaecyparissus

1.2m/4ft
Old English lavender (*Lavandula spica*)

2m/6ft 6in
Rosmarinus officinalis 'Miss Jessup's Upright'

2.5m/8ft
Box (*Buxus sempervirens* 'Handsworthensis')

Above The hedge of *Santolina neapolitana* in the foreground, in the author's garden, has been newly clipped. In the background, a taller hedge of golden yew can be seen. Virginian skullcap and houndstongue are coming into flower behind the santolina, and white violets, white fox-gloves and thyme are in bloom.

Right A long border edged with southernwood and catmint.

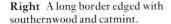

tough, coral-like, silver foliage. It can be clipped regularly throughout the growing season (though you will then lose the bright yellow button flowers), or trimmed like lavender in the late summer. *S. neapolitana* has looser, more feathery and graceful leaves. Both grow 80cm/32in high and have an aromatic, camphor scent. Set them 35cm/14in apart. The dwarf variety, *S.n.* 'Sulphurea', is very pretty and has lemon-colored flowers, and the less scented *S. virens* has bright yellow flowers that stand out against the strong green foliage.

Curry plant, with its pepper-scented silver leaves, needs a sheltered position but is generally hardy and grows up to 60cm/24in high. Set plants 30cm/12in apart and do not clip after midsummer as the summer growth is needed for protection during winter months.

However frequently wall germander is clipped, it usually manages to bloom during the summer. It makes a low (40cm/16in), handsome, glossy-leaved hedge, and grows well from cuttings. The flowers are bright pink. Set the plants 20cm/8in apart and keep clipping the terminal shoots to encourage bushiness.

All these herbs are reliably evergreen. Low, shrubby winter savory is hardy and long-lived but occasionally drops leaves during the winter. Garden thyme may not live as long, but can be clipped and makes an aromatic low hedge or border. Hyssop may lose all its leaves during a cold winter, but new ones appear during the spring. It, too, makes a scented, bushy hedge. Trim it quite hard in the spring, then wait until the rich blue flowers are over before clipping again. The dwarf form, *Hyssopus officinalis* 'Aristatus', has such a tightly compact habit that it is unlikely to need any clipping at all.

Two artemisias – southernwood and wormwood – make lush hedges during summer months, but be prepared to prune them severely in the late spring, although the twiggy stumps will be sadly bare for a month until vigorous new growth covers them again. Southernwood when pinched has an especially powerful scent, sweet and pungent – sometimes almost sickly-sweet.

Neither sage nor rue could be described as orthodox hedging herbs, but they both make good-sized, loose windbreaks up to 60cm/24in high, especially if they are well pruned in late spring. Green and red sages look good grown together (the variegated varieties don't grow at the same pace and are not quite so strong). *Ruta graveolens* 'Jackman's Blue' is particularly compact and has beautiful, steely-blue foliage.

Then there is the ubiquitous box. An extremely useful, hardy and dependable hedging shrub, box can grow 3m/10ft high. It can be clipped into fanciful shapes, and comes in variegated and dwarf varieties. Although it grows much more slowly than the other shrubby herbs, it makes a more permanent hedge. Dwarf box plants which are generally most suited to a herb garden should be spaced about 25cm/10in apart, and the leading shoots clipped to encourage bushy growth. The leaves have a dry, evocative scent.

HERBS FOR EDGINGS

Edgings of low-growing herbs may be more suitable for a small herb garden or for enclosing small beds. Around sunny beds plant hardy dwarf pinks, compact marjoram with its tight cushion of leaves, or chives (harvest the leaves regularly to keep growth steady and strong). Garlic chives are slightly taller and looser in habit, with a head of white flowers. Real garlic makes a good annual border.

The long-flowering varieties of *Viola cornuta* grow well in partial shade or sun; in dappled shade, grow little wild strawberry plants or the brighter forms with variegated leaves. Both prefer moist soil and will spread from the border onto the path, among gravel or stones.

Among the more decorative of the taller herbs most suitable as edgings are the flowering chamomiles (the low perennial or more upright annual varieties), and the neat, golden-leaved feverfew; both have daisy flowers that bloom through the summer.

There are several forms of golden marjoram, *Origanum vulgare* 'Aureum', which make bright edging herbs. One has large leaves, another has small round leaves, and another has pointed leaves tipped with gold. Since they all grow in spreading clumps they may need an annual trim in the late spring when the outer edges can be sliced off with a sharp-edged spade. If you wish the pink flowers to bloom each year cut the stems back as soon as flowering is over; otherwise trim back all leggy stems before flowering for neater, more formal edgings. (The leaves of golden marjoram and of many variegated herbs open green and only develop their bright colors with the first warm sun of early summer.)

Mixed box parterres and topiary in the *jardin d'ornement* at Château de Villandry. Viewed from above, it forms an elaborate page of Moorish calligraphy. This garden, and the *jardin d'amour* next to it, were laid out at the beginning of this century.

CULTIVATING HERBS

Each season in the herb garden is so different, and each month seems to be better than the last. The first flowering herbs of the year, the hellebores and pink- and blue-flowered lungworts, are especially welcome, standing out vividly against dark bare earth, or even snow. By midspring, the pure white star-flowers of woodruff have opened, and the hanging bells of Solomon's seal, strung along an arching stem. Colonies of broad-leaved lily of the valley and ramsons appear beneath the trees. Until they begin to flower, it is difficult to distinguish between them unless you crush their leaves: those of ramsons have a powerful garlic smell.

Ferny, aniseed-scented leaves of sweet cicely appear very early. Apart from the evergreens, this is the first culinary herb of the year, soon followed by purple shoots of lovage and glossy-green alexanders, bland bistort and sharp sorrel. In our garden there is a massed border of herbs that flower in late spring: blue-flowered comfrey, pink-flowered bistort and creamy sweet cicely.

The herb garden is at its neatest in early summer, and full of promise, with most plants still clearly seen and separated from one another. The leaves of fennel, lemon balm, motherwort and goat's rue are thick and glossy; southernwood and wormwood, recovered from spring pruning, are richly clothed with scented leaves.

By midsummer the garden becomes a riot, unless there has been some severe clipping. Most of the neat clumps will have lengthened into wildly leaning flowering stems. There is color everywhere. Self-sown marigolds and borage, bright orange and blue, have to be thinned out from the beds. Yellow elecampane flowers and sunflowers are taller than head-height. A hedge of wall germander is flowering bright pink. The garden is filled with scents, and banks of purple and white thyme are covered with bees.

The herb flowers of late summer and autumn are gold, tawny and red: golden rod, coreopsis and cone flower, bergamot and prince's feather. Among them are the steely-blue stems and heads of eryngo and stubby heads of jet-black poke root berries on brilliant red stems.

The beautiful, complex seedheads of herbs come as a surprise each autumn. The dried capsules of henbane develop in a one-sided row, like teeth. Tiny lidded dishes line the tall dead flower-stems of Virginian skullcap. Dark thornapple seeds are packed into large, prickly 'conkers'. Weld seedheads bend and twist crazily and there are yellow cartwheels of seeding dill.

Following the seasons, this part of the book takes each job in the herb garden in succession through the year, from preparing the ground and propagation to the final autumn harvest and the preservation of herbs. The last part of the book will, I hope, give a broad and clear idea of the choice of herbs to grow. The herbs are grouped according to height and color and to habitat, showing the way plants are adapted to shady, damp and dry soils in the wild, and how this knowledge can be applied to garden beds. The illustrated catalog which follows shows the tremendous range of herbs to choose from, each entry giving descriptions of the plants and notes on their cultivation and uses.

As well as the familiar herbs that are easily found as young plants or seeds in stores and garden centers and nurseries, I have listed unusual varieties that will need searching out. Look for them in specialist seed catalogs, in herb farms or in friends' gardens.

A spring herb garden with a bed of chervil in the foreground. Chervil seed will ripen by midsummer and can be sown then for an autumn crop. In the background are the first leaves of goat's rue, a border of chives and the tall leaves of Egyptian onion.

A Guide to Growing and Using Herbs

PREPARING THE GROUND

Most herbs are tougher and more resistant to disease than other garden plants, and are often able to survive and flourish in poor, thin soil, though bad drainage may defeat them. Those that grow wild on stony ground and are adapted to warm, dry conditions find it particularly hard to cope with cold, waterlogged soil. Their roots may become weakened, and they will then fall prey to molds and disease.

If the weather is reasonably dry, early spring is the best time to tackle and improve heavy soil. Ideally, herbs like a lightly enriched open soil; that is a soil that is coarse enough to contain air and fine enough to retain some water and which has sufficient nutrients to encourage steady, sturdy growth. Excessive feeding may result in too lush a growth for the nature of the plant, which not only weakens it, but also reduces the strength of its scent and flavor and the potency of its action.

Raised or mounded beds are especially suited to growing herbs on heavy clay soil, as the drainage is then more easily controlled and the lighter soil and larger surface area means that the earth will warm more quickly and also a little earlier in the year. A slight tilt toward the south will increase the warmth. Raised, narrow beds mean that access is easy for cultivation and harvesting, and the soil doesn't become compacted by treading. This method is not so suitable in areas of very low rainfall, where the earth may dry out too quickly.

Improving heavy soil

If you are faced with sticky, intractable clay, tackle the problem piece by piece. This will be made all the easier if you cultivate in small, easily accessible beds. In extreme cases, where the soil is very waterlogged, it may be worth laying drainage pipes or digging ditches at the lowest points in the garden and filling them with rubble, or spreading a layer of clinkers beneath each bed. Generally, the structure of the soil can be steadily and radically improved by adding bulky organic compost, straw-based manure and peat.

If the compost and manure are well rotted, it is best to

Top A herb garden in late spring. Thyme grows between the stepping stones with strawberries, fennel, sorrel, lovage and flowering rocket on the far side, and feverfew, comfrey and wormwood in the foreground.

Above The same garden at the height of summer.

dig or fork them in during the early spring, so that the nutrients are not washed down beyond reach of the herb roots by winter rains. If they have a stringy consistency, they are best applied in the autumn so that they can rot during the winter, which also helps aerate the soil. Both compost and manure attract earthworms, which play such a large part in helping to mix, enrich and lighten soil.

Peat bulks out and lightens heavy soils effectively, but it contains few nutrients and may make the soil slightly acid if used in great quantity.

On heavy acid soils, occasional applications of ground limestone will not only benefit most herbs and accelerate the breakdown of organic matter but are also thought to improve soil structure. Limestone should not be added at the same time as manure, and should be used in small quantities only, in early autumn. Leave it to lie for several months before digging in and preparing the soil for spring planting. Ashes from wood or peat fires also contain calcium and are beneficial.

PROPAGATION

Whether planning a new garden, or restocking and re-shaping an established one, spring is the time for choosing seed, for dividing and thinning old plants and, in late spring, for taking softwood cuttings.

Sowing seed

With a heated greenhouse, seed-sowing can begin early. Otherwise, for most of us, it is a matter of resisting the temptation that comes with the first fine spring days, and waiting until mid- or late spring before sowing seed, when the soil is thoroughly warmed.

Germinating seed indoors or in a warm greenhouse, in trays, peat pots, or soil or peat blocks has advantages. These are that tender herbs get an early start (important in cold climates with only a short frost-free season); that cropping can begin early; and that when seeds are precious or few they will be protected from outdoor pests and accidents. In a small garden there is the extra advantage of space-saving; seeds germinated indoors can be thinned out and the surplus seedlings given away.

The main disadvantage is that the germinating seed and seedlings require daily attention. Another disadvantage is that some herbs react particularly badly to transplanting and are best germinated where they are to grow throughout the season. Particularly sensitive to transplanting are those umbellifers that need to be prevented from flowering for as long as possible so that they produce good crops of leaves, such as chervil, parsley, coriander, dill, anise and cumin. Any root disturbance is likely to hurry them into premature flowering.

PROPAGATION INDOORS

soil blocks

seed flat

peat pots

Left Sow seed in flats, blocks or pots, in fine potting mix or a sterilized mixture of earth and sand.

Right Cover with a thin sprinkling of earth and water well (1). Cover seed tray with a sheet of glass or place the tray inside a polyethylene bag to keep a moist atmosphere. Lay newspaper over to exclude all light (2). As soon as the first signs of seedlings appear (3), remove all coverings and expose to light and air. Prick out well-developed seedlings into pots (4).

Use commercial potting mix, or a sterilized mixture of earth and sand to fill seed flats or, for least root disturbance, little peat pots.

Moisten the mix and sow the seed very thinly. If the seedlings grow too closely their delicate threadlike roots will tangle and break when they are pricked out.

Cover the seeds with potting mix or with the earth and sand mix. If the seeds are small, like marjoram seed, then only a light sprinkling of the mix will do. Larger seed, such as that of borage, will need a deeper covering.

Water the potting mix or soil covering lightly, using a fine rosed watering can, then cover first with glass or place in polyethylene bags to conserve the moisture, and then cover with newspaper to exclude all light. Put in a heated greenhouse or warm place in the house, perhaps near a stove, boiler or radiator.

Check the seed flats each day to watch for the first tiny shoots, and as soon as they appear remove the newspaper and bring the flats into a light and slightly cooler place. It is important to watch for these first signs, as otherwise you will suddenly find yourself with a flat filled with pale, bending, etiolated seedlings. (If this should happen, they may recover if you prick them out into another seed flat or into pots, bury half the limp stem in the potting mix and firm the soil well around each plant.)

Seedlings in peat pots or in peat blocks are left to grow on; those in seed flats will need to be thinned and pricked out. Handle them very lightly as any damage to the tender stems will encourage fungus or disease. Keep them in a light, cool but frost-free place until the ground is sufficiently warmed up outside for planting out.

The choice of what to sow indoors is a personal one. For myself, I sow sweet basil, sweet marjoram (and any other tender marjorams), and summer savory as early culinary herbs; any other interesting annuals such as pheasant's eye, safflower, flax, fenugreek, thornapple and henbane (these last two may also be sown at the end of the previous summer), and perennials for which I have only a limited number of seeds.

Sowing outdoors can begin as soon as the frosts are over and the ground is dry enough for the soil to be crumbly. If there is constant rain then spread plastic bags over the seed bed and weight them down at each corner. This method should allow the wind in but keep the rain out. In a few days the ground will be sufficiently dry for sowing to begin.

Rake the soil to a fine tilth, mark out drills, water them lightly and sow the seed thinly. If it is very difficult to break down lumpy soil, spread a layer of peat and light compost along the drill as a bed for the seeds, which will give them a better start. Mark each row clearly. By covering the drills with single cloches, or a plastic tunnel cloche after sowing, the seeds will be given an especially good start and will also be protected from late frosts. If you wish to grow some annuals in rows or blocks, use this method to sow, for example, coriander, dill, cumin and anise, and the biennial, caraway. (Do not use plastic cloches near the site of the garden bonfire; any hot, sparking debris might burn holes in the plastic.)

Hardy perennial herbs, such as thyme and pot marjoram, will flourish when sown outdoors. Thin them early, giving each one plenty of space to develop, and move the strong

PROPAGATION OUTDOORS

Rake the soil until it is fine and crumbly and draw a shallow drill (1). Water it well (2) and sow seed thinly (3). Cover lightly with fine soil and mark the seed bed.

Cover with a cloche if possible to hasten germination (4).

little plants to their permanent positions by late summer.

Many herbs self-seed well. Dill, borage, opium poppy and feverfew are especially prolific, and parsley, fennel, caraway, chervil and angelica can generally be relied upon to spread their own seed.

Root division

The most straightforward method of propagation is by dividing roots during the plant's dormant period, either in spring or autumn or in winter if the weather is mild. It is a method suitable for many herbaceous perennials such as monkshood, alkanet, marsh mallow and the chamomiles; herbs with creeping roots such as the mints, bergamot, woodruff and soapwort, and bulbous chives and everlasting onions. It will also check the spread of the most invasive herbs.

Dig up the plant and gently separate the roots or pry the bulbs apart. Some thick roots, such as those of lovage, may need slicing apart with a sharp knife. Plant the separated roots out in their new positions.

Root division will also prolong the life of old herbaceous herb plants that have begun to rot in the center of their crowns. Discard this center and plant out the healthy roots that are around the edge of the clump.

Softwood cuttings

Softwood cuttings are best taken in late spring or early summer. Many aromatic, shrubby herbs are easily propagated by this method: lavender, rosemary, sage, curry plant and santolina, for instance.

Choose a vigorous new shoot, 6–10cm/$2\frac{1}{2}$–4in long, that has no flower buds, and pull or cut it from the woody stem. Including a small piece of 'heel' of the harder bark seems to help the cutting take well. Dip the stem or heel in

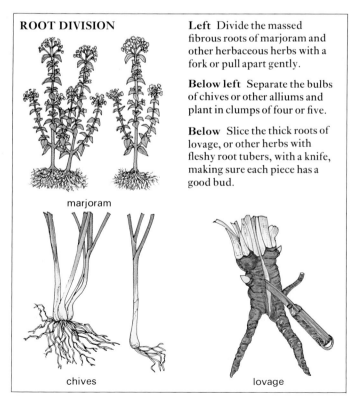

ROOT DIVISION

Left Divide the massed fibrous roots of marjoram and other herbaceous herbs with a fork or pull apart gently.

Below left Separate the bulbs of chives or other alliums and plant in clumps of four or five.

Below Slice the thick roots of lovage, or other herbs with fleshy root tubers, with a knife, making sure each piece has a good bud.

marjoram

chives

lovage

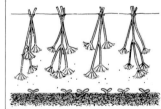

SPREADING UMBELLIFEROUS HERB SEED

Self-seeding herbs such as parsley, chervil and coriander can be encouraged to spread their seed onto dressed ground. String up heads of almost ripe seeds so that they hang upside down a few inches clear of the ground and drop their seed naturally.

TAKING A SOFTWOOD CUTTING

Select a soft-stemmed non-flowering twig and pull this from the parent plant. The cutting will take more easily if it has a heel attached – a sliver of bark from the parent stem Remove lower foliage from the cutting stem before pressing firmly into fine earth in a flower-pot. Several cuttings can be placed around the edge of each pot. Water well and stand in a shady place. Cover with a polyethylene bag to conserve moisture and hasten germination.

cuttings around edge of polyethylene-covered pot

heel of harder bark

hormone rooting powder if you wish, though most herbs will root without it.

Strip off the lowest leaves and push the cuttings around the edge of a flower pot, about four to a medium pot, firming the soil around them. This soil can either be a commercial potting mixture or garden earth, lightened and opened up with a 50 per cent addition of sand.

Water the cuttings well and set the pots on a shady windowsill indoors, or outside in the light shade cast by a hedge or shrub. A plastic bag fastened over the top of the pot will help conserve moisture and thus hasten the process, but this must be removed regularly to allow fresh air to circulate around the cuttings. When new growth appears, the roots will have developed. Move to a lighter position and plant out when well established.

It is also possible simply to push softwood cuttings into the shaded earth beneath the parent bush, remembering to keep them well watered, and then digging them up to replant once new growth has formed.

Semihardwood cuttings

Semihardwood cuttings are taken in early autumn. They are the longer shoots of the season's growth that are not yet quite woody, up to 30cm/12in long, with a small heel attached. The method is suitable for rosemary, lemon verbena, bay and myrtle, among other shrubby herbs.

Follow the instructions for softwood cuttings. Set the cuttings in a well-protected position outdoors, preferably under glass. They will develop roots very slowly, but by spring they should be producing strong new growth.

In a small garden herbs and cottage garden flowers grow together. Opium poppies, foxgloves and borage have self-seeded across paths and beds, golden thyme and golden marjoram cover the walls and low sinks hold sedums and lady's mantle.

PROPAGATING HERBS

Root division in spring is slightly preferable to autumn, but autumn is also satisfactory. Many herb seeds are oily and are best sown as soon as they are ripe, although they may germinate satisfactorily the following year. These seeds are indicated by noting them 'fresh'.

MIDSPRING

Sow under glass	basil, chervil, dill, marjoram, summer savory, sunflower
Layering	sage
Division of roots	American hellebore, bergamot, betony, bistort, calamints, catmint, comfrey, costmary, elecampane, fennel, goat's rue, lady's mantle, lemon balm, lovage, lungwort, marjoram, mints, monkshood, muskmallow, onion family, poke root, Roman chamomile, sea holly, sweet cicely, tansy, vervain, violet, white horehound, wintergreen, yarrow

LATE SPRING

Sow seed in open ground	anise, agrimony, bergamot, betony, borage, broom, calamints, caraway, catmint, chamomiles, cloud plant, coriander, cumin, curry plant, dill, elecampane, evening primrose, fennel, feverfew, fenugreek, flax, foxglove, houndstongue, hyssop, lemon balm, marjoram, meadowsweet, melilot, monkshood, mullein, muskmallow, onion family, orach, parsley, pinks/carnations, poke root, pot marigold, rocket, rosemary, rue, salad burnet, savories, sea holly, sunflower, tansy, thornapple, thymes, vervain, violet, white horehound, wintergreen, wood lavender

EARLY SUMMER

Sow seed in open ground	chicory, clary sage, meadow saffron (fresh), purslane, wallflower, weld
Softwood cuttings	curry plant, garden sage, lavender, pelargonium, rosemary, santolina, wall germander

MIDSUMMER

Sow seed in open ground	angelica (fresh), cowslip (fresh), daphne (fresh), hellebores (fresh),

Midsummer continued	marshmallow, melilot, pasque flower (fresh), rocket, woodruff (fresh)
Semihardwood cuttings	artemisia, bay, broom, curry plant, goat's rue, hyssop, lemon verbena, myrtle, pelargoniums, rosemary, rue, santolinas, thymes (shrubby varieties), wall germander
Division of corms	meadow saffron
Division of roots	thymes (creeping varieties)
Layering	calamints, hyssop, marjorams (perennials), pennyroyal, pinks/carnations, roses, sweet gale, thymes, winter savory

LATE SUMMER

Sow seed in open ground	burdock (fresh), caraway, chervil (fresh), henbane, honeysuckle (fresh), houndstongue, lovage (fresh), mandrake (fresh), parsley, poke root, sweet cicely (fresh), teazel, viper's bugloss, weld
Semihardwood cuttings	daphne, garden sage, lavender, winter savory
Division of roots	woodruff

EARLY AUTUMN

Sow seed in open ground	juniper (fresh), pot marigold, sweet gale (fresh)
Hardwood cuttings	bay, honeysuckle, roses
Division of roots	good King Henry, hellebores, licorice, meadowsweet, Roman chamomile (offsets), tarragon, valerian
Layering	wintergreen

LATE AUTUMN

Root cutting	mullein, yellow gentian

Layering

Many herbs spread naturally in the wild by layering, forming little clusters of roots wherever their stems come into contact with the ground. This process can be stimulated artificially by stapling the stem down and keeping the surrounding earth fairly moist until the roots are well developed, then cutting the new shoot from its parent.

Layer herbs during the growing season, from early to late summer; new roots should form within two months. Among the herbs that respond most readily to this method are the thymes, marjorams and sages, calamint, winter savory, hyssop, pennyroyal and clove carnation.

A variation of this type of propagation can be used for large old sage plants which develop woody stems with new growth only at the tips. Make an earth mound over the plant, leaving the new tips protruding. When roots have formed along the woody stem below the new growth, cut this part off the old stem and plant out. In this way, you can usually produce at least twenty vigorous new plants from one bush.

LAYERING HERB STEMS
Some herbs, such as thyme, have stems that root naturally when they come into contact with soft earth. Stapling the stem to the ground will stimulate the rooting process.

Old sage plants become woody, with bare stems with new growth at the top. Propagate new plants by mounding earth over the bush, leaving the tips protruding. The stems will produce roots.

low, flexible stems stapled down

leggy stems

a rooted stem

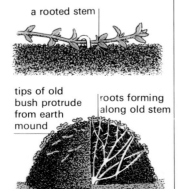

tips of old bush protrude from earth mound

roots forming along old stem

Planting out

When planting out young herb plants, or divisions or cuttings of plants in spring, it is always difficult to judge how much space is needed for each plant. Some perennials such as wormwood or southernwood, or annuals such as borage, melilot or prince's feather, can grow much larger and faster than expected and overwhelm smaller herbs that have been planted too close to them. On the other hand, many perennials such as fennel, licorice or sea holly may take several years to reach their full size. In this case, fill the space around young specimens with annuals.

Planting distance is a matter of experience – I still crowd my herbs far too closely – but it is always worth checking the size of mature herbs carefully before planting out seedlings. Remember, too, that those herbs with plenty of space to spread their roots and branches are the ones that will reach their full potential and finally make the most handsome shape.

GROWING HERBS UNDER GLASS

The growing season for herbs can begin earlier and end later if they have some form of protection from the cold. For culinary herbs and some of the most pleasant tisane herbs this is well worth while. Also, young seedlings and tender herbs such as basil will grow far better when sheltered from cold winds.

Cloches

Even during the coldest spring weather it is surprising how effectively a glass or polyethylene cloche, or a polyethylene tunnel, warms the soil. Set the cloches out at least a week before sowing the seed to warm the earth. By this time, the earth will be very dry, so lift the cloches and water the area thoroughly before making drills and sowing seed. Water the seed, cover the seed bed again and continue to water from time to time. The plastic or glass will hold in the moisture and create a damp atmosphere to encourage germination. Once the seedlings are up, lift the cloche, or the sides of the tunnel, occasionally to allow fresh air to circulate. (Large cloches give better circulation.)

Once strong plants have developed, and when the weather has become warmer and all danger of frost has passed, remove the cloches altogether. (In cold areas I would make an exception for sweet basil, which grows best if it is protected throughout the summer.)

Before frosts begin in the autumn, set cloches over the herbs again. Parsley, chervil, rocket and sorrel should then continue to produce some leaves throughout the winter, and mint, chives, coriander, cumin, basil, sweet marjoram, summer savory and purslane will continue to produce growth for a few weeks on into the winter.

The greenhouse

An unheated greenhouse is a real boon in the spring for protecting flats of young seedlings from frost and winds until the weather is warm enough for planting them out in the garden. Our own small greenhouse is packed with seed flats of herb and salad plants then. As soon as the frosts are over, herbs and salads are planted out and the greenhouse is filled with tomato plants interplanted with basil and with *Tagetes*, which are most effective against whitefly, the greenhouse scourge (see page 53). The tomatoes are mulched and watered with comfrey and stinging nettle fertilizer (see page 122).

In the autumn, when the tomatoes and basil are harvested (and bottled together), clumps of chives and runners of culinary mint and peppermint are planted in the greenhouse for winter flavorings and tisanes.

CLIPPING AND TRAINING

Most herbs are untamed wild plants that, in their native habitats, would be jostling with other species for root-holds on grassy banks or rocky screes, and they will take advantage of garden soil and sympathetic conditions to spread and grow fast. They will also recover quickly and even benefit from clipping or pruning (as they would in the wild, from browsing animals), soon developing fresh new growth and a more compact shape.

The first herbs that need quite fierce clipping in mid-spring are shrubby, aromatic plants. Their woody branches must be cut back to encourage strong foliage on new growth, and to prevent straining and splitting later on in the season.

Southernwood and wormwood require the most drastic pruning, and should be cut down to about 15cm/7in from the ground. Hardy sages and lavenders, santolinas and

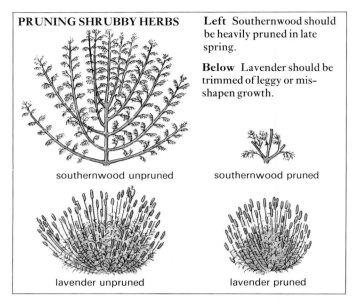

PRUNING SHRUBBY HERBS

Left Southernwood should be heavily pruned in late spring.

Below Lavender should be trimmed of leggy or mis-shapen growth.

southernwood unpruned

southernwood pruned

lavender unpruned

lavender pruned

curry plant need more careful clipping of old growth, though sages will benefit from fierce pruning if they are old and neglected.

Rosemary needs more delicate treatment. Avoid cutting old rosemary wood where possible. Some of the smaller woody herbs, such as garden thymes, winter savory, hyssop and wall germander, may need some trimming to help keep them healthy and vigorous.

Many soft-stemmed perennials will be developing flowering stems by early summer and some should be prevented or delayed from flowering to prolong leaf growth. Sorrel, particularly, will become rank and stop producing leaves as it comes into bloom. Caraway (if leaves rather than seeds are wanted), artemisias, and chamomiles (for lawns or paths), should have their flowering stems cut. Flowers of the annual salad herbs rocket, chervil, orach and fat hen should be nipped off. The lives of some early-flowering biennials, such as angelica and alexanders, can be prolonged by cutting down their flowering stems each year.

By midsummer, herbs such as perennial marjorams, mints and sweet cicely and salad burnet have flowered and begun to set seed, and their leaves will have become coarser and tougher. Cut them back, right down to their

A garden with the fresh growth of early summer. The low hedge of wall germander is covered with new yellow shoots, white violets are flowering and the dianthus is in bud. A young shrub of daphne is still blooming in the center of the bed. The southernwood (center right) and wormwood (at top of the picture) were both pruned hard four weeks earlier, but they are now thickly covered with lush, aromatic foliage. Between the bergamot and tarragon at the bottom of the picture grow two unusual foxgloves, *Digitalis grandiflora* (below) and the 'straw' foxglove, *D. lutea*.

basal leaves, and they will spring up lush and fresh. Some prolific herbs, such as comfrey and lemon balm, will give four or five good crops of leaves a season if cut this way.

Herb cuttings and prunings need never be wasted. If they are too old to dry for flavorings, or for scenting the house, save woody branches for aromatic firewood and use softer clippings on the compost pile.

Shaping herbs

The readiness of so many herbs to submit to clipping helps to keep some order in an informal herb garden. In a formal design, such clipping can be taken further, and shrubby herbs (those that are suitable for hedging) can be shaped into simple balls or cubes, providing punctuation marks or central points in curving designs, emphasizing corners, or flanking seats or steps. Box, though slow-growing, is the most adaptable and can be used for real topiary work. Sweet bay, juniper and myrtle respond well to clipping (bay is often grown as a neat standard). Low bushes of wall germander, winter savory, garden thymes and some artemisias, such as wormwood and its cultivars, can also be shaped.

Fast-growing climbers such as honeysuckle, hops and *Clematis flammula* can also be trained into formal shapes for the same purpose. Honeysuckle, particularly the early- and late-flowering Dutch varieties, can be trained into a standard or lollipop up a stake in a single season. Cut the side shoots, leaving only one or two stems to climb the stake, then twist the upper branches as they grow, around

strong wire that has been bent into a circle and fixed to the top of the stake. Herbaceous hops can be trained each season up a pole or wigwam of poles, or into more fanciful shapes, or to cover an arbor.

Supports

It is worthwhile setting supports against the taller herbaceous herbs early in the summer. Early supporting makes for good straight plants, which will not need to waste their strength by struggling against the wind; it also means that the plants will grow around the supports and camouflage them with their foliage.

Twiggy peasticks are especially suitable for herbs with untidy habits, such as *Achillea spp.*, dyer's chamomile, greater celandine and sea holly. Bamboo poles make longer-lasting supports. Stiff wires twisted into a semicircle and stem can be made or bought. These are pressed deep into the soil close to the plant at the beginning of the season, and then pulled higher little by little as the plant grows within the semicircle. On very heavy soils, a stake driven in with a mallet may be the only way to ensure a firm support.

MULCHING

In dry areas or on very well-drained soil, drought can be a problem during the summer. Mulching not only protects the surface of the soil from drying out, but insulates it and suppresses the growth of weeds. You can use organic or inorganic materials for mulching.

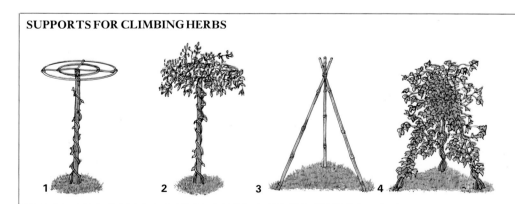

SUPPORTS FOR CLIMBING HERBS

1   2   3   4

A quick-growing honeysuckle can be trained into a standard by allowing two stems to grow up a pole (1); other stems should be cut off. Twist the branches as they grow around a circular wire frame (2).

A wigwam of poles (3) makes a good support for green or golden-leaved hops. The long stems grow fast from the perennial root each spring (4), dying down each autumn.

Calamintha grandiflora spreading in the shade of herbaceous herbs. This is the most ornamental of the calamints with large, deep-throated pink flowers and yellow-green toothed leaves that grow in pairs and have a deliciously fruity scent. Like other members of the family, it grows best in well-drained soil and will tolerate drought conditions. On the right grow the deeply divided leaves of musk mallow.

Organic mulching

When organic material is used, mulching will also improve the structure and fertility of the soil and encourage earthworms which will pull the material down into the soil. The only soils unsuitable for mulching are badly drained or heavily compacted soils that form a hard crust. Both these need to have organic matter dug into them to lighten and improve the soil (see page 109) before the surface can be mulched.

Mulching is an integral part of the 'no-dig' system, which is particularly suitable for the small, intensively cultivated beds in a herb garden. An indirect benefit is that the leaves of the plants are less likely to be splashed and muddied during heavy rain if the plant is bedded in a thick mulch. This will save washing the leaves before use.

Most herbs respond well to organic mulching, particularly those native to woodland and to rich or marshy ground, such as the mints, angelica and monkshood. Mulching will also encourage salad herbs such as sorrel, purslane, dandelion and corn salad to produce lush growth more quickly.

Mulching can be done at any time from early summer, when the earth has begun to warm up, and preferably after rain or heavy watering. The mulch should be spread around established plants or, most usefully, around young seedlings. It will also provide excellent frost protection for less hardy herbs, such as bay and lemon verbena, if spread during the autumn.

Cover the soil with up to 8cm/3in of light organic matter, quite open in texture, such as garden compost, spent mushroom compost, shredded bark, dried bracken or straw, or wood shavings. Lawn cuttings can be used, but dry them out for a couple of days before spreading them in a layer about 5cm/2in; if they are spread too thickly they

may heat up and damage young plants. Peat should also be used thinly as it is very absorbent and may hold rain or even draw moisture from the earth beneath. Make sure that there are no viable weed- or grass-seeds in any mulching material you plan to use.

Inorganic mulching

Mulching using quick-draining gravel or clinkers is ideal for herbs that are native to stony dry soil, such as the thymes, lavender, rosemary and sage. Its insulating effect will keep the soil warm at night and cooler during hot weather, and it will also encourage creeping thymes and chamomiles to spread across its hard surface.

HERBAL FERTILIZERS AND PESTICIDES

The interplanting of herbs with other plants, such as vegetables, for mutual protection or well-being has already been described on pages 53–54. For more immediate action against pests and disease in the garden, use the same beneficial companion herbs, either fresh or dried, as strong, health-giving and protective infusions or decoctions, to be watered or sprayed onto plants.

As a general rule, cover a double handful of fresh, or two tablespoonfuls of dried, herbs with about 1 liter/2 pints of boiling water and leave to infuse in a covered container for at least 15 minutes, or preferably all day. Strain and use the cooled infusion within the next few days, spreading the dregs as a mulch. If using the infusion against aphids or other leaf pests, add a teaspoonful of soft soap or mild washing-up detergent which helps the mixture adhere to the leaves of the infested plants. To deter underground pests, stronger infusions can be watered directly onto the soil.

Aromatic labiate herbs (members of the thyme family) make effective insect repellent sprays. For a stronger pest-icide, add a small quantity of more powerful herbs, tansy, wormwood, southernwood or feverfew, to the mixture. A light infusion of chamomile flowers or of couch grass

1 Pack an open-weave bag with leaves of comfrey and stinging nettles. Soak in rainwater for a month (**1**). Strain the liquid and use as a rich feed for developing plants (**2**). **2**

Make a strong infusion (**1**) of pest-repellent herbs (thyme, tansy, southernwood). Strain in a screen (**2**) and spray onto infected plants (**3**).

strengthens young seedlings and helps to protect them from the 'damping off' fungus that may attack newly germinated plants. An infusion of valerian root is said to attract and encourage earthworms.

For preventing or controlling attacks of rot, disease or insect pests use onion or garlic sprays. Either make an infusion of onion greens, chives, or bruised garlic cloves (4 cloves to 1 liter/2 pints) or liquidize the fresh greens or garlic with a little cold water, dilute and use direct.

Rhubarb or elder leaves, with their strong acid content, make good sprays against aphids and other pests, and they are usually available in bulk. Simmer 450g/1lb of leaves from either species in 1.5 liters/3 pints of water for 30 minutes in a covered pan (use an old one and avoid aluminum). Dilute with another 1.5 liters/3 pints of water, store in a cold place and use within a week.

The author's herb garden in early autumn. In the centre foreground are long, curving seed-heads of weld. Pot marigold, amaranthus, garlic chives and rose plantain are still flowering, and a shrubby southernwood and blue-stemmed field eryngo grow on the left. Angelica leaves turn yellow on the farthest side.

Comfrey is rich in potash, and stinging nettles are rich in iron; both contain considerable quantities of nitrogen. A nutritious and strengthening fertilizer is made by packing the leaves into a barrel or water butt, covering with water (rainwater if possible) and leaving for three or four weeks, or until they are decomposed. For smaller quantities, fill a small sack or open-weave bag with the leaves and leave them to soak in a bucket of water. Use the brown liquid as a feed for developing plants (tomato plants respond especially well to comfrey) and as a control against black fly and disease. Spread the rotted sludge as a rich mulch. Use the younger shoots rather than the older, lower leaves of stinging nettles.

COMPOSTING WITH HERBS

To turn a pile of rubbish into dark, rich, crumbling compost for the garden is a most satisfying job. By spreading or digging in compost, both the structure and texture of the soil are improved and plants are provided with more food, air and moisture. Adding herbs to the compost pile helps because they provide extra nutrients, and accelerate the process of fermentation of the pile.

Anything organic will eventually decompose in a normal environment; a compost pile speeds up the process by providing a much better environment, where the bacteria and fungi can do their work more efficiently. The bacteria need air, moisture, warmth and food, especially nitrogen and phosphates.

Make sure the container or retaining walls of the pile are well ventilated. The fibrous quality of much of the composting material will mean that there are plenty of air spaces within the pile, but if there is a quantity of fine material in the pile, such as grass cuttings, you need to push stakes into the pile at intervals to aerate it. Plant material generally provides sufficient moisture for the pile, but sprinkle the pile with water if it becomes too dry. Fresh green plant material and fresh manure, helped by strong brews of the most efficient composting herbs such as yarrow, valerian, stinging nettles and comfrey, will start off the heating process, which should eventually build up to a temperature that will kill most weeds (except perennial roots, which should not be added), and make a thorough job of decomposition.

Making a compost pile

Choose a sheltered site, away from drying winds and heavy rain, and fork the earth over. Ideally, the pile should be contained within retaining walls of wood, brick or metal, with gaps for ventilation, or with pig-wire or wire-network. The bottom layer should, if possible, be well-rotted compost from the previous pile, or fresh dung. Continue building up the pile with layers of kitchen waste, garbage, brown paper – anything organic can be used – plus plenty of garden rubbish, such as annual weeds and herb clippings.

One of the most valuable herbs for the pile is comfrey, since it is fast-growing and has nitrogen-rich leaves and plenty of bulk and fiber. Allow the leaves to wilt for a day to dry out excess moisture before adding them in layers to the pile.

Cover the pile when complete with planks or old carpets or corrugated iron, and leave it to do its work. For thorough decomposition, turn the pile once or twice, mixing the outer material into the hotter center. During summer, the pile should be ready within two months. In winter, it will take longer, up to four months at least.

HARVESTING

Although harvesting is traditionally associated with early autumn, herb harvesting begins in midsummer and continues through, with only seed and root harvesting as real autumnal jobs.

Herbaceous herbs like marjoram are available from spring to autumn, and evergreens like thyme throughout the year, but their flavor and effect vary tremendously according to the season. If they are to be harvested for drying or preserving, catch them at the perfect moment if you can, when their valuable oils are at full strength.

Leaves of aromatic herbs, dotted with oil glands, reach their peak just before the plant comes into flower. These include the basils, thymes, sages, mints, lemon balm and other labiates, artemisias, wild celery and lovage.

If either the whole herb or the flowering tops (that is, the flowering stem and upper leaves of the plant) are needed, collect them as their flowers are just beginning to open. Many medicinal herbs such as yarrow, agrimony, golden rod and St John's wort are collected for their flowering tops. Collect flowerheads with special care as they must not be bruised. They should be freshly opened, not overblown or marked. Whole flowers of mullein, chamomile, safflower and carnation are used, and the petals of marigold and rose. Cut lavender flowers with a long stem.

The only time seeds can be collected is when they are almost ripe, just before they fall to the ground. Cut the whole stem and invert the head of seeds, or seed pods, each into its own brown paper bag. Do this for all those seeds that are to be stored for sowing the following year, and

also for those for culinary use such as dill, fennel, lovage, caraway and coriander.

Roots are generally at their best in the autumn, when they are plumped out with food stored for the winter months. Roots that should be harvested at that time include dandelion, burdock, licorice and aromatic elecampane.

Although the root can be gathered in any weather, other parts of the herb should be harvested on a dry day, ideally in the morning, when the dew has evaporated but before the sun has begun to affect the plant. Unless you are hand-

THE HERB HARVEST

The ideal seasons are given here for harvesting a selection of some of the most useful culinary, medicinal and scented herbs, although many herbs can be harvested throughout the year. The best conditions for harvesting are on a sunny morning after the dew has dried.

LATE SPRING alexanders *leaves and stems*; angelica *stems, leaves*; bistort *leaves*; borage *leaves*; caraway *leaves*; chervil *leaves*; fennel *leaves*; feverfew *leaves*; good King Henry *leaves, young flower spikes*; ground ivy *flowering herb*; lady's bedstraw *flowering herb*; rocket *leaves*; rosemary *leaves*; salad burnet *leaves*; sorrel *leaves*; sweet cicely *leaves*; woodruff *flowering herb*

EARLY SUMMER alchemillas *leaves*; allium *leaves and bulbs*; basil *leaves*; bay *leaves*; catmint, catnep *leaves*; dill *leaves*; elder *flowers*; houseleek *leaves*; lemon balm *leaves*; lemon verbena *leaves*; lovage *leaves*; meadowsweet *leaves*; mullein *leaves and flowers*; nasturtium *leaves*; parsley *leaves*; pot marigold *flowers*; rose *petals*; salvias *leaves*; tarragon *leaves*; thymes *leaves and flowering herb*; violet *flowers*; woad *leaves*; wood sage *flowering herb*

MIDSUMMER agrimony *flowering herb*; angelica *seed*; anise *leaves*; chamomile *flowers*; fenugreek *leaves*; golden rod *flowering herb*; lavender *flowers*; lime tree *flowers* *and bracts*; marjorams *leaves and flowering herb*; meadowsweet *flowers*; melilot *flowering herb*; mints *leaves*; motherwort *flowering herb*; purslane *leaves*; St John's wort *flowering herb*; summer savory *leaves*; sweet cicely *seed*; weld *flowering herb*; white horehound *flowering herb*; yarrow *flowering herb*

LATE SUMMER bearberry *leaves*; bilberry *berries*; caraway *seed*; chervil *leaves*; coriander *seed*; cumin *seed*; dill *seed*; elderberries; fennel *seed*; fenugreek *seed*; garlic *bulb*; hop *flowers*; horseradish *root*; juniper *berries*; lovage *seed*

EARLY AUTUMN angelica *root*; anise *seed*; bistort *root*; burdock *root*; dandelion *root*; elecampane *root*; licorice *root*; madder *root*; marshmallow *root*; orris *root*; sea holly *root*; Solomon's seal *root*; sweet cicely *root*; sweet flag *root*; yellow gentian *root*

LATE AUTUMN chervil *leaves*; chicory *root*; corn salad *leaves*

ling very small quantities, gather herbs of only one species at a time and set these to dry before going back to gather others.

Cut the herbs down with a knife or scissors and handle them gently, laying them in a basket rather than cramming them in a bunch. Most herbs can be harvested several times in a season. Keep soft-stemmed perennials vigorous by cutting them back by about a third, and leave a strong basal growth on annuals.

Sort them through in the shade or indoors, picking out earth and weeds. Washing the herbs should not be necessary, particularly if they have been mulched, but if they are really dirty rinse them briefly and lightly and make sure they are thoroughly dry before tying them in bunches. An electric fan or hair dryer will help speed this process.

PRESERVING HERBS

Many herbs with aromatic leaves and a strong texture, such as sage, rosemary and thyme, dry well as they have little moisture content. Those with juicier leaves such as basil, borage or comfrey are not so easy and take longer to dry. If the drying takes too long, many of the properties and flavors of the herb are lost, so drying should take place in the shortest time that is possible without overheating or damaging the herb.

Freely circulating air is essential for drying herbs. They should be hung in a shaded place away from direct sunlight, which bleaches and reduces their properties, and, if possible, they should be given some heat.

Preparation

Tie long-stemmed herbs, such as sage, rosemary and artemisias, into loose bunches with not more than ten stems to the bunch. Mint and lemon balm, with their juicier leaves, should be tied into bunches of only five stems. Whole plants of bushy herbs, such as summer savory and thyme, can be tied in pairs.

Soft-stemmed herbs, such as woodruff, ground ivy and lady's bedstraw, the leaves of lovage, the whole plant of small herbs such as eyebright and parsley piert, and the flowerheads of chamomile, lime and mullein should be laid out in a drying tray or flat. If you are drying small quantities, spread the herbs on cheesecloth, or brown paper which has holes or slits cut into it, and lay this on a wire cooling tray (the kind of rack used for cooling cakes or bread), or on wire-network or a garden screen. Anything will do provided that it allows a free current of air to circulate around the plants.

Seedheads or pods should be left in their brown paper bags and hung in an airy place – not in artificial heat – for at least three weeks, until thoroughly ripened and dry and falling from their heads or pods.

Roots will need some artificial heat for them to be thoroughly dried. Wipe or wash them clean. Cut narrow roots, such as those of marsh mallow, into manageable lengths, and slice larger roots into thick pieces. Tie them into bunches or lay the pieces on drying trays.

Drying

Hang the bunches, or set the drying trays, in a well-ventilated, thoroughly drafty, dark garret or garden shed, or a shady room in the house, near an open window. Do not leave them in a small, steamy kitchen or bathroom. For a quicker and therefore more efficient operation, hang them in a heated cabinet with the door left open, or above a boiler. Best of all, dry them on racks in a very cool oven with the door open. The temperature should not rise above 33°C/90°F. This quick oven method is also best for drying delicate flowers.

For really fast drying, a microwave oven may be used. Small-leaved herbs will take about a minute; larger, juicier herbs about three minutes.

For dealing with herbs in large quantities it is worth making a drying cabinet. This can be a simple structure, designed to hold trays on which the herbs are dried. The trays can be made by stretching cheesecloth across wooden frames. Use a greenhouse heater or a small electric heater to provide warmth.

On a larger scale, a dark outbuilding can be used as a drying shed. A wood or solid fuel stove can provide steady warmth, and drying trays can be set around the walls in tiers, with bunches of larger herbs hanging from the ceiling.

As soon as the herbs are thoroughly dried they should be stored; otherwise, they may begin to reabsorb moisture. Leaves are ready when they have become brittle and break easily. Either store them on the twig or strip off the leaves.

A SHED FOR DRYING HERBS

The best method for drying herbs in large quantities is in a purpose-built drying shed with racks for loose herbs and a solid fuel or wood-fired stove to provide a steady heat. Drying trays, made by stretching cheese-cloth across wooden frames, slot into the racks in tiers. The more delicate soft-stemmed or large-leaved herbs, herb flowers and flowering tops are dried in the trays, while tougher plants and roots can be hung from hooks or tied to bamboo poles slung horizontally across the width of the racks. Air should circulate freely around the shed.

For drying herbs on a much smaller scale, just one or two racks will be needed. Use an electric heater to speed the drying process.

Don't crumble them unnecessarily. Flowers are ready when they rustle like tissue paper. Roots should have lost all elasticity and should snap, rather than bend, between the fingers.

Store the dried herbs, or the leaves, flowers or roots, in airtight jars or pots. If the containers are glass, or are at all transparent, keep them in a dark place. If the glass should mist at all, or if there is any trace of dampness inside the containers, take the herbs out at once and continue to dry them a little while longer.

Remember to label and date the containers. When storing a new crop, throw any remnants of last year's on the compost pile.

Herbs with fine or delicate leaves, such as fennel, dill, basil, chives and chervil, do not dry well but they can be frozen. Seal them in small plastic bags, just a few sprigs at a time, and freeze. Another method is to put the sprigs, chopped into smaller pieces, into the individual compartments of an ice tray, then topping them up with water and freezing them. Strong-flavored herbs can be preserved in oil, vinegar, syrup or brandy; many medicinal herbs are taken in this way, too. Basil lasts for several years when

PRESERVING HERBS
Glass jars hold mint and tarragon for flavoring vinegar, basil leaves preserved in oil and herb flowers in syrip. Sealed plastic bags contain sprigs for freezing. Chopped herbs are frozen in ice cubes. A box contains chive-flavored salt.

packed into a jar, mixed with sea salt and covered with olive oil. The leaves eventually blacken, but the flavor is usually rather good.

Tarragon and mint can be preserved in olive oil, although they will not last as long by this method. Traditionally, they are preserved in vinegar. Fill jars with their leaves and cover with good quality wine vinegar, white or red, omitting the salt. Alternatively, instead of using vinegar as the preservative, use the herbs to flavor it, a few sprigs to the bottle. Try using chive flowers which will color white wine vinegar a rosy pink.

Syrups are made either with herb flowers, such as elderflowers or carnation flowers, or with the stem (angelica), or with aromatic roots, such as eryngo, sweet cicely or elecampane. These can be further flavored with lemon or orange peel or spiced with cardamom, cinnamon, nutmeg or cloves. They will keep in the refrigerator for a few weeks, or can be kept for longer in sterilized jars.

Herbs can be steeped in brandy, covered tightly, and either strained after a month or left in the bottle. These are usually taken in small quantities as digestives or cordials. Bitters, such as sliced gentian root, need plenty of spicing to make them palatable. Add a little sugar to the brandy with the seeds of dill, caraway and anise.

Finally, here is one of the best ways of preserving onion flavoring and at the same time using up excessive quantities of chives. Chop the chives into short lengths, mix them with a roughly equal quantity of sea salt and spread them thinly in a large cookie sheet. Leave them in a very low oven with the door open until the chives are completely dry, then store them in covered pots. The strongly flavored salt mixture can be used to flavor soups, stews, roast meats and omelets, for example.

PREPARING FOR WINTER

By late summer or early autumn, growth has slowed down, and it is time for the final trimming and clipping of shrubby herbs and hedges. They will then need several more frost-free weeks to develop protective shoots against winter cold.

There are bound to be some winter casualties, so take semihardwood cuttings of precious or tender herbs now (see page 113).

In cold areas, pot up tender or half-hardy herbs such as lemon verbena, the more delicate lavenders and marjorams, Balm of Gilead, pineapple sage and the basils and bring them indoors, or into a greenhouse or onto a sheltered balcony. If they are growing in a sheltered position in a warmer area, mature specimens may survive the winter if their roots are protected with straw, or dried bracken. Other herbs that may need some protection when growing in cold, exposed places are French tarragon, southernwood and the less hardy thymes, particularly the variegated varieties. Cover the soil around young bay trees and myrtle bushes with straw to help to protect their roots from frost-damage.

For winter supplies of culinary herbs, plant rooted runners of mint and clumps of chive bulbs in the greenhouse, or, if they are to be taken indoors, in flowerpots. Leave them outside in their pots for several weeks in early autumn to become strong and well established, taking them indoors before the first frost.

Several special lavenders and rosemaries need protection during the winter. Fringed lavender, *Lavandula dentata*, which flowers in late autumn, needs to come indoors or into a cool greenhouse, where it makes a good partner for pineapple sage. Pale, woolly lavender, *L. lanata*, and the hardier *L. stoechas* can overwinter on a protected veranda or balcony. The white- and pink-flowered rosemaries are often less hardy than those with blue flowers and need some winter protection.

Growing Herbs in Containers

A wide range of herbs can be grown in containers of every sort and size on a balcony or roof garden or in a patio or courtyard garden. There is great scope for designing and grouping the herbs and for using containers in an imaginative way. Single plants of bright-flowering herbs grown in pots also have a useful place in a larger garden because they can be moved to fill temporary gaps in beds, and permanent troughs or sinks filled with a mixture of herbs can be used to give height in a garden and to act as focal points. However, all herbs in containers will need regular watering.

Drainage is also an important factor. The earth in the container will need to be enriched and may need some salts added in urban areas where soil tends to become acid.

Herb-growing on a balcony or roof garden may be hampered by high winds. Erect a temporary screen of fine network which will protect young plants from prevailing winds, and include in the design for the area a windbreak or trellis, which can soon be covered by a fast-growing honeysuckle.

Another consideration is the weight of the containers. Use lightweight pots and troughs of plastic or fiberglass and position them around the edges of the roof or to the sides and rear of a balcony. Check the weight-bearing capacity of both before you plan your planting.

With containers on firm ground – in a courtyard or basement garden, or on a patio or terrace – most herbs can be grown so long as their containers are sufficiently large. With invasive herbs such as the mints, tansy or comfrey grow only one species to each container. Otherwise, mixed plantings can be successful. Begin with a well-shaped tall or shrubby herb at the center, plant lower herbs around it and lastly plant hanging or leaning varieties to cover the outer rim of the pot.

You may like to mix bright-flowered herbs among shrubby varieties: marigold, bergamot and nasturtium all grow easily in troughs or tubs. Grow purple sage, silver wormwood, rue and golden marjoram for their rich-colored foliage.

For those with no garden but with space on an enclosed balcony or a sunny windowsill, herbs can be grown successfully in pots, troughs or boxes. By choosing suitable species that will tolerate conditions indoors, it is possible to have herbs for flavoring, for tisanes and for scent all the year round, with the added pleasure of watching them develop through every stage of their growth in a way that is seldom possible with plants in a garden.

The first thing to consider is the position of the container. Most herbs need sunlight for at least half the day, and some ventilation but no direct drafts. They dislike sudden changes in temperature, and the fluctuating heat and cooking fumes in a small kitchen will not suit them, nor will the hot and dry atmosphere directly above a radiator. An ideal indoor situation for a row of pots or a box of herbs would be on a sunny windowsill in a reasonably airy and slightly humid room or, failing that, on a windowsill facing east or west.

The container itself should be deep enough to accommodate the roots of the plants; 20cm/8in would be the minimum depth. Drainage should be especially good, so cover the bottom of the pot with broken crocks or stones.

HERBS GROWN IN POTS
An attractive group of various pots suitable for a patio or balcony. They contain lush herb plants – giant chives, lemon balm, thyme, sage and marjoram.

The soil needs to be richer than normal garden earth as the herbs have such a limited quantity to feed from and soon exhaust the nutrients. Either buy the balanced potting mixture that is sold in garden shops or make your own. I mix one half of spent mushroom compost with a blend of equal quantities of fibrous loam, peat and coarse sand or grit. Feed the herbs at least every six weeks during the growing season, using an organic fertilizer if possible.

Overwatering is always a danger with indoor plants. A good soaking once or twice a week is enough. Stand the pot in slightly tepid water until all the soil is moistened but not saturated. For the rest of the week stand the pot or tray on gravel as the dangers of overwatering are then lessened and excess water can drain off easily. If the atmosphere in the room is dry, occasionally spray the herb leaves with tepid water.

All indoor herbs should be cropped with care. Cut the outer sprigs for use and always leave plenty of vigorous growth on the plant.

As for the choice of herbs to grow, obviously very large herbs are generally unsuitable for indoor pots. Perennials will have a shorter life indoors, though they may flourish. Many annuals will grow happily to maturity indoors.

Of the culinary herbs, both the sweet and bush varieties of basil grow particularly well indoors. Coriander should produce lush leaves, too, for curries or salads, though the seedheads may not develop so well as those growing outside. As a perennial, fennel grows too large for indoor pots, but try treating it as an annual, sowing seed and cropping the 20cm/8in high young plants for their fine, aniseed flavor.

Bushy perennial culinary herbs, thyme, winter savory, sage and rosemary, should last for several years if they are kept trimmed and given a rich soil mixed with plenty of grit or coarse sand. Soft-stemmed perennials such as mint and tarragon may become rather damp and moldy as they reach maturity. Keep a steady supply of cuttings available to replace the older plants. A collection of mints, or just the basic spearmint or Bowles' mint, need a cool, light position or they will weaken and rot.

For onion flavoring, grow a clump of everlasting onions with their coarse, hardy leaves that survive the winter well.

Several herbs that are used for making delicious and health-giving tisanes grow well indoors. My favorite is lemon verbena with its graceful, arching, woody stem and sharply lemon-flavored leaves. Give it a pot to itself (25–30cm/10–12in deep), and don't worry if some leaves fall in the autumn – more will appear in the spring. One of the most useful tisane herbs, especially for winter colds and 'flu, is black peppermint which should produce leaves throughout the year indoors. This is a hungry herb that needs plenty of feeding – probably about once a month – and a moist, well-composted soil, though too much moisture will encourage a damp fungus.

Many scented herbs are tender and, while needing to be protected indoors during the winter, will be happy to stay indoors throughout the year. Among the easiest of all pot plants to grow are the scented-leaved pelargoniums. They take well from cuttings, need little watering during the winter, survive in a dry atmosphere and with only indirect light, and make good lush growth. Their flowers are often undistinguished, but the leaves have a great variety of scents and are used in potpourris and to flavor milk puddings, custards and creams, fruit jellies and preserves.

Some of the highly scented, tender sages make large shrubby plants indoors. Pineapple sage, *Salvia rutilans*, for instance, has leaves with a quite startlingly fruity scent and bright red flowers that bloom in the winter; it is easily grown from cuttings. There is also a tender lavender with long, rather drooping branches that does well indoors in a hanging basket or large pot. This is the fringed lavender, *Lavandula dentata*, with pale, soft flowers that bloom in the autumn and toothed leaves that have a scent reminiscent of balsam.

I grow several species of basil for their scent rather than for their culinary uses, though they are not especially decorative. Sacred basil, *Ocimum sanctum*, for instance, which has rather hairy leaves and a spicy scent, and lemon basil, *O. citriodorum*, with sharper leaves and a citrus scent.

All these perennial herbs become more vigorous and long-lived if they can be set outside for a while during the summer, especially if they are grown in porous clay pots and sunk into the earth where they can live a more natural life for a month or two.

A Guide to Choosing Herbs

HERBS FOR THE SHADE

A shady garden, or a bed beneath a tree or in the heavy shade cast by a house or wall, may not seem ideal for growing herbs. In fact, there are many woodland herbs, especially those with medicinal uses, that grow well in shade and are very ornamental and others that tolerate or prefer dappled shade.

Plants that grow in woods generally need to flower early, before they are shaded by leaves overhead and may not be able to flower for years at a time if the light is too dim.

This means that annuals do not stand much chance, and neither do those plants that depend on sexual reproduction. Therefore many woodland plants are able to reproduce in another way, by vegetative reproduction, in other words spreading by bulbs, creeping stems or runners. This is why in shady places there are colonies of plants, such as bugle, woodruff, pennyroyal and ground ivy, and the taller, pale-flowered valerian.

Food storage is important, too, in an unpredictable environment. Solomon's seal and lily of the valley have thick underground rhizomes that spread and form new plants and also store food; ramsons store food in their bulbs; hellebores and mandrake have massive roots for food storage, which also contain the most potent of their poisonous alkaloids.

So a heavily shaded herb bed will most happily contain woodland perennials. It will be at its brightest from late winter to late spring, from the flowering of the first hellebores and lungwort, followed by woodruff and violet, then wood strawberry, Solomon's seal, lily of the valley, bistort and Jacob's ladder.

A few other plants will flower later and prefer a more dappled shade: angelica and monkshood in early summer, and then the curious figwort and scrambling wood sage with its long camouflaged spikes of yellow-green flowers.

There is a great choice of ground cover among so many creeping, spreading herbs, and some, for instance, bugle and bistort, may need to be cut back or held in check. Plant one or two of the larger herbs among them such as the hellebores, valerian, monkshood, angelica, Jacob's ladder, sweet cicely and mandrake. Many of these have particu-larly beautiful foliage, which will be especially important once the spring flowering is over. Take this into consideration when planning the bed.

Herbs for heavy shade

Ajuga reptans, bugle
Allium ursinum, ramsons
Atropa belladonna, deadly nightshade
Convallaria majalis, lily of the valley
Galium odoratum, woodruff
Helleborus spp., the hellebores
Hydrastis canadensis, golden seal
Mandragora officinarum, mandrake
Mentha pulegium, pennyroyal
Oenothera biennis, evening primrose
Polygonatum multiflorum, Solomon's seal
Polygonum bistorta, bistort
Pulmonaria officinalis, lungwort
Valeriana officinalis, valerian
Viola odorata, sweet violet

Herbs for partial shade

Aconitum napellus, monkshood
Alchemilla vulgaris, lady's mantle
Angelica archangelica, angelica
Chelidonium majus, greater celandine
Digitalis purpurea, foxglove
Fragaria vesca, wild strawberry
Gaultheria procumbens, wintergreen
Geum urbanum, wood avens
Glechoma hederacea, ground ivy
Meum athamanticum, spignel
Myrrhis odorata, sweet cicely
Polemonium caeruleum, Jacob's ladder
P. reptans, abscess root
Scrophularia nodosa, figwort
Teucrium scorodonia, wood sage
Trillium erectum, birthroot

Herbs that tolerate some shade

Allium schoenoprasum, chives
Althaea officinalis, marsh mallow
Anthriscus cerefolium, chervil
Apium graveolens, wild celery
Arctium lappa, burdock
Ballota nigra, black horehound
Chenopodium bonus-henricus, good King Henry
Colchicum autumnale, meadow saffron
Digitalis purpurea, foxglove
Dipsacus fullonum, teazel
Eruca sativa, rocket
Filipendula ulmaria, meadowsweet
Galega officinalis, goat's rue
Galium verum, lady's bedstraw
Hyoscyamus niger, henbane
Hypericum perforatum, St John's wort
Lonicera periclymenum, honeysuckle
Malva moschata, musk mallow
Melissa officinalis, lemon balm
Mentha spp., the mints
Parietaria officinalis, pellitory of the wall
Petroselinum spp., the parsleys
Phytolacca americana, poke root
Portulaca oleracea, purslane
Primula vulgaris, primrose
Rubia tinctorum, madder
Rumex acetosa, garden sorrel
Smyrnium olusatrum, alexanders
Symphytum officinale, comfrey

HERBS FOR DAMP GROUND AND PONDS

Herbs that grow wild on river banks and in marshy places or water meadows have to deal with an unpredictable environment, and are usually perennial. Unlike woodland herbs, they are likely to grow tall and to blossom from early summer onward, often with bright flowers to attract pollinating insects.

Only a few of these herbs demand a watery or really muddy place in the garden. Grow them in a fairly sheltered corner, away from drying winds, and in a reasonably water-retentive soil. Most of them are happy in a dappled shade and will grow in spreading clumps or colonies and, as many are strong and tenacious, you may need to cut back their roots at least once a year. There are few flavoring herbs among them but most have medicinal or domestic uses and some can be eaten as salad herbs.

Three herbs are particularly suitable for a shallow pond in a herb garden. They should all be firmly planted in mud, with their roots submerged and anchored down with pebbles. There is the sweet flag, which is grown for its sweetly scented, crinkle-edged leaves rather than for its uncommon, curving flowerhead, and the yellow flag, which has elegant flowers in early summer. The bogbean flowers at the same time and is a smaller plant with intensely bitter leaves (much valued formerly as a tonic), and lovely fringed blossoms of a faint blue-pink. This looks well grown on its own against a darkly shaded background – I have seen it looking very attractive planted in old copper, against dark stones.

In a really heavy damp clay soil, plant comfrey and elecampane, two of the most tolerant of herbs. Both are large and grow in spreading clumps. In an acid, damp soil, plant sweet gale with its bitter aromatic leaves.

Among herbs associated with river banks are Virginian skullcap, sneezewort, fleabane (which spreads very fast in the garden) and water figwort. All are herbaceous and grow up to 75cm/30in high. Soapwort with pink flowers, lush leaves and lanky stems has a more sprawling habit. (There is also gipsywort, *Lycopus europaeus*, used in the past as a dye and a medicine, but it is a pest in the garden, its swollen pale-purple shoots spreading like wildfire.)

Taller herbs that grow wild in ditches, and on low marshy ground, include meadowsweet, hemp agrimony and valerian, all with fragrant flowers in early summer, and the taller boneset which flowers later.

Bistort and sweet cicely are among the first, and most welcome, edible herbs to appear in the spring, and they grow naturally together in damp meadows in northern countries. The broad succulent leaves and pink spike-flowers of bistort provide a good background for the feathery, sugary leaves and creamy flowers of sweet cicely. They grow well in dappled shade beneath trees in the garden or in an orchard.

Achillea decolorans, mace
A. ptarmica, sneezewort
Acorus calamus, sweet flag
Althaea officinalis, marsh mallow
Angelica archangelica, angelica
Eupatorium cannabinum, hemp agrimony
E. purpureum, gravel root
Filipendula ulmaria, meadowsweet
Gillenia trifoliata, Indian physic
Hydrastis canadensis, golden seal
Inula helenium, elecampane
Mentha aquatica, water mint
Menyanthes trifoliata, bogbean
Myrica gale, bog myrtle
Myrrhis odorata, sweet cicely
Nasturtium officinale, watercress
Polemonium caeruleum, Jacob's ladder
Polygonum bistorta, bistort
Pulicaria dysenterica, fleabane
Rumex acetosa, garden sorrel
Sanguinaria canadensis, bloodroot
Saponaria officinalis, soapwort
Scrophularia aquatica, water figwort
Scutellaria spp., the skullcaps
Symphytum officinale, comfrey
Trillium erectum, birthroot
Valeriana officinalis, valerian

HERBS FOR DRY GROUND

A rough, stony garden makes an ideal environment for most aromatic flavoring herbs, many of which grow wild in hot, dry places, along the mountainsides bordering the Mediterranean and in harsh scrubland. There, in scorching sun and hot, drying winds, wild thymes, rosemaries and marjoram, savories and sages, develop their volatile oils and powerful flavors. The oils are drawn from their leaves by the heat of the sun to form a protective vapor around the plant, and this, together with the often fiercely pungent flavor of the leaves and their spiky tips and leathery surfaces, repels browsing animals. The toughness of the leaves and their grayish colors help herbs to retain precious moisture that would otherwise be evaporated by the sun and dispersed by winds.

Bear this habitat in mind when planting these herbs in the garden. They must have sharp drainage, otherwise their roots may rot, and they should not be given too rich a soil or they will produce excessively lush foliage and may weaken and die. Imitate their natural environment by providing them with a stony, well-drained bed, in a sunny position, and by occasionally forking in some well-rotted compost – say, every two years. If the garden slopes, you could build a rocky bank for extra drainage, or grow the herbs through a thick mulch of gravel.

Other herbs grow wild in poor, thin soil along road verges: mugwort, yarrow, plantain and species of mallow, and on dry embankments there are teazel, mullein, viper's bugloss, evening primrose and the *Chenopodium* family. These tough, tolerant plants will thrive in dusty corners of the garden that might otherwise be thought unusable, such as around garbage cans or rubbish piles.

Herbs that grow along dry banks have often adapted to drought by developing long tap roots to enable them to reach for water. They include pasque flower, centaury, salad burnet, burnet saxifrage and foxglove. Other herbs, like lady's bedstraw, calamint and wild marjoram, have adopted a scrambling habit and many fibrous roots. Among rocks and over walls, wallflower and pellitory of the wall send long thread roots deep into crevices for moisture and anchorage, and houseleek and roseroot store water in their thick, succulent leaves. These all grow well on thin, fast-draining soil, and on walls and rockeries.

Aromatic shrubby herbs for dry, sunny soil
Artemisia spp., the artemisias
Helichrysum angustifolium, curry plant
Hyssopus officinalis, hyssop
Lavandula spp., the lavenders
Phlomis fruticosa, Jerusalem sage
Rosmarinus officinalis, rosemary
Salvia spp., the sages
Santolina spp., the santolinas
Satureja montana, winter savory
Thymus spp., the thymes

Herbs for dry places
Artemisia vulgaris, mugwort
Balsamita vulgaris tanacetoides, costmary
Calamintha spp., the calamints
Chamaemelum nobile, Roman chamomile
Chamomilla recutita, German chamomile
Cheiranthus cheiri, wallflower
Cytisus scoparius, broom
Dianthus spp., the carnations
Digitalis purpurea, foxglove
Dipsacus fullonum, teazel
Echium vulgare, viper's bugloss
Eryngium maritimum, sea holly
Foeniculum vulgare, fennel
Galium verum, lady's bedstraw
Genista tinctoria, dyer's greenweed
Hypericum perforatum, St John's wort
Inula conyza, ploughman's spikenard
Isatis tinctoria, woad
Juniperus communis, juniper
Malva moschata, musk mallow
Marrubium vulgare, white horehound
Melilotus officinalis, melilot
Nepeta spp., catnep/catmint
Oenothera biennis, evening primrose
Origanum spp., the marjorams
Parietaria officinalis, pellitory of the wall
Pimpinella saxifraga, burnet saxifrage
Plantago spp., the plantains
Reseda luteola, weld
Ruta graveolens, rue
Salvia pratensis, meadow clary
Sambucus nigra, elder
Sanguisorba minor, salad burnet
Scrophularia nodosa, knotted figwort
Sedum rosea, rose root
Sempervivum tectorum, houseleek
Stachys officinalis, betony
Tanacetum parthenium, feverfew
T. vulgare, tansy
Verbascum thapsus, mullein
Verbena officinalis, vervain

Herbs for a rockery
Alchemilla alpina, alpine lady's mantle
Centaurium erythraea, centaury
Hyssopus officinalis 'Aristatus', rock hyssop
Pimpinella saxifraga, burnet saxifrage
Primula veris, cowslip
Pulsatilla vulgaris, pasque flower

HERBS FOR COLOR

The colors of flowers and foliage are as important as the variations of hue and texture of foliage.

I have listed herbs according to color to help in planning a border or garden of mixed or single-colored herbs. Unless stated otherwise, color categories refer to the flowers of the plants.

Red
Adonis annua, pheasant's eye
Amaranthus hypochondriacus, prince's feather
Cynoglossum officinale, houndstongue
Dianthus caryophyllus, clove carnation
Monarda didyma, bergamot
Paeonia officinalis, peony
Rosa gallica officinalis, apothecary's rose
Salvia rutilans, pineapple sage

Blue
Alkanna tinctoria, alkanet
Borago officinalis, borage
Cichorium intybus, chicory
Eryngium maritimum, sea holly *stem*
Isatis tinctoria, woad *leaves*
Linum usitatissimum, common flax
Lobelia inflata, Indian tobacco
Polemonium caeruleum, Jacob's ladder
Rosmarinus officinalis, rosemary
Ruta graveolens, rue *leaves*
Salvia uliginosa, bog sage
Scutellaria lateriflora, Virginian skullcap

Blue-purple and mauve
Aconitum napellus, monkshood
Ajuga reptans, bugle
Aquilegia vulgaris, columbine
Echium vulgare, viper's bugloss
Glechoma hederacea, ground ivy
Hyssopus officinalis, hyssop
Lavandula spp, the lavenders

Nepeta cataria, catnep
Pulmonaria officinalis, lungwort
Salvia pratensis, meadow clary
Symphytum officinale, comfrey
Thymus vulgaris, thyme
Viola odorata, sweet violet
Viola tricolor, wild pansy

Pink
Agastache anethiodora, anise hyssop
Allium schoenoprasum, chives
Althaea officinalis, marsh mallow
Calamintha officinalis, common calamint
Centaurium erythraea, centaury
Colchicum autumnale, meadow saffron
Crocus sativus, saffron
Daphne mezereon, daphne
Digitalis purpurea, foxglove
Eupatorium cannabinum, hemp agrimony
Malva moschata, musk mallow
Menyanthes trifoliata, bogbean
Origanum spp., the marjorams
Papaver somniferum, opium poppy
Phytolacca americana, poke root
Polygonum bistorta, bistort
Saponaria officinalis, soapwort
Teucrium chamaedrys, wall germander
Thymus drucei 'Annie Hall', thyme
T.d. coccineus 'Pink Chintz', thyme

Green-yellow
Alchemilla vulgaris, lady's mantle
Anethum graveolens, dill
Foeniculum vulgare, fennel
Galium verum, lady's bedstraw
Helleborus spp., the hellebores
H. niger, Christmas rose
Levisticum officinale, lovage
Reseda luteola, weld
Ruta graveolens, rue
Smyrnium olusatrum, alexanders
Teucrium scorodonia, wood sage
Veratrum viride, white hellebore

Yellow
Acorus calamus, sweet flag
Anthemis tinctoria, dyer's chamomile
Arnica montana, arnica
Carthamus tinctorius, safflower
Cheiranthus cheiri, wallflower
Chelidonium majus, greater celandine
Cytisus scoparius, broom
Filipendula ulmaria 'Aurea', meadowsweet *leaves*
Galium verum, lady's bedstraw
Genista tinctoria, dyer's greenweed
Gentiana lutea, yellow gentian
Hamamelis virginiana, witch hazel
Helianthus annuus, sunflower
Helichrysum angustifolium, curry plant
Hypericum perforatum, St John's wort
Inula helenium, elecampane
Isatis tinctoria, woad
Laurus nobilis 'Aurea', bay *leaves*
Melilotus officinalis, melilot
Melissa officinalis 'All Gold', lemon balm *leaves*
Oenothera biennis, evening primrose
Origanum vulgare 'Aureum', marjoram *leaves*
Phlomis fruticosa, Jerusalem sage
Primula veris, cowslip
P. vulgaris, primrose
Pulicaria dysenterica, peabane
Salvia glutinosa, Jupiter's distaff
S. officinalis 'Icterina', sage *leaves*
Sambucus nigra 'Aurea', elder *leaves*
Santolina spp., santolina
Sedum rosea, rose foot
Solidago virgaurea, golden rod
Tanacetum parthenium 'Aureum', feverfew *leaves*
T. vulgare, tansy
Taraxacum officinale, dadelion
Thymus drucei coccineus 'E. B. Anderson', thyme *leaves*
Verbascum thapsus, mullein

White and cream
Allium tuberosum, garlic chives
A. ursinum, ramsoms
Chamaemelum nobile, Roman chamomile
Convallaria majalis, lily of the valley
Dictamnus albus, white dittany
Digitalis purpurea, foxglove
Eupatorium purpureum, gravel root
Filipendula ulmaria, meadowsweet
Galega officinalis, goat's rue
Galium odoratum, woodruff
Gaultheria procumbens, wintergreen
Glycyrrhiza glabra, licorice
Iris florentina, orris
Lilium candidum, madonna lily
Malva moschata, musk mallow
Myrrhis odorata, sweet cicely
Polygonatum multiflorum, Solomon's seal
Sambucus nigra, elder
Sanguinaria canadensis, bloodroot
Symphytum officinale, comfrey
Tanacetum parthenium, feverfew
Thymus drucei 'Albus', thyme
Valeriana officinalis, valerian
Viburnum opulus, guelder rose

Purple
Ajuga reptans 'Atropurpurea', bugle *leaves*
Amaranthus hypochondriacus, prince's feather
Atriplex hortensis rubra, red orach *leaves and flowers*
Digitalis purpurea, foxglove
Echinacea angustifolia, cone flower
Foeniculum vulgare, bronze-leaved fennel *leaves*
Liatris odoratissima, vanilla plant
Mentha × piperita, black peppermint *leaves*
M. raripila rubra, red raripila *leaves*
Ocimum basilicum 'Dark Opal', basil *leaves*

Plantago major, purple-leaved great plantain
Salvia officinalis 'Purpurascens', sage *leaves*
Serratula tinctoria, sawwort
Stachys officinalis, betony
Thymus drucei, thyme

Orange
Calendula officinalis, pot marigold
Coreopsis tinctoria, coreopsis
Tagetes lucida, cloud plant
Tropaeolum majus, nasturtium

Variegated foliage
Ajuga reptans 'Multicolor', bugle
Buxus sempervirens 'Elegantissima', box
B.s. 'Latifolia Maculata'
Melissa officinalis 'Aurea', lemon balm
Mentha × gentilis 'Variegata', ginger mint
M. suaveolens 'Variegata', pineapple mint
Myrtus communis 'Variegata', myrtle
Pelargonium crispum 'Variegatum', pelargonium
P. graveolens 'Lady Plymouth'
Rumex sanguineum, bloody dock
Ruta graveolens 'Variegata', rue
Salvia officinalis 'Tricolor', sage
S.o. 'Icterina', sage
Sambucus nigra 'Aurea-variagata', elder
Scrophularia aquatica 'Variegata', water figwort
Silybum marianum, milk thistle
Thymus × citriodorus 'Aureus' and 'Silver Queen', lemon thyme
T. drucei coccineus 'Doone Valley'
T. vulgaris 'Silver Posie'

Silver or gray foliage
Althaea officinalis, marsh mallow
Artemisia absinthium 'Lambrook Silver', wormwood
A. borealis, old lady
A. lactiflora, white mugwort

A. maritima, sea wormwood
A. pontica, Roman wormwood
A. schmidtiana
A. stelleriana, dusty miller
Balsamita vulgaris tanacetoides, costmary
B.v. tomentosum, camphor plant
Dianthus caryophyllus, clove carnation
Eryngium maritimum, sea holly
Helichrysum angustifolium, curry plant
Lavandula spp., the lavenders
Marrubium vulgare, white horehound
Nepeta cataria, catnep

N. mussinii, catmint
Origanum dictamnus, dittany of Crete
Papaver somniferum, opium poppy
Phlomis fruticosa, Jerusalem sage
Salvia officinalis, sage
S. sclarea 'Turkestanica', clary sage
Santolina chamaecyparissus and *S. neapolitana*, santolina
Sedum rosea, rose root
Thymus drucei coccineus, 'Lanuginosus', thyme
T. fragrantissimus, thyme
Verbascum thapsus, mullein

TALL HERBS

The height of plants plays an important part in the planning of the herb garden. Tall herbs can be a central focal point in a small garden, or mark corners, steps or seats, or act as part of a protective enclosure or windbreak. Small deciduous trees in a medium sized garden can shelter spring flowering herbs, and evergreen shrubs give interest throughout the year. Or you may like to fill a bed entirely with large, statuesque or well-shaped herbaceous herbs massed together.

Use the list below as a reference when planning the garden. I have included elder as it is such a useful tree, all parts having effective medicinal properties, but it does grow tremendously fast and tends to suppress the growth of plants beneath it, so don't grow it in a small garden. (Plants are listed here in height order, with tallest first.)

Small deciduous trees and shrubs
Tilia cordata, small-leaved lime, 11m/34ft (responds well to heavy pollarding and plaiting)
Sambucus nigra, elder, 8m/26ft
Viburnum opulus, guelder rose, 4m/13ft
Euonymus europaeus, spindle, 3m/10ft
Hamamelis virginiana, witch hazel, 3m/10ft

Small evergreen trees and shrubs
Laurus nobilis, bay, 7m/23ft
Myrica cerifera, bayberry, 4m/13ft
Myrtus communis, myrtle, 3m/10ft
Juniperus communis, juniper, 3m/10ft
Buxus sempervirens, box, 3m/10ft
Rosmarinus officinalis, rosemary, 2.5m/8ft

Cytisus scoparius, broom, 1.5m/5ft
Lavandula angustifolia, lavender, 1.2m/4ft
Rosa gallica officinalis, apothecary's rose, 1.2m/4ft
Phlomis fruticosa, Jerusalem sage 1.2m/4ft
Artemisia absinthium, wormwood, 1m/3ft
Artemisia abrotanum, southernwood, 90cm/36in
Santolina spp., the santolinas, 80cm/32in
Salvia officinalis, sage, 75cm/30in
Helichrysum angustifolium, curry plant, 60cm/24in

Tall herbaceous perennial herbs
Phytolacca americana, poke root, 3m/10ft
Eupatorium purpureum, gravel root, 2.5m/8ft
Inula helenium, elecampane, 2m/6ft 6in
Levisticum officinale, lovage, 2m/6ft 6in
Galega officinalis, goat's rue, 1.5m/5ft
Myrrhis odorata, sweet cicely, 1.5m/5ft
Valeriana officinalis, valerian, 1.5m/5ft
Symphytum officinale, comfrey, 1.5m/5ft
Artemisia vulgaris, mugwort, 1.5m/5ft
Gentiana lutea, yellow gentian, 1.5m/5ft
Veratrum viride, white hellebore, 1.5m/5ft
Tanacetum vulgare, tansy, 1.5m/5ft
Lilium candidum, madonna lily, 1.5m/5ft
Nepeta cataria, catnep, 1.4m/4ft 6in
Glycyrrhiza glabra, licorice, 1.2m/4ft

Eupatorium cannabinum, hemp agrimony, 1.2m/4ft
Filipendula ulmaria, meadowsweet, 1m/3ft
Foeniculum vulgare, fennel, 1m/3ft
Althaea officinalis, marsh mallow, 1m/3ft
Allium cepa 'Proliferum', tree onion, 1m/3ft
Verbena officinalis, vervain, 1m/3ft
Eryngium maritimum, sea holly, 60cm/24in

Tall biennial herbs
Angelica archangelica, angelica, 2m/6ft 6in
Verbascum thapsus, mullein, 2m/6ft 6in
Digitalis purpurea, foxglove, 1.5m/5ft
Dipsacus fullonum, teazel, 1.5m/5ft
Reseda luteola, weld, 1.5m/5ft
Isatis tinctoria, woad, 1.3m/4ft 4in
Salvia sclarea, clary sage, 1.2m/4ft
Cynoglossum officinale, houndstongue, 1m/3ft
Oenothera biennis, evening primrose, 1m/3ft

Tall annual herbs
Helianthus annuus, sunflower, 4m/13ft
Anethum graveolens, dill, 1.5m/5ft
Atriplex hortensis rubra, red orach, 1.5m/5ft
Melilotus officinalis, melilot, 1.3m/4ft 4in

Heights given are those for mature trees and shrubs

A Catalog of Herbs

Unless stated otherwise, seed should be sown in spring and roots divided in spring or autumn. Details of propagation and harvesting are on pages 114 and 123. NOTE The remedies mentioned in the index are intended as a source of reference only, and not as prescriptions.

ACHILLEA millefolium

Yarrow, milfoil *Compositae*
Widespread on roadsides and wasteground in temperate climates. A tough, hardy perennial, variable to 60cm/24in high, with long, narrow, aromatic, much-divided leaves and flat clusters of white or pink-tinged flowers blooming throughout much of the year.
CULTIVATION Sow seed or (more easily) divide creeping root. Yarrow is tolerant of most soils but prefers sun.
USE Young leaves are edible and nutritious, and can be used as a salad herb. A traditional wound herb, its astringent leaves can be used as a poultice or infused for a healing wash. Infuse whole herb for a tonic tea, especially for fevers and colds. Ancient herb of divination. Good compost activator and fertilizer.

A. ptarmica   Sneezewort
Has similar habit and cultivation to *A. millefolium*, yarrow, but prefers moist, acid soils. Leaves are narrow, saw-toothed and aromatic; the flowers are fewer and larger than those of yarrow.
USE As yarrow. The dried, powdered leaves formerly taken as a medicinal snuff against headaches.
VARIETY *A. p.* 'The Pearl' has decorative white double flowers but less aromatic leaves.
Note *A. decolorans*, mace, is similar to sneezewort but has slightly larger leaves; leaves are used as a flavoring.

ACONITUM napellus

Monkshood, wolfsbane
Ranunculaceae
Native on high ground in Europe and Asia in shady places, *A. napellus* is now commonly cultivated in gardens. A hardy perennial up to 1m/3ft tall, it has dark, deeply divided leaves and a spike of deep blue helmeted flowers in summer.
CULTIVATION Sow seed or divide roots. Grow in a moist, semi-shaded position.
USE All parts poisonous. Formerly used as a painkiller and powerful sedative. Now used as a homeopathic remedy for asthma and anxiety.

ACORUS calamus

Sweet flag   *Araceae*
Hardy perennial, native to eastern countries but naturalized elsewhere in temperate climates. Grows in shallow water and marshy places. Up to 1m/3ft high with sword-shaped leaves that have crinkled margins and a curving head of tiny green flowers that grow from the side of the stem in midsummer. It will only flower when planted in water.
CULTIVATION Divide knobbly rhizome. Plant in rich wet soil.
USE Whole plant formerly used as an aromatic flavoring and scented strewing herb. Today root is chewed or taken as infusion or decoction against indigestion.

ADONIS annua

Pheasant's eye, red chamomile
Ranunculaceae
A hardy European annual that grows in fields and open ground. About 30cm/12in high, it has finely divided leaves and a pretty red buttercup-shaped flower with a dark center in summer.
CULTIVATION Grow from seed in sunny position.
USE All parts poisonous. A medicinal herb, it has a powerful action on the heart, as does similar but perennial and yellow-flowered *A. vernalis*.

AGASTACHE anethiodora

Anise hyssop, North American mint   *Labiatae*
Native of N. America, similar to mint in appearance and habit. About 1m/3ft high with long spikes of pink flowers in mid- to late summer.
CULTIVATION Sow seed or divide creeping root. Grow in sunny position.
USE Leaves make pleasant tea with mintlike properties. Excellent bee herb.

AGRIMONIA eupatoria

Agrimony   *Rosaceae*
Scented perennial, native to Europe. Common in grassy places and open ground, it grows about 60cm/24in high with rough-textured leaflets and a spire of little yellow flowers, followed by burrs.
CULTIVATION Sow seed or divide roots. Grow in well-drained, sunny position.
USE Infuse whole herb to make either a pleasant, faintly aromatic tonic and astringent tisane, good for sore throats, or a healing wash for wounds.

AJUGA reptans

Bugle   *Labiatae*
Widespread in light woodland and moist meadows in temperate climates. A creeping hardy perennial with dark, wrinkled, ovate leaves and erect stems of blue flowers during early summer.
CULTIVATION Sow seed or divide offshoots. Plant as ground cover or in paths. It is tolerant of shade.
USE Traditional wound herb. Bruise leaves as a poultice or infuse them as a healing wash.
VARIETIES Many including *A. r.* 'Atropurpurea' with dark purple leaves and *A. r.* 'Multicolor' (*A. r.* 'Rainbow') with bronze, pink and cream variegated leaves.

ALCHEMILLA vulgaris

Lady's mantle   *Rosaceae*
Hardy perennial, growing in grassy places in northern temperate climates. About 30cm/12in high, with rounded, lobed, downy leaves and clusters of yellow-green flowers from late spring.
CULTIVATION Sow seed or divide roots. Grow in light shade.
USE A highly astringent styptic and tonic. Infusion of leaves or decoction of root can be taken to control excessive menstrual flow or against diarrhea, or used as external wash for wounds and boils.
SIMILAR SPECIES *A. alpina*, alpine lady's mantle, is low-growing and decorative. It has delicate leaflets with silvery silky undersides. Identical properties to those of *A. vulgaris. A. mollis* is an easily cultivated species that self-seeds lavishly.

ALKANNA tinctoria

Alkanet, dyer's bugloss
Boraginaceae
Native of S. Europe, widely

naturalized. A hardy perennial about 30cm/12in high, with long, rough, hairy leaves and small bright blue flowers in spring.
CULTIVATION Sow seed or divide roots. Grow in any soil, in sun or light shade. It self-seeds freely.
USE Root formerly used as wound herb, now solely as source of red dye or coloring agent when mixed with oil or alcohol.

ALLIUM *Liliaceae*

Large group of bulbous perennials, cultivated and developed over thousands of years. Those listed below are hardy and have long, pungent-smelling leaves and round heads of flowers.
CULTIVATION All grow best in deeply worked rich soil, in sun.
USE They contain, in varying degrees, important vitamins and minerals, trace elements and sulfur, and have antiseptic and cleansing properties. Used as pot-herbs and flavorings. Can also be applied externally as a poultice to soothe boils, inflammations and insect stings.

A. cepa 'Proliferum'   Tree onion, Egyptian onion
Variety of the common garden onion, *A. cepa*. Grows 1m/3ft high with thick, hollow stems and leaves and a head of bulblets that fall in late summer to root and grow into new plants.
CULTIVATION Can also be propagated like shallots or chives, by division of parent bulbs.
USE Leaves used as green-onion flavoring; bulblets for soups or as pickles.

A. fistulosum   Welsh onion
Generally evergreen, it grows like chives in a spreading clump but with coarse hollow leaves about 60cm/24in high, and occasional tightly packed heads of little white flowers from late spring.
CULTIVATION Sow seed or divide roots.
USE Steady supply of green leaves with onion flavor.

A. perutile Everlasting onion
Similar to *A. fistulosum*, but does not flower.

A. sativum   Garlic
Flat leaves about 30cm/12in high and heads of white or pink flowers in summer of second year.
CULTIVATION Divide the garlic bulb and plant each clove in early spring in rich, sheltered soil. Harvest bulbs in early autumn as leaves become yellow.
USE An important, rich and pungent flavoring for a wide range of foods. A powerful antiseptic and disinfectant, it can be taken internally to prevent or treat infections and externally as a treatment for wounds, stings, etc.

A. schoenoprasum   Chives
About 30cm/12in high with fine, hollow leaves and round pink flowerheads with papery bracts in summer. Multiplies rapidly and forms compact clump.
CULTIVATION Sow seed or divide bulblets. Keep well watered and feed each year with compost.
USE Leaves have delicate onion flavor. Use fresh in soups, sauces, salads and egg dishes. Immerse flowers in white wine vinegar for fine-flavored pink vinegar. Dry leaves in cool oven with sea salt and crush to store as chive salt.
VARIETIES *A. s.* 'Sibiricum' is the giant variety of chives, taller, stouter and well flavored.

A. tuberosum   Garlic chives
Narrow flat leaves 60cm/24in high and heads of pretty, white, star-shaped flowers in late summer.

CULTIVATION Sow seed or divide clumps of little bulbs.
USE Garlic-flavored leaves used as flavoring.

A. ursinum   Ramsons
European native in damp, shaded woods, with broad leaves and starry white flowers in spring.
CULTIVATION Sow seed or divide creeping roots and grow in moist shady soil. It spreads easily to make good ground cover.
USE Edible leaves as garlic flavoring.

ALTHAEA officinalis

Marsh mallow   *Malvaceae*
A tall, hardy perennial widespread in marshes and estuaries near the sea. Over 1m/3ft high, with stems and lobed leaves that are thickly downy. Small pale pink flowers bloom in late summer.
CULTIVATION Sow seed or divide long roots. Plant in light, damp soil.
USE Edible, but flavor is faint. Decoction of roots mainly used as soothing medicine for coughs, bronchitis; a mild laxative and diuretic. Fresh, crushed leaves or root reduce inflammation. Other mallow species share emollient properties.

AMARANTHUS hypochondriacus

Prince's feather   *Amaranthaceae*
Native to Central America. A tender annual, up to 1.5m/5ft high, with long pointed leaves and dense upright racemes of dark red flowers in summer.
CULTIVATION Sow seed in rich soil and sunny position. For large specimens, sow early under glass and plant out after danger of frost is past.
USE Infuse astringent leaves as a wash for ulcers and swellings.

Achillea millefolium

Achillea ptarmica

Achillea decolorans

Angelica
archangelica

Artemisia
abrotanum

Artemisia absinthium

ANETHUM graveolens

Dill *Umbelliferae*
Much cultivated hardy annual
growing 1.5m/5ft high with fine
threadlike leaves and large decorative umbels of yellow flowers in
early summer, followed by
aromatic seeds.
CULTIVATION Sow seed in sunny
sheltered position in good, light
soil.
USE Leaves have refreshing,
subtle, sour flavor; use with fish
and pickles, salads and vegetables. Seeds are warming and
pungent; use to flavor root
vegetables, vinegars and sweets,
also a good digestive and anti-
flatulent medicine.

ANGELICA archangelica

Angelica *Umbelliferae*
Native to N. Europe and Russia,
often naturalized elsewhere. A
monumental hardy biennial
growing 2m/6ft 6in high, it has a
stout, hollow stem, glossy leaflets
with thickly inflated leaf-stem
bases and large umbels of yellow-
green flowers in early summer.
All parts are strongly aromatic.
CULTIVATION In autumn, sow
fresh seed or divide offsets. Plant
in light shade. May survive for
several years if prevented from
flowering.
USE Candy young stems for pungent cake decoration or add fresh
as flavoring for stewed fruit. Use
seeds to flavor liqueurs. All
parts act as aromatic tonic,
stimulant and digestive. Formerly
reputed to be powerful protection
against infection.
Note *A. sylvestris*, wild angelica,
is a smaller, less striking herb with
similar but weaker properties.

ANTHEMIS tinctoria

Dyer's chamomile, golden
marguerite *Compositae*
Decorative hardy herbaceous

perennial, 1m/3ft high, with
yellow daisy flowers in summer
and aromatic, toothed leaves.
CULTIVATION Sow seed or divide
roots; grow in sunny position.
USE Yellow dye obtained from
flowers. Once used as a tonic.

ANTHRISCUS cerefolium

Chervil *Umbelliferae*
Native to Asia and E. Europe. A
hardy annual that grows up to
60cm/24in high, with delicate,
anise-scented leaves and white
umbels of flowers from early
summer.
CULTIVATION Sow seed in midspring or late summer. Ideally,
grow in dappled shade and moist
rich light soil, to prevent it running too quickly to seed. Self-
seeds freely.
USE Use fresh to flavor egg and
other light savory dishes. Traditionally taken in spring to cleanse
the blood and aid digestion.

APHANES arvensis

Parsley piert *Rosaceae*
Widespread small hardy annual
of variable height that grows in
dry stony places. Slightly astringent downy leaves and tiny yellow
flowers from early summer.
CULTIVATION Sow seed in thin,
stony soil.
USE A traditional remedy for bladder stones. (It used to be called
parsley breakstone.) Infuse whole
herb as a diuretic and remedy for
bladder and kidney complaints.

APIUM graveolens

Smallage, wild celery
Umbelliferae
Variable hardy biennial locally
common near the sea and estuaries. Shiny leaves and ridged
stems have pungent celery scent
and flavor. Produces a head of
off-white flowers in summer of
second year.

CULTIVATION Sow seed in moist
soil. It tolerates some shade.
USE Both whole plant and seeds
are slightly bitter; can be used as
appetizer and general tonic.
Leaves have powerful celery
flavor for soups, etc.
VARIETY *A. g.* 'Dulce' has sweeter
flavor but less valuable
medicinal properties.

AQUILEGIA vulgaris

Columbine *Ranunculaceae*
Native to Europe, introduced in
N. America. A familiar, decorative hardy perennial 60–80cm/
24–32in high, with trifoliate
leaves and complex spurred
mauve or blue flowers in early
summer.
CULTIVATION Sow seed in spring
or autumn or divide roots
and plant in well-drained moist
loam. Tolerates partial shade.
USE All parts **poisonous**, with
action similar to related monkshood. Whole plant was used as an
antiseptic and sedative.

ARCTIUM lappa

Burdock *Compositae*
Large-leaved hardy biennial
1m/3ft high, common in temperate climates, with small purple
flowers in late summer and
hooked burrs.
CULTIVATION Sow fresh seed in
autumn in sun/semishade and
rich soil.
USE Leaves used for beer-making.
Decoction of roots/leaves for skin
troubles, dandruff.

ARCTOSTAPHYLOS
uva-ursi

Bearberry *Ericaceae*
Hardy perennial evergreen under-
shrub of N. Europe and N.
America, with leathery leaves,
hanging pink flowers and small
red berries. Grow in sun/semi-
shade on acid soil.

CULTIVATION Propagate by woody cuttings or layering. Harvest leaves in late summer.
USE Leaves are astringent, antiseptic; contain tannin. Used to treat bladder and kidney infections.

ARMORACIA rusticana

Horseradish *Cruciferae*
Long-leaved hardy perennial 1m/3ft high, common in temperate climates. Loose panicle of white flowers from midsummer, long fleshy root.
CULTIVATION Plant sections of root in spring in sun/semishade and rich soil. Once established, it is difficult to eradicate.
USE Grate raw root for a strong sauce which aids digestion.

ARNICA montana

Arnica *Compositae*
Hardy perennial, 30–60cm/ 12–24in high, from mountains in central Europe. Stem of yellow daisy flowers grows from rosette of long leaves from midsummer.
CULTIVATION Grow in sun and loamy acid soil.
USE All parts **poisonous**. Dried flowers and/or root are used to make salve or tincture for sprains and bruises. Homeopathic remedy for bruises and exhaustion. Related American species used in the same way.

ARTEMISIA *Compositae*

Large, widely distributed family, many with strongly scented decorative leaves. Those listed here are all perennial and hardy, need sun and a light open composted soil. Most are inedible, with the notable exception of *A. dracunculus*, tarragon.

A. abrotanum Southernwood
About 90cm/36in high. Woody stem and finely divided, power- fully scented leaves. Small yellow flowers in mid- to late summer are seldom produced in cool climates.
CULTIVATION Take soft or semiwoody cuttings. Clip back hard in late spring.
USE Infusion of leaves used as wash to clear skin. Strong infusion can be used as pesticide. Leaves deter moths.

A. absinthium Wormwood
About 1m/3ft high. Deeply cut, very bitter scented leaves with downy underside. Loose panicle of small yellow flowers.
CULTIVATION Take soft or semiwoody cuttings or sow seed or divide root. Clip hard in late spring.
USE Leaves and flowers used fresh or infused for an insecticide.
VARIETIES *A.a.* 'Lambrook Silver' has finer, silvery leaves.

A. borealis Old lady
About 50cm/20in high. Finely cut aromatic pale gray leaves.

A. camphorata
Similar habit to southernwood, but smaller, with threadlike leaves and camphor scent.

A. dracunculus French tarragon
About 1m/3ft high. Smooth, strongly flavored leaves. The soft stem dies down in winter. It seldom flowers. Do not confuse with robust, coarse-flavored *A.d.* 'Inodora', Russian tarragon.
CULTIVATION Grow in well-drained, sunny position from cuttings or divided roots. Protect from frost and damp during winter.
USE Important culinary herb, hot-flavored with subtle pungency. Use with chicken, fish, potato and in butter sauces.

A. maritima Sea wormwood
Low, shrubby plant with strongly scented, finely divided downy silver leaves.
USE As wormwood.

A. pontica Roman wormwood
Smaller than wormwood, with filigree silvery leaves and a more delicate scent. Spreading roots.

A. stelleriana Dusty miller
Pale gray ovate lobed leaves with panicles of small yellow flowers in late summer. Has a spreading, trailing habit. Will grow in semishade.

A. vulgaris Mugwort
A familiar roadside weed, 1.2m/ 4ft high, with broad, cut leaves, dark green above and downy beneath. Small rusty yellow panicles of flowers.
CULTIVATION Sow seed or divide root; grow in sun/semishade. May become invasive.
USE Leaves have coarse, bitter flavor; were used to flavor beer and to stimulate appetite.

ASARUM canadense

Wild ginger *Aristolochiaceae*
Low, spreading hardy perennial of N. America, Russia and Far East, with large kidney-shaped leaves rising on hairy stalks from creeping roots; dull purple flowers in summer.
CULTIVATION Plant divided roots in moist rich shaded soil.
USE Aromatic root used fresh or dried as ginger.

ATRIPLEX hortensis rubra

Red orach *Chenopodiaceae*
Cultivated hardy annual of unknown origin. Variable height to 1.5m/5ft. Arrow-shaped red leaves with violet, mealy stalks and a purple spike of small flowers from late spring.

Artemisia dracunculus

Artemisia pontica

Artemisia vulgaris

Chamaemelum nobile

Chamomilla recutita

CULTIVATION Best grown fast from seed in rich ground. Self-seeds freely.
USE Eat young mild-flavored leaves in salads or cooked as spinach.

ATROPA belladonna

Deadly nightshade, belladonna
Solanaceae
Bushy hardy perennial, 1–2m/3–6ft 6in high, of Europe and S. Britain. Oval pointed leaves, dull-purple bell-shaped flowers and shiny black berries.
CULTIVATION Sow seed or divide roots in semishade and rich limy soil. Young plants need moisture and protection from frost.
USE All parts **very poisonous**. Powerful alkaloids hyoscyamine and atropine extracted from leaves and roots. Homeopathic remedy for sudden pain.

BALSAMITA vulgaris tanacetoides

Costmary, alecost *Compositae*
Originally from the East, a hardy perennial grown for its broad minty scented leaves. Straggling habit. Yellow button flowers bloom in sunny position, from midsummer, but plant will tolerate semishade.
CULTIVATION Divide root.
USE Leaves scent potpourri. Infuse for a weak tonic tea or a rinse for hair or clothes; also use as insect repellent. Crushed fresh leaf soothes stings.

B.v. tomentosum Camphor plant

Similar to above, but with smaller camphor-scented leaves and white-rayed flowers from midsummer.

BORAGO officinalis

Borage *Boraginaceae*
Hardy annual from S. Europe, of very variable height to 1m/3ft. Large, wrinkled, bristly leaves; drooping star-shaped blue flowers from late spring; stout stem.
CULTIVATION Sow seed or self-seeds freely. Tolerant of soil and some shade.
USE Young leaves make pleasant, cooling salad. Flowers pretty in salads and drinks.

BRASSICA nigra

Black mustard *Cruciferae*
Formerly widely cultivated (new strains more suitable for modern farm machinery). Hardy annual, 1–2.5m/3–8ft high, with bristly lobed leaves, yellow flowers from midsummer and long pods of dark seeds.
CULTIVATION Sow seed in sun and rich soil. Harvest and dry ripe pods.
USE Powerfully pungent seeds used as mustard ingredient and externally as rubefacient. Plant may irritate tender skins.

BRYONIA dioica

White bryony *Cucurbitaceae*
Hardy deciduous climber, native of European hedgerows, with 4m/13ft stem, vine-shaped leaves, small pale green flowers, red berries and a very thick root.
CULTIVATION Plant fresh berries or root in sun/semishade in limy soil. Provide support.
USE Acrid root formerly used against leprosy, as purgative and irritant and as cheap substitute for mandrake root.

BUXUS sempervirens

Box *Buxaceae*
Hardy perennial shrub/small tree in temperate climates. Grows 3m/10ft high with small glossy scented leaves and tiny yellow-green flowers in late spring.
CULTIVATION Take cuttings in spring or autumn, grow in sun/semishade. Prefers a limy soil. Slow growing but responds well to clipping and shaping; ideal for hedging.
USE Leaves and wood formerly used as narcotic and vermifuge. Hard, dense wood used for turning.
VARIETIES Many including *B.s.* 'Elegantissima', with silver-edged leaves and dense habit; 'Latifolia Maculata', 1.8m/6ft high, with variegated yellow leaves; 'Suffruticosa', a dwarf form which is suitable for edging.

CALAMINTHA officinalis

Common calamint, mountain balm *Labiatae*
Perennial with straggling stems 30cm/12in long; native to roadsides and sunny banks in Britain and Europe. Soft, scented, paired leaves and thymelike, rosy flowers from midsummer.
CULTIVATION Sow seed or divide root in sunny, light soil.
USE Infusion of minty, aromatic leaves makes pleasant tonic tea.
Note Several *Calamintha* species are suitable for growing on banks or in paving: *C. grandiflora* has larger, purple-pink flowers; *C. nepetoides* has small white flowers and a neater habit.

CALENDULA officinalis

Marigold, pot marigold
Compositae
Half-hardy annual of S. Europe, 50cm/20in high. Oblong, pale leaves, large orange flowers from late spring. Becomes leggy in shade.
CULTIVATION Grow in sun, in any soil, from seed. Self-seeds freely.
USE Petals flavor soups and salads, are antiseptic, soothing and promote perspiration.
Note There are many hybrids which have less medicinal value.

CARTHAMUS tinctorius

Safflower, dyer's saffron
Compositae
Annual, 1m/3ft high, widely
cultivated, origin unknown.
Prickly thistlelike leaves; shaggy
orange-yellow flowers.
CULTIVATION Grow in sun, in
good open soil, from seed in
permanent position; does not
transplant well.
USE Petals once used medicinally.
Main use is as a yellow dye.

CARUM carvi

Caraway   *Umbelliferae*
Native to Asia and parts of Europe,
a hardy biennial about 1m/3ft
high. Grows like a carrot with a
strong tap root, and much-divided
feathery leaves the first year, and
white flowers in the second.
CULTIVATION Sow seed in spring
or late summer in good soil and
sun. Harvest fresh seed.
USE Add fresh leaves to salads,
soups; dried seeds are warmly
aromatic as flavoring for cakes,
breads, liqueurs, etc.; fleshy roots
are edible and can be cooked like
carrots. Seeds make excellent
digestives and dispel flatulence.

CEDRONELLA canariensis

Balm of Gilead   *Labiatae*
Native to the Canaries and
Madeira. Half-hardy shrubby
perennial about 1m/3ft high, with
strongly scented leaves and pale
mauve flowers in summer.
CULTIVATION Sow seed or take
cuttings. Protect from frost.
Grows well in a pot.
USE Scented leaves in potpourri.

CENTAURIUM erythraea

Centaury   *Gentianaceae*
European hardy annual or bien-
nial, height variable to 30cm/12in.
Rosette of leaves and stem of five-
petaled pink flowers in summer.
CULTIVATION Sow seed in spring

or autumn in dry sunny position.
USE Infuse whole plant for a bitter
tonic and digestive.

CHAMAEMELUM nobile

Roman chamomile   *Compositae*
A creeping hardy perennial up to
25cm/10in high, with finely cut
fruit-scented leaves and daisy
flowers blooming throughout
summer.
CULTIVATION Sow seed in spring
or plant offsets in spring or
autumn. Tolerant of acid soils
and a little shade. For a thick mat
or lawn do not allow to flower, and
clip as necessary, or grow the non-
flowering *C.n.* 'Treneague'. There
is also a pretty double-flowered
form.
USE Infuse dried flowers for a
calming sedative tisane, an antiseptic cleanser and a hair rinse, or
crush them for a soothing poultice. Use in garden as compost
activator.

CHAMOMILLA recutita

German chamomile   *Compositae*
As above, but annual and up to
50cm/20in high, with a more
upright habit and petals that
droop around the hollow yellow
center of the flower. Similar uses.

CHEIRANTHUS cheiri

Wallflower, wall gilliflower
Cruciferae
Native to Europe, a hardy perennial that grows in walls and stony
places. It has narrow leaves and
sweet-scented, yellow four-
petaled flowers that bloom in
spring. Compact habit, about
45cm/18in high.
CULTIVATION Sow seed in spring
or autumn or take cuttings in early
autumn. Grow in light soil in
sunny position.
USE Formerly a medicinal plant;
wallflower oil, 'Cheirinum', was
used against ulcers and palsy.

CHELIDONIUM majus

Greater celandine   *Papaveraceae*
Native to Europe, widespread as a
garden escape. A hardy perennial,
unrelated to lesser celandine,
found on wasteground, roadsides
and walls. Grows 90cm/36in high,
with decorative lobed leaflets and
yellow flowers that bloom throughout summer. When broken, stems
ooze acrid yellow juice.
CULTIVATION Sow seed or divide
roots. Tolerates poor soil and
semishade.
USE All parts **poisonous**. Juice
formerly used for eye ailments;
used today for removing warts.

CHENOPODIUM
Chenopodiaceae

A family that includes many hardy
annual and colonizing weeds with
unremarkable flowers and edible
leaves and seeds.
CULTIVATION Best grown fast from
seed on rich ground to encourage
tender foliage.

C. album   Fat hen
Up to 1m/3ft high, with green
flowers and lanceolate leaves.
USE All parts can be added to
soups, stews, salads, etc.

C. ambrosioides   American
wormseed, Mexican tea, epazote.
At least 1.2m/4ft high, with broad
indented leaves and thick spikes
of green flowers that turn bright
red in late summer.
USE Pungent fresh leaves give
distinctive flavor to Mexican
bean dishes and tortillas, but
seeds should not be eaten. Seeds
make a powerful vermifuge and
insect repellent.

C. bonus-henricus   Good
King Henry
Perennial whose arrow-shaped
leaves and green flower spikes
appear in spring.

*Chenopodium
album*

*Chenopodium
bonus-henricus*

CULTIVATION Sow seed or divide roots and grow on rich soil. Will tolerate semishade.
USE Leaves provide a spinach substitute. Young flower spikes in spring may be steamed.

C. botrys Ambrosia, Jerusalem oak
About 60cm/24in high. Leaves have wavy margins; thick heavy green flower spikes in summer curve under their own weight.
USE Whole pungently scented plant can be used in dried flower arrangements or twisted into wreaths.

CICHORIUM intybus

Chicory, French endive
Compositae
Widely cultivated perennial 1.5m/5ft high, with large toothed leaves, stiff stems of sky-blue flowers in summer and a thick taproot.
CULTIVATION Sow seed in rich soil in late spring. From autumn through winter lift roots, cut off leaves to within 2cm/1in of root and force sweet new growth in a bucket of sand or earth in a dark place. Of the many other varieties, some need no blanching but taste rather bitter.
USE As salad. Bitter root of *C.i.* 'Magdeburg', 'Brunswick' or 'Witloof' can be dried and ground as a coffee substitute.

CLEMATIS vitalba

Traveller's joy   Old man's beard   *Ranunculaceae*
Hardy woody perennial in south of England and Europe, clambering along hedgerows with stems many meters long. Leaves are pinnate, flowers pale green and scented, fruit in clusters with pale hairy plumes.
CULTIVATION Propagate from semisoftwood cuttings or layerings or sow seed and plant in sun or semishade, against support.
VARIETIES Other varieties have similar properties and may be poisonous to some degree, but also highly ornamental. *C. flammula*, virgin's bower, has panicles of sweetly scented white flowers in autumn and grows up to 3m/10ft. *C. recta*, upright virgin's bower, has the most powerful medicinal action. It is herbaceous and only 1m/3ft high with white flowers.

CNICUS benedictus

Blessed thistle   *Compositae*
Hardy annual, native to the Mediterranean. The branched stem with harsh spiny heads of yellow flowers from midsummer grows 60cm/24in high above dark, white-veined, prickly leaves.
CULTIVATION Sow seed in autumn or spring in sunny position. Self-seeds freely.
USE A traditional medicine was made from the flowering tops, popular as a tonic for nursing mothers but it is an emetic in large doses. Use young leaves in salads.

COLCHICUM autumnale

Meadow saffron, naked ladies
Liliaceae
Hardy perennial autumn crocus. The rosy purple flowers rise after leaves have withered.
CULTIVATION Sow seed or plant corms in moist, semishaded position.
USE Corm and seeds **poisonous**; they contain powerful alkaloids including colchicine and have been used to treat rheumatism.
VARIETIES There is a white form, *C.a.* 'Album', and also some double forms.

CONVALLARIA majalis

Lily of the valley   *Liliaceae*
Familiar hardy perennial garden plant with pairs of broad leaves and a 30cm/12in stem of sweet-scented white bell-shaped flowers in spring.
CULTIVATION Sow fresh seed or divide creeping roots in autumn. Plant in good, moist, lightly shaded position.
USE Flowers **poisonous**; used to make strong drug to regulate heartbeat, also used in perfume manufacture.

COREOPSIS tinctoria

Coreopsis   *Compositae*
Hardy annual from N. America, 75cm/30in high, with deeply cut leaves and many daisy flowers of yellows, burnt oranges and terracotta in late summer.
CULTIVATION Sow seed in spring and grow in sunny position.
USE Flowers give excellent yellow or orange dye.

CORIANDRUM sativum

Coriander   *Umbelliferae*
Hardy annual native to S.E. Europe, growing 60cm/24in high. Lower leaves broader than thread-like upper leaves; heads of pink flowers in summer followed by round seeds. Whole plant strongly aromatic: leaves pungent, dried seeds scented like orange peel.
CULTIVATION Sow seed in spring in good soil and sunny position. Keep well watered to encourage lush leaf growth from base. Harvest seeds in autumn.
USE Add chopped fresh leaves plentifully to curries and hot chili dishes; blend with yogurt and fresh Indian chutneys. Seeds flavor marinades, curries, stews, sweetmeats; also make good digestives. Roots are pounded with garlic in Thai food.

CROCUS sativus

Saffron   *Iridaceae*
The wild saffron crocus grows in E. Europe and Asia. The cultivated form has extra large red styles, rich purple autumn flowers and three stamens which distinguish it from *Colchicum autumnale*, the poisonous meadow saffron, which has pink flowers and six stamens.
CULTIVATION It takes several years to flower from seed, so plant corms in well-drained light soil in sunny position. To harvest, collect orange stigmas and styles from open flowers (35,000 flowers yield 225g/8oz saffron).
USE Flavor rice and meat dishes, soups and stews with scented stigmas and styles. An infusion of these has been used to reduce fevers and to induce menstruation; also considered an aphrodisiac. The strong yellow dye is soluble.

CUMINUM cyminum

Cumin   *Umbelliferae*
Native to countries bordering the Mediterranean, a tender annual 30cm/12in high with threadlike leaves and sparse pale flowers in summer followed by aromatic seeds.
CULTIVATION Sow seed in late spring in sheltered sunny position; harvest fresh seeds.
USE Powerfully flavored seeds valuable in Middle Eastern and Indian dishes, especially with curries, lamb and yogurt. Similar warming, digestive and anti-flatulent effect as dill and caraway.

CYNOGLOSSUM officinale

Houndstongue   *Boraginaceae*
Hardy stalwart European biennial, most common near the sea, with long broad pointed leaves. Flowers are small and maroon red.
CULTIVATION Sow seed in spring or autumn in sunny position and good soil.
USE Blanch leaves or crush root

for an external medicine to soothe and relieve painful inflammation and piles.

CYTISUS scoparius

Broom *Leguminosae*
Widespread hardy shrub growing on sandy heathland. Up to 1.5m/5ft high, with long green stems, tiny trifoliate leaves and bright yellow pealike flowers in early summer. Many garden varieties.
CULTIVATION Sow seed in spring or take cuttings in late summer.
USE Flowering tops contain narcotic **poisonous** principle. Formerly used as a tonic and against ague.

DAPHNE mezereon

Daphne *Thymelaeaceae*
A hardy perennial shrub, native to deciduous woodland in Europe and W. Asia. Up to 1.5m/5ft high, with clusters of rich pink, highly fragrant flowers on bare branches in early spring, followed by blunt leaves, then scarlet berries in autumn.
CULTIVATION Take cuttings in late summer and plant in sheltered, sunny position.
USE All parts **poisonous**. Bark and root have long history of use for scrofulous and ulcerous skin conditions and as a purgative.
VARIETY There is a white-flowered form, *D.m.* 'Alba'.

DATURA stramonium

Thornapple *Solanaceae*
Half-hardy annual naturalized weed from Near East. Height variable to 1.2m/4ft; toothed leaves have fetid smell; solitary white trumpet-shaped, sweet-scented flowers from midsummer; distinctive spiny fruit.
CULTIVATION Sow seed under glass in spring. Plant out in pots or sheltered position in rich soil after frost is past.

USE All parts **poisonous**; they contain narcotic principles and poisonous alkaloids. Formerly, dried herb was smoked to remedy asthma and chest complaints.

DIANTHUS caryophyllus

Clove carnation *Caryophyllaceae*
Native to S. Europe, ancestor of the many hardy garden carnations. A short-lived perennial with long, narrow, gray-bloomed leaves and rich pink, clove-scented flowers in midsummer.
CULTIVATION Sow seed in spring or layer in late summer. Plant in sunny well-drained position.
USE Cut bitter heels from petals and use to scent and flavor salads, syrups and preserves and in potpourri. Traditionally a comforting and cheering herb.
VARIETY An old favorite is *D.c.* 'Crimson Clove', grown in herb and cottage gardens for over 500 years.

DICTAMNUS albus

White dittany, burning bush *Rutaceae*
Hardy perennial from rocky hillsides in Asia and S. Europe. Grows 1m/3ft high, with dark lush leaves and spikes of pink or white orchidlike flowers in midsummer. Whole plant warmly aromatic and seed pods occasionally give off a volatile oil that can be ignited on a still evening.
CULTIVATION Takes several years to flower from seed, sown fresh in late summer. Plant in sunny well-drained position in limy soil; avoid disturbing roots.
USE Traditionally used against pestilence and infection.
VARIETY *D.a.* 'Purpureus' has pink flowers streaked with purple.

DIGITALIS purpurea

Foxglove *Scrophulariaceae*
Native to dry places in W. Europe,

a familiar hardy biennial, occasionally perennial, up to 1.5m/5ft, with a spike of pink or white tubular flowers from early summer. Leaves are large, soft and wrinkled. There are many ornamental varieties.
CULTIVATION Sow seed in spring or late summer in well-drained position. It self-seeds well.
USE All parts **poisonous**. Valuable glycosides, which regulate and strengthen the heartbeat, are extracted from the leaves.
Note Another important medicinal species, *D. lutea*, has pale yellow flowers in summer and smooth, glossy leaves.

DIPSACUS fullonum

Teazel *Dipsacaceae*
Handsome widespread hardy biennial, 1.5m/5ft high, with rosette of long leaves in first year and prickly stem of cylindrical pale mauve flower heads and spiny bracts in the summer of the second.
CULTIVATION Sow seed in autumn or spring in well-drained sunny position; self-seeds readily.
USE A decoction of the root was used medicinally to cleanse and soothe. Rainwater caught in the cupped leaf bases was a traditional skin cleanser. Form with hooked bracts and longer flower-heads traditionally used to tease or raise the nap on cloth.

ECHINACEA angustifolia

Cone flower *Compositae*
Hardy herbaceous perennial from N. America, 60cm/24in high, with long narrow leaves. Flowers throughout late summer with purple petals and high central cone.
CULTIVATION Sow seed in spring; divide roots in autumn or spring.
USE A decoction of the root is used as a strong antiseptic.

Datura stramonium

*Eupatorium
cannabinum*

*Eupatorium
perfoliatum*

*Eupatorium
purpureum*

ECHIUM vulgare

Viper's bugloss *Boraginaceae*
Widespread hardy biennial or
short-lived perennial of coarse
and curious habit, 60cm/24in
high. Darkly spotted stems,
lanceolate leaves and curving spike
of flowers that open pink from
early summer and turn blue.
CULTIVATION Sow seed in late
summer in well-drained sunny
position or divide roots. It self-
seeds readily.
USE Infuse leaves for a cooling
tonic. Formerly used against
snake bite.

ERUCA sativa

Rocket *Cruciferae*
Hardy annual from S. Europe.
It has toothed leaves and pale
cream, purple-penciled flowers
in summer.
CULTIVATION Sow seed in well-
watered, rich soil at intervals
through spring and early summer
to ensure steady supply of leaves.
Pinch out flowering stem to
encourage lush growth.
USE Tasty, warming salad herb.

ERYNGIUM maritimum

Sea holly, eryngo *Umbelliferae*
Widespread on European sea-
shores. A perennial with long,
branched roots. Variable height
to 45cm/18in, with prickly thistlelike leaves; from midsummer,
steely blue flowers among spiky
bracts. There are many cultivated,
ornamental forms.
CULTIVATION Sow seed in autumn
or spring or divide roots in
autumn. Plant in light, well-
drained soil in sunny position.
Harvest roots in autumn.
USE Boil and candy the slightly
sweet, aromatic roots as cough
sweet, nerve tonic and diuretic.
Note *E. campestre*, field eryngo,
has smaller flowerheads and
similar properties.

EUONYMUS europaeus

Spindle tree *Celastraceae*
Native to Europe and W. Asia, a
small, elegant deciduous tree or
shrub up to 3m/10ft high. Small
green flowers in early summer
followed by decorative four-lobed
pink capsules with orange seeds.
CULTIVATION Sow fresh, slow-
germinating seed in autumn or
take hardwood cuttings. Plant in
sun or semishade.
USE All parts **poisonous**. Dried
bark formerly used externally to
treat skin complaints. Wood was
carved into spindles and skewers.

EUPATORIUM cannabinum

Hemp agrimony *Compositae*
Native to ditches and damp roadsides in Europe, a hardy perennial,
up to 1.2m/4ft high, with lanceolate leaves and rounded heads of
pinky-mauve flowers from mid-
to late summer. All parts have a
resinous scent.
CULTIVATION Divide roots. Plant
in good moist soil in semishade.
USE Whole herb taken in large
doses acts as an emetic; in small
doses as a bitter tonic and laxative.
Attracts butterflies.

E. perfoliatum

Boneset, thoroughwort
Native to marshy places in N.
America, a hardy perennial, variable height to 1.5m/5ft, with pairs
of pointed leaves joined at the
base and a head of gray-white
flowers in late summer.
CULTIVATION Divide roots and
plant in good moist soil.
USE Whole herb taken in large
doses acts as an emetic; in small
doses infusion effective as treatment for colds and fevers. Attracts
butterflies.

E. purpureum

Gravel root, Joe Pye weed
Native to open woodland in N.

America, a handsome, hardy
perennial, up to 2.5m/8ft high,
with whorls of lanceolate, vanilla-
scented leaves and clusters of
pink-tinged or creamy flowers in
late summer.
CULTIVATION Sow seed in spring
or divide roots. Plant in rich soil.
It tolerates some shade.
USE Decoction of astringent root
is a treatment for fevers, and a
diuretic.

EUPHRASIA officinalis

Eyebright *Scrophulariaceae*
Tough-stemmed hardy annual
native to grasslands in temperate
climates. Variable height to
20cm/8in, with toothed leaves
and, in summer, pale patterned
complex flowers with yellow spot
on lower lip.
CULTIVATION Difficult to cultivate
as it is semiparasitic on grasses.
USE Infuse whole herb as mildly
soothing and astringent eyewash.

FILIPENDULA ulmaria

Meadowsweet *Rosaceae*
Common perennial in temperate
climates in moist places. Grows
1m/3ft high, with tough reddish
stems, dark toothed leaves that
smell freshly of disinfectant when
crushed, and clusters of scented
creamy flowers in midsummer.
CULTIVATION Sow seed or divide
roots. Plant in moist semishaded
position.
USE Infusion of flowers treats
fevers, acidity and heartburn.
Infusion of leaves treats diarrhea.
Strong decoction of astringent
root used as external wash for
wounds and ulcers.
VARIETIES Decorative double and
variegated forms include *F.u.*
'Aurea' with pale golden leaves.

FOENICULUM vulgare

Fennel *Umbelliferae*
Native to the Mediterranean,

naturalized elsewhere, a handsome perennial, to 2m/6ft 6in high, with finely cut leaves and a yellow umbel of flowers in summer.
CULTIVATION Sow seed in spring in sunny position, or detach offsets. It self-seeds readily.
USE Good aromatic culinary herb. Use the leaves raw, the stems cooked, to flavor fish, chicken, etc.; warming, pungent seeds flavor breads, stews, liqueurs, and act as excellent digestive.
VARIETIES There is a decorative bronze-leaved variety, and also the annual, *F.v.* 'Azoricum', Florence fennel, whose swollen stem base is a delicious vegetable.

FRAGARIA vesca

Wild strawberry   *Rosaceae*
Woodland plant of temperate climates. Low-growing hardy perennial with silky ovate toothed leaves and small white flowers in spring followed by juicy red berries. Leaves give musky scent as they die in autumn.
CULTIVATION Divide runners; grow in semishade and moist soil.
USE Fruit are edible and delicious. Infusion of leaf or root makes a bitter tonic with astringent properties, a useful treatment for diarrhea.

GALEGA officinalis

Goat's rue   *Papilionaceae*
Native to grassland in S. Europe and Asia Minor, a hardy perennial of sprawling habit. Up to 1.5m/5ft high, with graceful pinnate leaves and white or pale purple flowers in midsummer.
CULTIVATION Sow seed or divide roots. Plant in moist semi-shaded tion and stake well.
USE Leaves are fed to stock to encourage milk production; mildly acidic flowers are used to curdle milk for cheesemaking.

GALIUM *Rubiaceae*

Easily recognized by their long weak stems and regular whorls of leaves, most are hardy perennials and were used as wound herbs; red dye was also made from their roots.

G.odoratum   Woodruff
Widespread in woodland in temperate climates. Stems seldom rise higher than 30cm/12in, leaves are comparatively broad and glossy. Bright white starry flowers bloom in spring. Whole herb richly scented and scent increases as herb dries.
CULTIVATION Sow fresh seed in late summer or divide creeping roots; plant in shady, loamy soil.
USE Deliciously hay-scented dried herb. Taken in infusion, it is said to relieve stomach pains. Also, a traditional flavoring for white wine and excellent addition to potpourri. A favorite medieval garland herb.
Note Related dyer's woodruff, *Asperula tinctoria*, has finer leaves. Tiny squinancywort, *Asperula cynanchica*, is traditional treatment for quinsy or sore throat.

G. verum   Lady's bedstraw
Common in temperate climates, on dry banks and grassland. Wiry stems may grow 1m/3ft high, with whorls of fine dark leaves and massed panicles of tiny, scented, yellow flowers in mid- to late summer.
CULTIVATION Sow seed or (more easily) divide roots. Plant in well-drained sunny position.
USE Infuse whole herb as a mild treatment for wounds and a diuretic. Formerly used to curdle milk. As herb dries scent increases; it was used as stuffing for mattresses and pillows, hence its name (traditionally used in Christ's crib).

GAULTHERIA procumbens

Wintergreen   *Ericaceae*
Hardy perennial N. American evergreen of low shrubby habit with glossy leaves, solitary white bell-flowers in midsummer and autumnal scarlet berries.
CULTIVATION Propagate from seed, cuttings or layerings in spring or early autumn. Plant in acid soil and semishaded position.
USE Strongly aromatic leaves can be infused as a gargle for sore throats and as a poultice; oil distilled from leaves is used to soothe inflammations and rheumatism. Also used as a toothpaste flavoring.

GENISTA tinctoria

Dyer's greenweed   *Leguminosae*
Low hardy deciduous shrub, generally about 1m/3ft high, widespread in grassy places in temperate countries. Small leaves, dark and glossy; bright yellow pealike flowers in midsummer.
CULTIVATION Sow seeds in spring or take cuttings in late summer and plant in well-drained sunny position.
USE Similar poisonous principles to those in common broom; formerly used as diuretic and emetic. Flowering tops give good yellow-green dye.

GENTIANA lutea

Yellow gentian   *Gentianaceae*
Native to mountain pastures in Europe and Asia, a hardy perennial growing at least 1.5m/5ft high with strongly veined leaves and clusters of showy yellow flowers in late summer.
CULTIVATION Very slow to develop from seed, so plant root cuttings in enriched moist soil in sheltered sunny position in late autumn.
USE Very large fleshy root has extremely bitter properties, as do most members of gentian family.

Galium odoratum

Asperula cynanchica

Galium verum

Glechoma hederacea

Gratiola officinalis

Helichrysum angustifolium

Used in very small quantities to flavor aperitifs and as fortifying tonic and digestive. Root and leaves make antiseptic wound treatment.

GEUM urbanum

Wood avens, herb bennet
Rosaceae
Hardy perennial common in woodlands and on shady banks of temperate Europe. Variable height to 60cm/24in, with cut, toothed leaves, unassuming yellow flowers through summer and faintly aromatic root.
CULTIVATION Sow seed or divide roots and grow in semishade. It self-seeds well.
USE Mildly antiseptic and astringent leaves and root can be infused as tonic or remedy for sore throats and fever, or as a refreshing washing water. Has been thought of value against infection.

GILLENIA trifoliata

Indian physic *Rosaceae*
Native to woodland in the USA, a low hardy perennial whose stems of sparse pink flowers reach 80cm/32in.
CULTIVATION Divide creeping root and grow in moist semishade.
USE Very bitter roots used by American Indians in small doses as digestive tonic and in large doses as emetic.

GLECHOMA hederacea

Ground ivy *Labiatae*
Hardy perennial, common in temperate woodlands. Its downy kidney-shaped leaves grow from creeping stems, and it has rich blue or purple long-throated flowers from late spring throughout summer.
CULTIVATION Easily propagated from pieces of rooting stem; plant in well-drained soil in semishade.
USE Pleasant, slightly bitter,

aromatic infusion of whole herb is a tonic and treatment for colds, coughs, kidney troubles and menstrual pains. Crush fresh herb as a poultice for bruises. Traditional ale flavoring.

GLYCYRRHIZA glabra

Licorice *Leguminosae*
Shrubby hardy perennial of S.E. Europe and Asia. Up to 1.2m/4ft high, with graceful leaflets that droop in the dark, pale blue-white pea-flowers from mid-summer and long pods of hard seeds.
CULTIVATION Divide root in autumn; grow in sheltered sunny position in deeply worked soil. Harvest mature roots in autumn.
USE Sweet-tasting root flavors confectionery and beverages; decoction is invaluable for coughs, bronchitis and gastric ulcers. Used medicinally for at least five thousand years.

GRATIOLA officinalis

Hedge hyssop *Scrophulariaceae*
Native to damp places in Europe, easily overlooked hardy perennial 30cm/12in high with opposite lanceolate leaves and single pale pink flowers growing from leaf axils in late summer.
CULTIVATION Sow seed or divide roots and plant in damp, half-shaded position.
USE All parts **poisonous**. Extremely powerful and toxic, it acts upon the heart, as does related foxglove; formerly used as a drastic purgative.

HAMAMELIS virginiana

Witch hazel *Hamamelidaceae*
Graceful small deciduous tree. Its scented yellow flowers in late autumn have petals like twisted ribbons.
CULTIVATION Best propagated by layering in autumn. Grow in

moist loam and light shade.
USE Decoction of bark and leaves is highly astringent; use externally to treat sprains, bruises, inflammations, varicose veins. Distilled essence produced commercially.
SIMILAR SPECIES *H. mollis*, Chinese witch hazel, flowers in early spring from bare twigs; prefers a sunny position. Not used medicinally.

HELIANTHUS annuus

Sunflower *Compositae*
A hardy annual native to central N. America. Now a familiar garden plant and crop, up to 5m/16ft high, with rough leaves and broad heavy flowerheads with yellow petals in summer.
CULTIVATION Sow seed in good soil and sunny position.
USE Edible, highly nutritious seeds also give good quality oil. Formerly used against coughs and bronchitis.

HELICHRYSUM angustifolium

Curry plant *Compositae*
A subshrub, native to S. Europe, a half-hardy perennial evergreen, up to 60cm/24in high; powerfully pepper-scented silver leaves and mustard-yellow flowers in summer. Scent strongest after rain.
CULTIVATION Sow seed in spring or take cuttings in late spring or summer. Grow in well-drained, sunny position. Clip in late spring to prevent legginess. Protect the roots from frost in colder districts.
USE Taste is less interesting than scent; leaves are included in spicy potpourri mixtures and everlasting flowers are dried for winter decoration.
SIMILAR SPECIES *H. italicum* is smaller, 30cm/12in high.

HELLEBORUS

Ranunculaceae

Native to woodland, handsome

evergreen hardy perennials blooming in winter or early spring.
CULTIVATION Sow fresh seed in summer in rich loam and shady position; avoid disturbing roots. Most self-seed readily (especially *H. foetidus*).
USE All parts **poisonous**. The rhizomes have been used for many thousands of years as purgatives and sedatives.

H. corsicus (H. lividus corsicus)   Corsican hellebore 60cm/24in high, with handsome thick spiny three-lobed leaves and pale green cup-shaped flowers in midspring.

H. foetidus   Stinking hellebore 75cm/30in high, with dark, narrow-cut leaves. Clustered green flowers are often red-rimmed.

H. niger   Christmas rose 45cm/18in high, with lobed leaves; early-flowering, white, saucer-shaped blooms.

H. orientalis   Lenten rose 60cm/24in high, with lobed leaves and flowers varying from cream to dark purple, often freckled within.

H. viridis   Green hellebore 30cm/12in high, with deciduous palmate leaves and green flowers.

HUMULUS lupulus

Hop   *Cannabinaceae*
Native to temperate climates in hedgerows and open woodland, vigorous, hardy, fast-growing herbaceous perennial climber, with rough, vine-shaped leaves. Male and female flowers are on separate plants. Females grown for highly aromatic papery cone flowers.
CULTIVATION Propagate from cuttings or suckers. Plant in rich deep soil in open sunny position.
USE Bitter young leaves and shoots are edible. Powdery glands among female flower bracts contain bitter principle; whole flowers used to flavor and preserve beer. Infuse flowers and leaves as a tonic and gentle sedative and digestive tisane. Flowers can be applied as a soothing poultice; also dried and stuffed in pillows against insomnia.
VARIETY The golden hop, *H.l.* 'Aureus', has bright yellow leaves.

HYDRASTIS canadensis

Golden seal   *Ranunculaceae*
Hardy woodland perennial from USA. About 30cm/12in high with a few deep-cut hairy leaves and one green flower rising in late spring from a long rhizome.
CULTIVATION Divide root in autumn and plant in moist, shady position. Harvest roots in autumn.
USE All parts **poisonous** in large doses. Dried root acts strongly on mucous membranes. Taken by American Indians against catarrh and gastric troubles and as a bitter tonic and digestive. Root gives good yellow dye.

HYOSCYAMUS niger

Henbane   *Solanaceae*
Widespread but local on waste-ground, a hardy biennial or annual of variable height to 1m/3ft. All parts slightly hairy and fetid; leaves toothed; pale yellow finely penciled flowers in early or late summer, followed by rows of curious seed capsules.
CULTIVATION Sow seed in spring or autumn; plant in sunny position. Eccentric germination.
USE All parts **poisonous**. Powerful alkaloids, including hyoscyamine, extracted from leaves. Still in use as an anaesthetic. Formerly chewed against toothache. Poultice of leaves can be applied to rheumatic joints.

HYPERICUM perforatum

St John's wort   *Guttiferae*
Hardy woodland perennial, common in temperate climates. Up to 1m/3ft high, with small star-shaped yellow flowers from mid- to late summer and pairs of leaves dotted with tiny glands.
CULTIVATION Divide fibrous roots in autumn and plant in semi-shade. Harvest flowering tops and leaves.
USE Red oil obtained from these is a strong, astringent, healing, antibiotic treatment for wounds, inflammations and aching joints. Mild tisane is a treatment for coughs and insomnia. Flowering tops give an orange dye.

HYSSOPUS officinalis

Hyssop   *Labiatae*
Native to S. Europe, a hardy bushy evergreen perennial or small shrub, about 90cm/36in high, with narrow aromatic leaves and rich purple-blue scented flowers in mid- to late summer. Also pink- or white-flowered forms.
CULTIVATION Seeds slow to germinate; sow in spring or divide roots or take cuttings; grow in light soil and sunny position. Trim in late spring to prevent legginess. A good hedging shrub.
USE Small quantities of bitter leaves flavor fatty foods, stuffings, sausages, etc., and act as a digestive. Flowering tops flavor liqueurs. Infuse flowers and leaves as tisane with antiseptic and cleansing effect on sore throats. Use externally, as a wash for wounds and bruises. Good bee plant.
VARIETY *H.o.* 'Aristatus', rock hyssop, is a compact dwarf variety.

Humulus lupulus

Hyoscyamus niger

INULA conyza

Ploughman's spikenard
Compositae
A hardy perennial that grows wild on limy soils in dry places in temperate climates. About 1m/3ft high, with long, pointed leaves and clusters of insignificant dusky yellow and purple flowers from midsummer.
CULTIVATION Sow seed or divide root. Will tolerate some shade.
USE Whole plant is faintly aromatic, particularly the root, which was formerly used as an antiseptic, fumigant and insect repellent.

I. helenium Elecampane
Native to Europe and Asia, a statuesque hardy perennial, 2m/6ft 6in high, with very large basal leaves, downy beneath, and smaller upper leaves; yellow daisy flowers bloom from midsummer.
CULTIVATION Sow seed in spring or divide root. Plant in moist, semishaded position. Harvest aromatic root in autumn.
USE Pungent, bitter root formerly used as culinary flavoring. Contains powerful antiseptic oil and has long history as treatment for bronchitis and catarrh and in decoction as a wash for skin diseases, acne, etc. (Sometimes known as scabwort.)

IRIS florentina

Orris, Florentine iris *Iridaceae*
Native to S. Europe, one of the oldest hardy cultivated plants, with sword-shaped leaves and white, violet-tinged flowers in early summer on stems up to 75cm/30in high.
CULTIVATION Divide rhizomes in late spring; plant in rich soil and sunny position and avoid disturbing.
USE Formerly used as a purgative. Highly fragrant root is of great value in perfumery and as scent fixative in potpourri; used to be smoldered to scent rooms and powdered to scent clothes and hair.
Note *I. pseudacorus*, yellow flag, native to Europe and Asia, and *I. versicolor*, blue flag, native to N. America, have powerfully acrid rhizomes formerly used as purgatives.

ISATIS tinctoria

Woad *Cruciferae*
Native to S. Europe and W. Asia, a hardy biennial with a rosette of long dark leaves and a flowering stem 1.3m/4ft 6in high. Small yellow flowers in early summer followed by dark hanging seed pods.
CULTIVATION Sow seed in spring or late summer on rich, well-drained ground and in sunny position. Self-seeds readily.
USE Astringent leaves are used externally to stop bleeding; gives good blue dye.

JUNIPERUS communis

Juniper *Cupressaceae*
Widespread shrubby perennial, native to heaths and mountains in Asia, N. America and Europe. Variable height to 3m/10ft. Bark, narrow leaves, tiny green-yellow flowers (in early summer) and fleshy berries (which take several years to ripen) are all strongly aromatic. Varieties include dwarf, prostrate and creeping forms.
CULTIVATION Can be grown from fresh seed but easier to take cuttings in autumn. Plant in sun or semishade.
USE A few berries (or strictly, cones) give resinous flavor to marinades, stews, etc., and to gin. Smoldering leaves and wood flavor barbecued meat and fish. Strongly antiseptic. It is also a traditional fumigant. Decoction of berries can be used as a remedy for urinary troubles, but should only be taken under supervision.

LAURUS nobilis

Bay *Lauraceae*
Native to S. Europe, grows to about 7m/23ft in temperate climates but 15m/50ft in warmer regions. A sturdy, hardy tree with glossy evergreen aromatic leaves, small flowers and black berries.
CULTIVATION Take cuttings in late summer and grow in sheltered sunny position and well-drained soil. Protect young tree during cold winters. Responds well to clipping once or twice a year.
USE Add strongly flavored leaves to stews, marinades, pâtés, etc., or infuse in milk for puddings and custards. Use with restraint. Leaves and especially berries have strongly antiseptic and mildly narcotic effect; oil from them is used as a remedy for bruises and rheumatism. Leaves and branches act as fumigants and insect repellents.
VARIETY *L.n.* 'Aurea' has golden-yellow leaves.

LAVANDULA *Labiatae*

Over 20 species of highly fragrant shrubby evergreen perennials from S. Europe. They have narrow leaves and spikes of scented flowers.
CULTIVATION Can be grown from seed, but cuttings take easily in spring or late summer. Plant in sunny, well-drained position. Respond well to clipping and shaping and ideal for hedging.
USE Leaves can be used with restraint as flavoring for stews and marinades; flowers scent conserves and jellies. Oil from flowers and stems powerfully antiseptic; can be used externally only on wounds, bruises, aching joints and insect bites, and for headaches. Use dried flowers in potpourri and as scented insect repellent among clothes.

L. angustifolia Old English lavender
The largest and most hardy lavender, up to 1.2m/4ft high and broad, with pale leaves and mauve flowers from mid- to late summer.
VARIETIES Many, including *L.a.* 'Hidcote Giant' with rich dark-purple flowers; the dwarf 'Hidcote', only 45cm/18in high; the paler and less compact dwarf 'Munstead' and 'Twickel Purple'; the compact Dutch lavender, and pink- and white-flowered forms.

L. dentata Fringed lavender
A half-hardy lavender, about 75cm/30in high, with toothed leaves and a delicate balsam scent. Soft, pale lilac flowers bloom in late autumn. Best grown in a pot and brought indoors during winter.

L. lanata Woolly lavender
Another tender lavender needing winter protection. Rather broad soft downy leaves and dark violet camphor-scented flowers blooming in late summer.

L. stoechas French lavender
Half-hardy in cold climates; about 60cm/24in high, with a more resinous lavender scent and conspicuous, ornamental purple bracts topping each flower spike in summer. There are several forms.
CULTIVATION Grow in a pot for moving indoors, or in a sheltered sunny position outside.

LEONURUS cardiaca

Motherwort *Labiatae*
Native to wasteground in Europe, a tough hardy perennial about

1.5m/5ft high, with palmate lobed veined leaves, dark above and downy beneath, and whorls of dusky purple flowers in summer.
CULTIVATION Sow seed or divide roots. Plant in open sunny position. Self-seeds readily.
USE Whole herb slightly astringent. Infuse as calming, sedative tonic. Name suggests its soothing effect on the heart.

LEVISTICUM officinale

Lovage   *Umbelliferae*
Native to the Mediterranean, a stout hardy perennial, up to 2m/6ft 6in high, with strongly aromatic pinnate leaves and umbels of yellow flowers in midsummer.
CULTIVATION Sow fresh seed or divide root. Plant in good loamy soil and sunny position.
USE Leaves have strong, earthy, celery flavor and are used in salads, soups, stews and vegetarian dishes. Seeds are warming and aromatic in meat dishes, soups, breads and cheese dishes. Seeds contain oil with digestive, antiseptic, cleansing, soothing properties; take for sore throats and catarrh.
Note *Ligusticum scoticum*, Scotch lovage, has similar but more pungent flavor and shorter, more compact habit.

LILIUM candidum

Madonna lily   *Liliaceae*
Cultivated since ancient times, a hardy perennial growing 1.5m/5ft high, with narrow shining leaves and sweet-smelling white flowers in midsummer.
CULTIVATION Plant bulbs shallowly in early autumn in good soil and sunny position, though lower stems of plants should be shaded if possible. Avoid disturbing. Harvest bulbs in late summer.

USE Bulbs contain much mucilage and are slightly astringent. Use externally, freshly bruised or boiled, on ulcers, corns and inflammations, and on minor burns.

LINUM usitatissimum

Common flax, linseed   *Linaceae*
Pretty, much-cultivated hardy annual, 50cm/20in high, with narrow leaves and blue flowers in summer.
CULTIVATION Sow seed in spring in open, sunny position.
USE Seeds, if taken internally, are an irritant and are now used only in veterinary medicine; pulped, they are used externally as a poultice for inflammations and boils. Oil from seeds is used commercially in paint and varnish. Stems are used to make cloth.

LIPPIA triphylla

Lemon verbena   *Verbenaceae*
Native to S. America, a woody half-hardy deciduous shrub growing 1.5m/5ft high in temperate climates. Graceful, pointed, sharply lemon-scented leaves and a sparse panicle of pale mauve flowers in summer.
CULTIVATION Take cuttings in summer, keep under cover during winter and plant out in late spring in sunny, sheltered position, preferably against a sunny wall. Protect roots during frost.
USE Leaves flavor cakes, fruits, etc.; fresh or dried leaves make a deliciously lemon-flavored tisane that acts as a gentle sedative and is a remedy for nausea and flatulence.

LOBELIA inflata

Indian tobacco   *Lobeliaceae*
Native to N. America, a hardy annual, 60cm/24in high with scattered pale blue flowers from mid- to late summer and toothed leaves.

CULTIVATION Sow seed in spring or autumn in sunny position.
USE Whole herb used against asthma and as an expectorant, but its very powerful action is the subject of controversy and it should be taken only under proper supervision. An important medicine to American Indians and early American settlers.
Note Other lobelias have similar properties. *L. syphilitica* is perennial and taller, with showier flowers. The root was formerly taken against dysentery and syphilis and is used today in homeopathy.

LONICERA periclymenum

Honeysuckle, woodbine   *Caprifoliaceae*
Native to temperate Europe and Asia, a familiar woodland climber. Hardy perennial and deciduous, with ovate leaves and fragrant, long, pale yellow, pink-flushed flowers followed by red berries. Woody stems twist up to about 6m/20ft high.
CULTIVATION Sow fresh seeds or take cuttings or layerings. Grows best in enriched soil, lightly shaded. Prune or thin old wood, if necessary, in spring. Can be trained as a standard.
USE Berries act as an emetic and can be poisonous. Infusion of leaves and flowers formerly taken for nervous diseases and headaches but no longer recommended. Antiseptic and astringent flowering tops have been used externally against skin infections.
VARIETIES These include the early summer-flowering Dutch varieties, *L.p.* 'Belgica' and the late summer-flowering 'Serotina'.
Note There are many other species such as the vigorous hybrid *L. americana* and the evergreen Japanese honeysuckle,

Inula
helenium

Inula
conyza

Lavandula
dentata

Lavandula
stoechas

L. japonica, and its variety 'Halliana', which has pale cream sweetly scented flowers.

MALVA moschata

Musk mallow   *Malvaceae*
Widespread on dry banks and roadsides, a handsome scented hardy perennial, 80cm/32in high, with lower leaves kidney-shaped, upper leaves deeply divided, and pink or occasionally white flowers from midsummer.
CULTIVATION Sow seed or take cuttings in spring. Plant in well-drained light soil in sun or semi-shade.
USE All mallows have edible leaves and seeds but are chiefly valuable for their emollient properties. All parts, especially the root, treat coughs and bronchitis, are gently laxative and make soothing poultices.

MANDRAGORA officinarum

Mandrake   *Solanaceae*
Native to S. Europe, a perennial with a rosette of wrinkled leaves 60cm/24in long, single, dusky yellow bell-flowers in late spring and very large yellow fruit.
CULTIVATION Sow fresh seed or divide roots. Plant in sheltered, sunny semishaded position.
USE All parts **poisonous**. An ancient anesthetic herb, the large taproot is especially potent. Leaves are used as an ingredient in soothing ointments and as a poultice for ulcers. Much superstition in the past surrounded the harvesting of the root.

MARRUBIUM vulgare

White horehound   *Labiatae*
Native to Europe and often naturalized elsewhere, an aromatic hardy perennial that grows in waste places. About 75cm/30in high, with wrinkled, pale, hairy leaves and whorls of off-white flowers throughout summer.
CULTIVATION Sow seed or divide root. Plant in well-drained sunny position.
USE Infusion of flowering plant or leaves is astringent and mucilaginous; an ancient cough and laxative medicine and a treatment for bronchitis and lung troubles. Profoundly bitter, so take with honey or as throat lozenges.
Note Black horehound, *Ballota nigra*, has similar habitat and habit but has small purple flowers, dark leaves and a most unpleasant smell. Formerly used as a sedative and anti-emetic.

MELILOTUS officinalis

Melilot   *Leguminosae*
A former fodder crop now widespread and naturalized on roadsides and wasteground. Hardy annual or biennial, about 1.2m/4ft high, much branched with graceful leaflets and yellow flowers from mid- to late summer, the whole sweetly scented, especially as it dries.
CULTIVATION Sow seed in autumn or spring; grow in sunny position and harvest flowering tops.
USE Infusion of flowering tops considered a mild expectorant, digestive and antiseptic. One of the best bee herbs.
Note *M. alba* has white flowers.

MELISSA officinalis

Lemon balm   *Labiatae*
Native to S. Europe, a hardy herbaceous perennial 1m/3ft high, with deliciously lemon-scented, toothed leaves and inconspicuous white flowers in summer.
CULTIVATION Sow seed or divide root. Tolerant and easy to cultivate in sunny position. Self-seeds. Cut down flowering tops to encourage fresh young leaf growth.
USE Fresh leaves give minty lemon flavor to stuffings, fruit salads, etc. Infusion of leaves makes refreshing lemon tisane, valuable against fevers, colds, nausea and upset stomach; also as a scented washing water. Fresh leaves soothe insect bites and are slightly antiseptic.
VARIETIES *M.o.* 'Aurea' is variegated and 'All Gold' has golden foliage.

MENTHA   *Labiatae*

Strongly scented hardy perennials with squared stems, pointed leaves and whorls of flowers in summer; they hybridize freely.
CULTIVATION Easily propagated from pieces of creeping root. Although tolerant, grows best on rich moist soil and in light shade. Often invasive and needs containing in bottomless buckets or between half-buried slates or stones. Cut down flowering tops to encourage fresh leaf growth. Leaves dry well.
USE Delicious, refreshing culinary herbs used fresh or dried with vegetables, yogurt, lamb and pulses, and in drinks; also as a scented tisane which has digestive and antiseptic properties.

M. aquatica   Water mint
Grows in damp meadows and on river banks. Has purple-tinged pungently scented leaves and stem.

M. arvensis   Corn mint, field mint
Prefers drier position; grows in fields and grassland. Slightly hairy coarsely scented leaves. Effectively prevents milk from curdling.

M. × gentilis 'Variegata'
Ginger mint
Bright yellow and green variegated leaves, shorter habit and a spicy scent.

M. × piperita   Black peppermint
Long, purple-tinged leaves and purple stem, tall habit and powerful peppermint scent.
USE Makes excellent tisane for soothing nerves and preventing nausea and indigestion. Peppermint oil is antiseptic; chew leaves to ease toothache, take infusion to relieve headache; also used to flavor candies, toothpaste.
VARIETIES There are many with different scents, including *M. × p.* 'Citrata' (eau-de-Cologne or bergamot mint), white peppermint and a curled form, 'Crispa'.

M. pulegium   Pennyroyal
A creeping mint with small rounded shining leaves, a strong peppermint scent and erect flowering stems of mauve blossoms.
CULTIVATION Prefers a moist, slightly shaded position. Ideal for growing between stones or as a carpeting herb.
USE Fresh leaves are an insect repellent. Dried herb formerly used to purify water on long voyages. There is a more erect form.

M. raripila rubra   Red raripila
Similar to black peppermint but with red-tinged rounded stubby leaves.

M. requienii   Corsican mint
Creeping mint with tiny round leaves, very small mauve flowers and a strong peppermint scent. Flourishes between paving in slightly shaded and fairly dry position.

M. spicata   Spearmint
The most commonly grown culinary mint with pointed well-flavored leaves. Very prone to

rust fungus: with a large crop
it is worth burning the dead
surface growth in autumn to
destroy rust spores (cover thinly
with dry straw and set alight).
Leaves dry very well.

M. suaveolens Apple mint
Fruitily scented, slightly rounded
downy leaves. The smaller cultivar *M.s.* 'Variegata', pineapple
mint, has a rich fruity scent and
smaller, very pretty variegated
cream and pale green leaves.

M. × villosa 'Alopecuroides'
Bowles' mint
Large, vigorous and finely flavored. Versatile with food and
seldom troubled with rust. Stems
over 1m/3ft high; big, rounded,
slightly downy leaves. A good all-
round variety.
Note Among the many other mint
varieties are 'Buddleia' with long
pale purple flowerheads, 'Eucalyptus' with eucalyptus scent, and
'Lavender' with soft, gray leaves.

MENYANTHES trifoliata

Bogbean, buckbean
Menyanthaceae
Hardy aquatic perennial in temperate climates. Has creeping
submerged rhizomes, trifoliate
leaves and pink, fringed flowers
in late spring.
CULTIVATION Divide root in spring
or autumn and plant in pond or
marshy ground.
USE Infuse dried leaves, take in
small quantities as appetizer and
as bitter tonic to cleanse blood and
skin, in spring. Use bruised leaves
externally as a poultice for
inflammations.

MEUM athamanticum

Spignel, meu or baldmoney
Umbelliferae
Native to high ground in northern
countries, a pretty perennial

about 50cm/20in high, with
feathery aromatic leaves and white
or purple-tinged flowers in
summer.
CULTIVATION Sow seed or divide
root. Plant in well-drained soil in
sun or light shade.
USE Whole herb, especially the
root, has pleasant aromatic
flavor reminiscent of lovage or
fennel. Roots are used as a digestive and stimulant.

MONARDA didyma

Bergamot, bee balm, oswego tea
Labiatae
Native to N. America, a hardy
herbaceous perennial, 1m/3ft
high, with highly fragrant broad
pointed leaves and heads of
curious, decorative, red flowers
from midsummer. There are
many varieties with different
colored flowers and less sweetly
scented leaves.
CULTIVATION Sow seed or divide
roots. Plant in good moist soil
and sunny position.
USE Float sweetly scented leaves
in drinks or add to ordinary tea
leaves. Infused, they make a
refreshing tisane that relieves
flatulence, nausea and menstrual
pain; also used to scent rinsing
and washing water.

MYRICA cerifera

Bayberry, candleberry, wax
myrtle *Myricaceae*
Native to damp places in N.
America, an evergreen or semi-
evergreen shrub or small tree up
to 4m/13ft high, with tough sharp
aromatic leaves, small pale
green flowers from late spring
and clusters of gray wax-
encrusted nutlets in late summer.
CULTIVATION Propagate from
seed, layers or suckers. Plant in
moist peaty lime-free soil.
USE Decoction of bark or leaves
can be used as a gargle for sore

throats or taken in very small
doses as tonic or against diarrhea.
Nutlets are scalded and wax
skimmed off to make sweetly
perfumed candles.
Note Related *M. gale*, the European sweet gale or bog myrtle,
also provides scented wax. Its
leaves have been used to flavor
and preserve 'gale beer'.

MYRRHIS odorata

Sweet cicely *Umbelliferae*
Native to high ground in temperate Europe and Russia, a hardy
perennial, 1.5m/5ft high, with
downy finely divided leaves smelling of licorice and aniseed;
creamy flowers in spring and long
dark oily fruit.
CULTIVATION Sow fresh seed in
autumn or divide root. Plant in
shady, moist position.
USE Fresh leaves have sugary
anise flavor and are pleasant in
salads and as sweetener in fruit
tarts. Chop unripe fruit to flavor
creams and custards. Boil or steam
large fleshy roots as vegetable. A
warming herb whose strong oils
are a tonic, digestive and mild
antiseptic: take infusion of leaves
or decoction of root.
Note The similar N. American
Osmorhiza longistylis has the
same properties.

MYRTUS communis

Myrtle, common myrtle
Myrtaceae
Thought to originate from W.
Asia, the evergreen myrtle is now
common in the Mediterranean
region. It grows about 3m/10ft
high, with glossy dark aromatic
leaves and pretty white flowers in
midsummer, followed by blue-
black berries.
CULTIVATION Can be grown from
seed but best propagated from
layers or cuttings in summer.
Plant in sunny, sheltered position;

Mentha requienii

Mentha spicata

Mentha suaveolens 'Variegata'

Mentha × piperita

Ocimum
basilicum

Ocimum
basilicum
'Dark Opal'

Ocimum
citriodorum

Ocimum
minimum

Ocimum
sanctum

protect young plants from frost. Adapts well to pots. Can be clipped and shaped.
USE Dried flower buds and berries have spicy flavor and are used in stuffings and stews. Leaves and smoldering wood give aromatic flavor to game dishes. Oil of myrtle is strongly antiseptic, formerly used to treat bronchitis. Dried flowers scent potpourris.
VARIETY *M.c.* 'Variegata' has variegated cream and green leaves.
Note *M.c. tarentina* is shorter, with a more compact habit and smaller leaves.

NASTURTIUM officinale

Watercress   *Cruciferae*
Common water plant in limy districts in temperate climates. It has glossy pinnate leaves; white flowers throughout summer.
CULTIVATION Sow seed or divide roots in summer. Plant in moist compost or in muddy shallow stream or grow indoors in porous pot set in saucer of water.
USE Chop hot, fresh-flavored leaves into salads or add to soups. Rich in minerals and vitamin C; a good tonic herb. Poultice of bruised leaves cleanses and freshens skin.

NEPETA cataria

Catnep   *Labiatae*
Native to Europe and Asia, a perennial about 1.4m/4ft 6in high. Soft and downy leaves resemble stinging nettles; dingy white flowers in late summer.
CULTIVATION Sow seed or divide roots. Plant in moist soil in an open position; it tolerates semi-shade.
USE Aromatic infusion of leaves is a mild, pleasant digestive and cough remedy and promotes perspiration.
Note *N. mussinii*, the common garden catmint, is generally

supplanted by its hybrid *N. × faassenii*. This is shorter, about 60cm/24in high, with smaller scented wrinkled leaves and decorative spikes of mauve-blue flowers throughout summer. It has similar properties.

OCIMUM   *Labiatae*

Subtropical species usually grown as tender annuals in temperate climates. All possess powerfully aromatic, spicily scented leaves and spikes of labiate flowers.
CULTIVATION Sow seed from spring to summer in frost-free position. Plant out in sheltered, sunny, well-drained, composted soil. Good results when grown under glass or on sunny window-sill. Pinch out flowers to encourage lush leaves.
USE Among the best culinary herbs, especially associated with tomatoes, vegetables, and pasta and rice dishes. Elusive flavor changes when leaves are dried; best preserved in oil or by deep freezing. Medicinally, oils from leaves are antiseptic, stimulant and digestive.

O. basilicum   Sweet basil
The most popular culinary basil, 20cm/8in high, with white flowers and finely flavored, large, toothed, succulent leaves.
VARIETY *O.b.* 'Dark Opal' has rich purple leaves and a spicier flavor.

O. citriodorum   Lemon-scented basil
Smaller than sweet basil, with more pointed leaves, a bushier habit and a lemon scent.

O. crispum   Lettuce leaf basil
Very large crinkled leaves similar in flavor to sweet basil.

O. kilimandsharium
Camphor basil

From Kenya, over 1m/3ft tall and camphor-scented.

O. minimum   Bush basil
About 25cm/10in high, with a compact habit and small leaves similar in flavor to sweet basil. Grows well in pots.

O. sanctum   Sacred basil, holy basil
About 40cm/16in high, with hairy leaves and stems and an aromatic clove scent. Sacred in the Hindu religion.

OENOTHERA biennis

Evening primrose   *Onagraceae*
Native to N. and S. America but widely naturalized elsewhere on wasteground, a hardy biennial with a rosette of long leaves and a stem over 1m/3ft high of yellow, delicately scented, cup-shaped flowers with flimsy petals that open at dusk throughout summer. There are many different species and hybrids.
CULTIVATION Easy to grow from seed or divide roots or offsets. It self-seeds freely and is tolerant of most soils and some shade.
USE Root can be boiled as a vegetable. Leaves and outer layer of stem are sedative, astringent and demulcent, used to treat whooping cough, asthma and stomach upsets. An oil extracted from seeds contains essential fatty acids and is currently being investigated for its considerable medicinal properties.

ORIGANUM   *Labiatae*

A large and widespread group of mainly perennial herbs with highly aromatic leaves and tubular flowers through summer.
CULTIVATION Sow seed or divide root. Plant in well-drained soil in a sunny position.
USE Many are important culinary

herbs that dry well, with leaves that contain strongly flavored, warming oil. Much used in soups, stews, roasts, etc. Medicinally an antiseptic, tonic and digestive herb, soothing and settling the stomach. Excellent bee and butterfly plant.

O. dictamnus   Dittany of Crete
Native to Crete, a tender perennial, 30cm/12in high, with small rounded leaves and flowers among drooping, rose-pink bracts. Strongly aromatic leaves and stems are covered with pale, woolly down and have a pungent flavor. Has low, shrubby habit.

O. heracleoticum   Winter marjoram
Tender perennial, native to Cyprus. Has low, creeping habit; downy, deliciously scented leaves and white flowers on erect stems.

O. majorana   Sweet marjoram, knotted marjoram
Grown as annual in temperate climates, 50cm/20in high, with rounded, strongly scented leaves and pale flowers emerging from tightly knotted bracts.
USE Leaves give fine flavor to light dishes, stuffings and sauces; also make a scented, warming tisane. Strong infusion can be used to scent washing waters.

O. onites   Pot marjoram
Hardy, spreading perennial, up to 60cm/24in high, with well-flavored leaves and pink or white flowers.

O. vulgare   Wild marjoram oregano
Very variable, widespread, hardy perennial, about 60cm/24in high, with paired leaves and rosy-pink flowers. Flavor varies tremendously according to climate and

habitat; best in hot sun and stony soil.
CULTIVATION Cut hard back in summer to encourage leaf growth.
VARIETIES Several including *O.v.* 'Aureum', golden marjoram, whose bright leaves may become 'scorched' during a hot summer. There is also a gold-tipped form. 'Compactum' is delightful, with well-flavored, small, close-growing leaves, though it seldom flowers.

PAEONIA officinalis

Peony   *Paeoniaceae*
A long-lived herbaceous hardy perennial, native to S. and W. Europe. Grows up to 1m/3ft high and has lobed leaves cut into segments, and single, rich red flowers with yellow stamens in early summer. There are many beautiful varieties.
CULTIVATION Sow seed in spring or divide root in early autumn; plant in rich loam. It tolerates some shade. Avoid disturbing.
USE Flowers and root **poisonous**. Root was widely used in past against convulsions and nervous diseases, as a sedative and 'against lunacy'. Seeds commonly used in Middle Ages as hot pepper substitute.

PANAX pseudoginseng

Chinese ginseng *Araliaceae*
A hardy perennial in woodland of China and Korea, *P. pseudoginseng* has a large, thick root and a single stem about 60cm/24in high bearing palmate leaves. Small umbels of green-yellow flowers in summer.
CULTIVATION Grow from seed in rich, shaded soil; it takes several years to develop.
USE Decoction of root has been accorded almost mythical powers for thousands of years and has complex constituents which

appear to adapt to bodily needs.
Note The American gingseng, *P. quinquefolius*, has similar properties.

PAPAVER somniferum

Opium poppy   *Papaveraceae*
Cultivated for several thousand years, a hardy annual of variable height to 1.2m/4ft, with white, pale pink or mauve flowers throughout summer.
CULTIVATION Sow seed in sunny position. Self-seeds readily.
USE Dried seeds of this and other species are used as flavoring for breads, cakes, etc. Thick juice obtained from seed capsule contains dangerous and addictive **poison**, opium, from which valuable medicinal drugs such as morphine are obtained.

PARIETARIA officinalis

Pellitory of the wall   *Urticaceae*
Hardy native of Europe and a widely naturalized weed growing in cracks in walls and on stony wasteground. Variable height to 75cm/30in, with red stems, glossy pointed leaves that dull with age, and tiny green flowers throughout summer.
CULTIVATION Sow seed or divide root. Once established, difficult to eradicate.
USE Infusion of flowering plant is valuable for bladder complaints, cystitis, etc., and is a gentle laxative.

PELARGONIUM *Geraniaceae*

A large genus of tender, shrubby, evergreen perennials which includes the popular scented-leaf species. Just a few are listed here.
CULTIVATION Generally, grow in pots indoors or bring under shelter for the winter. Can be propagated from seed but also takes well from cuttings, par-

Origanum majorana

Origanum vulgare

Origanum vulgare 'compactum'

Petroselinum
crispum

Petroselinum
crispum 'Neapolitanum'

Cryptotaenia
japonica

Aethusa
cynapium

ticularly in late summer. The flowers are usually insignificant and should be nipped out to encourage leaf growth.
USE The fragrant, lobed leaves have a great variety of scents and can be used to flavor custards, creams and fruit dishes; also dried for potpourri.

P. crispum
Small, tightly curled, balm-scented leaves; its variegated form, *P.c.* 'Variegatum', has foliage margined with cream-white.

P. graveolens
A common, vigorous species with rough, rose- and lemon-scented leaves; *P.g.* 'Lady Plymouth' is its variegated form.

P. tomentosum
Broad, soft, downy leaves smelling deliciously of peppermint when crushed.

PETROSELINUM
Parsley   *Umbelliferae*
Origin uncertain, as it has been so long in cultivation. All species are biennial, with a flowering stem up to 1m/3ft, deeply cut leaves, flowers in summer in yellow-green umbels, dark seeds and taproots.
CULTIVATION Self-seeds well, but to hasten germination of sown seed, soak seed bed with boiling water, scatter seed and cover only lightly with soil. Grow in sun or light shade and nip off flowers to prolong leafy growth.
USE Important culinary herb. Use the leaves fresh, the stems to flavor soups and stews. Rich in vitamins A, B, C and minerals, it is a tonic and digestive herb.

P. crispum   Curled parsley
Most familiar and decorative,

with bright green, moss-curled leaves. *P.c.* 'Neapolitanum', Italian parsley, French parsley, plain-leaved variety, hardy and highly nutritious but with slightly coarser flavor. *P.c.* 'Tuberosum', Hamburg parsley, the hardiest variety, plain-leaved, with large, edible, well-flavored roots which can be boiled like parsnips.
Note The unrelated, perennial *Cryptotaenia japonica*, Japanese parsley or mitsuba, has a similar but fainter flavor and broad, pale, trifoliate leaves. *Aethusa cynapium*, fool's parsley, is a weed with very similar looking but **poisonous** leaves, often confused with parsley or chervil. Can be identified by scentless leaves and narrow bracts hanging beneath umbel of flowers.

PHYTOLACCA americana
Poke root, pokeweed, pokeberry
Phytolaccaceae
Enormous hardy herbaceous perennial from N. America. Over 3m/10ft high and 2m/6ft 6in wide, with many hollow, often purple stems, large pale oblong leaves and long racemes of tightly clustered pink-white flowers in late summer, followed by berries which turn from pink to black.
CULTIVATION Sow seed or divide root. Grow in sun or light shade in deep, rich soil.
USE All parts **poisonous**. Root and sometimes berries used by American Indians as an emetic and remedy for venereal disease. Its powerful principles and alkaloids are being investigated.

PIMPINELLA anisum
Anise   *Umbelliferae*
Delicate annual, about 50cm/20in high, native to Mediterranean region. Has broad, basal leaves, finely cut upper leaves, small

white flowers in late summer and curved seeds that may not ripen in cool climates.
CULTIVATION Sow seed in late spring in light soil and sunny, sheltered position. Do not transplant.
USE Fragrant leaves can be used fresh in salads and light dishes. Powerfully aromatic seeds flavor fish, cream sauces, cakes, biscuits, fruit and various alcoholic liqueurs. Acts as strong digestive; also as an antiseptic and stimulant. Oil of anise is used in cough mixtures and lozenges.
SIMILAR SPECIES *P. saxifraga*, burnet saxifrage, grows wild throughout Europe in sunny, dry places. Pinnate leaves and umbel of white flowers. Decoction of acrid root formerly used as antiseptic and sedative. Use as a gargle or wound wash.

PLANTAGO major
Great plantain   *Plantaginaceae*
Perennial weed widespread in most temperate climates. Broad ribbed leaves grow from the base, with a 50cm/20in stem of tiny green flowers throughout summer. There is a cultivated form with dark purple leaves.
CULTIVATION Sow seed or divide root. Will grow in almost any situation; withstands treading.
USE Among the first recorded medicinal herbs, an astringent vulnerary taken in infusion for urinary troubles; especially effective as poultice or ointment for wounds, ulcers, stings and insect bites. Emollient seeds swell in water and were used as eye lotion and laxative.
Note Similar properties have been attributed to other plantain species. The curious rose plantain has similar leaves to *P. major* but with green flowerlike leafy inflorescences in summer.

P. psyllium   Flea seed
Native to the Mediterranean region, a hardy annual about 60cm/24in high, with wiry, hairy stems, threadlike leaves and little round flowerheads throughout summer, followed by glossy brown seeds.
CULTIVATION Sow seed in a dry, sunny position.
USE Emollient seeds have most effective medicinal action as eye lotion and laxative.

POLEMONIUM caeruleum

Jacob's ladder, Greek valerian
Polemoniaceae
Native to Europe, often cultivated in gardens, a hardy herbaceous perennial up to 1m/3ft high, with paired leaflets and blue flowers in spring.
CULTIVATION Sow seed or divide root. Plant in moist, semishaded position.
USE In ancient times whole herb, especially the astringent root, taken in wine as remedy for fevers, palpitations and nervous hysteria.
Note *P. reptans*, abscess root, grows in N. American woodlands and has a similar appearance, with clusters of drooping blue flowers. Decoction of astringent root taken for coughs, fevers and lung complaints.

POLYGONATUM multiflorum

Solomon's seal, David's harp
Liliaceae
Hardy native of woodlands in N. Europe. Up to 1m/3ft high, with curving stems, ribbed leaves and creamy bell flowers in spring. There are dwarf and variegated varieties.
CULTIVATION Sow fresh seed or divide creeping roots. Plant in light, loamy soil in semishade.
USE Root is astringent and rich in mucilage. Crush and use as a poultice for inflammations, bruises and wounds. Do not take internally.

POLYGONUM bistorta

Bistort   *Polygonaceae*
A hardy perennial growing in damp grassland on high ground in temperate Europe and Asia. Has creeping roots, broad leaves, and stems up to 1m/3ft high of pink flowers in late spring. Many varieties.
CULTIVATION Propagated easily by dividing root. Grow in moist, shaded position. It spreads fast.
USE Early spring leaves make pleasant salad or steamed vegetable. Decoction of roots makes powerful astringent remedy for coughs, sore throats and dysentery; also a mouthwash for ulcers and a healing wash for wounds.

PORTULACA oleracea

Purslane   *Portulacaceae*
Much cultivated hardy annual, low and succulent, with fleshy rounded leaves and tiny yellow flowers in late summer.
CULTIVATION Sow seed in light soil and open position from spring through summer for successive crops. Keep well watered.
USE Deliciously cooling salad herb. Older leaves can be boiled. Rich in vitamin C.
VARIETY There is a golden-leaved form, *P.o.* 'Sativa'.

PRIMULA veris

Cowslip   *Primulaceae*
A hardy perennial in grassland of temperate Europe and Asia, it has rosette of wrinkled leaves and, in spring, a flower stem up to 30cm/12in high topped with a cluster of richly scented yellow, orange-centered flowers.
CULTIVATION Sow fresh seed or divide root. Plant in well-drained, sunny position.

USE Flowers have sedative soothing properties when taken as an infusion or in wine. Whole herb, especially root, can be taken for coughs, bronchitis. Flowers formerly used as cosmetic.

P. vulgaris   Primrose
Habitat similar to cowslip, with rosette of leaves–but shorter flower stem and paler, larger, solitary and less fragrant flowers. Cultivate as cowslip. Has similar properties.

PULICARIA dysenterica

Fleabane   *Compositae*
Native to damp grassland in Europe, a pretty, herbaceous hardy perennial about 75cm/30in high, with downy lanceolate leaves and yellow daisy flowers in late summer. It spreads fast.
CULTIVATION Divide roots and plant in sun or semishade.
USE A fumigant herb, whose astringent leaves taste of soap and smell fruitily antiseptic. A strong infusion can be used as an insect repellent.

PULMONARIA officinalis

Lungwort, Jerusalem cowslip, spotted dog   *Boraginaceae*
Hardy perennial in European woodland, 30cm/12in high, with large silver-spotted evergreen leaves and spring flowers that open pink and change to blue.
CULTIVATION Forms a spreading clump that can easily be divided, or propagate from seed. Grow in moist, lightly shaded position.
USE In common with many other members of the borage family, leaves contain much mucilage and are used in infusion for coughs and lung complaints.
Note There are many species, including *P. angustifolia*, which has large, bright blue flowers; *P. rubra* and its cultivar 'Bowles

Polygonum bistorta

Rosmarinus officinalis

Rosmarinus officinalis 'Benenden Blue'

Rosmarinus lavandulaceus

Red' with pink flowers; *P. longifolia*, with very long, sharply pointed leaves; and *P. saccharata*, which has broader leaves heavily splashed with silver.

PULSATILLA vulgaris

Pasque flower   *Ranunculaceae*
Hardy perennial, native to dry, calcareous grassland in Europe. Grows up to 30cm/12in high, and has pinnate leaves covered with silver hairs and large rich purple bell-shaped flowers, with golden stamens, that bloom in spring.
CULTIVATION Sow seed or divide rhizome. Plant in well-drained, open, sunny position, in limy soil.
USE All parts **poisonous**. Whole herb acrid and highly irritant; large dose can cause convulsions and death. Small dose acts as a sedative and nervine. A homeopathic treatment for measles.

RESEDA luteola

Dyer's rocket, weld   *Resedaceae*
Native to calcareous soil in Europe, a hardy biennial with a rosette of long, wavy-edged leaves the first year and a 1.5m/5ft stem of small, yellow-green flowers grouped in a spike during summer of the second year.
CULTIVATION Sow seed in light soil and sunny position.
USE Whole flowering plant gives strong clear yellow dye.

RHAMNUS cathartica

Buckthorn, purging buckthorn *Rhamnaceae*
Native to hedges and scrub in N. Europe and Asia, a hardy shrubby deciduous tree about 4m/13ft high, with rounded, veined leaves, small green flowers from late spring and red berries that blacken as they ripen.
CULTIVATION Takes easily from cuttings; makes good hedging.

USE Bark and berries fiercely purgative and were formerly used as a drastic laxative.
Note A species from N. America, *R. purshiana*, also known as Cascara, sagrada or holy bark, is a larger tree with narrower leaves. Its dried bark has less violent laxative properties.

ROSA gallica officinalis

Apothecary's rose, Provins rose *Rosaceae*
Derived from the ancient *R. gallica*, a hardy shrub rose up to 1.2m/4ft, with semidouble deep pink-red richly scented flowers with golden stamens followed by red hips.
CULTIVATION Take cuttings in late summer to plant out the following autumn in a sunny position in good loam. Mulching is beneficial. Prune lightly after flowering. Has few thorns and is suitable for hedging.
USE The petals dry well, retaining their scent, and are highly antiseptic and astringent. Was often taken as an electuary (made by simmering the petals in honey) for sore throats, mouth ulcers and lung disease. Prime ingredient in potpourri.
VARIETY *R.g.* 'Versicolor' (*R.g.* 'Rosa Mundi') is striped deep pink and white.
OTHER OLD ROSE SPECIES Varieties of *R. damascena*, the Damask rose, have an extremely rich scent. *R. moschata*, the musk rose, can grow 6m/20ft high and has a subtle, musky perfume. Varieties of *R. rubiginosa*, sweet briar or eglantine, have single, pale pink flowers in late spring, and scented leaves, and can be trained along a fence or used as hedging.

ROSMARINUS officinalis

Rosemary   *Labiatae*
Much cultivated perennial half-

hardy evergreen shrub from Mediterranean regions. Has spiky highly fragrant leaves and mauveblue flowers in early summer. May grow over 2m/6ft 6in high in sheltered, sunny position.
CULTIVATION Sow seed or propagate (easily) from cuttings. Plant in light, well-drained soil. Grows well in pots. Can be shaped and grown as a hedge. Protect from frost in cold areas.
USE Use powerfully flavored leaves with discretion with broiled and roast meats, fish, milk puddings and creams. A digestive and strengthening herb; also soothing and antiseptic. Oil is used on aching joints and as insect repellent; distilled water or infusion used as cosmetic and hairwash or rinse.
VARIETIES These include the whiteflowered *R.o.* 'Albiflorus', the pink-flowered 'Roseus', and 'Miss Jessup's Upright' which grows tall, like a column. *R.o.* 'Benenden Blue' has fine leaves leaves and rich blue flowers, and there is a variable form with golden variegation in the leaves.
Note *R. lavandulaceus* is slightly less hardy, with a low, trailing, almost prostrate habit.

RUBIA tinctorum

Madder   *Rubiaceae*
Much cultivated ancient dye plant of uncertain origins. A hardy perennial, it spreads to about 60–100cm/24–40in, with long scrambling stems and whorls of large leaves, which are rough and prickly. Pale yellow-green flowers in early summer.
CULTIVATION Sow seed or divide creeping roots. Plant in deeply worked, well-drained soil.
USE Powdered root was used to treat bladder complaints. Fleshy rootstock gives a good-colored red dye.

RUMEX acetosa

Garden sorrel *Polygonaceae*
Common in moist grassland of
Europe and Asia, a hardy perennial with broad, lush leaves and
stems 1m/3ft high of red
flowers.
CULTIVATION Sow seed or divide
root. Plant in rich moist soil in
sun or semishade. It self-seeds
readily. Cut back flowering stems
to encourage leaf growth.
USE Valuable, sharp-tasting salad
herb available from early spring;
excellent cooked in soups and
sauces. A nutritious tonic herb
with cooling and cleansing
properties.

R. obtusifolius Common
broad dock
Most valuable when used
externally for skin complaints.

R. sanguineum Bloody dock
The most decorative for the herb
garden.

R. scutatus French sorrel
Has small, rounded leaves and a
low, spreading habit. Cultivate
and use as for *R. acetosa*.

RUTA graveolens

Rue *Rutaceae*
Handsome evergreen hardy
perennial from S. Europe. Grows
65cm/26in high, with ornamental
rounded lobed leaves and complex
yellow-green flowers.
CULTIVATION Sow seed or take
cuttings and grow in well-drained
sunny position. Can be trimmed
to shape in late spring, and makes
a loose hedge.
USE Formerly an important
medicinal herb, but inadvisable
to use without supervision.
Powerful, bitter oil in leaves can
be toxic and lead to abortion;
makes a strong disinfectant and
insect repellent. Handling plant

may cause a rash on tender skins.
VARIETIES *R.g.* 'Jackman's Blue',
with blue-bloomed leaves, is the
most decorative and commonly
grown. *R.g.* 'Variegata' has
variegated leaves.

SALVIA *Labiatae*

Besides the common *S. officinalis*
there are over 700 species, many
aromatic with culinary or medicinal value, and with tubular
deep-throated flowers from early
summer. Most species grow wild
in dry warm stony places and
prefer well-drained garden soil
and a sunny position.

S. glutinosa Jupiter's distaff
Native to damp subalpine woods
in the Alps and N. Turkey, a
hardy perennial, about 90cm/36in
high, with long wrinkled leaves
and a spike of pale yellow lightly
penciled flowers in late summer.
The whole herb has a warm aroma
and exudes a scented gum in
summer.
CULTIVATION Sow seed or divide
root. Plant in sheltered, sunny
position.

S. officinalis Common sage
Native to the Mediterranean
coast, a shrubby, woody, strongly
aromatic perennial with pointed
rough-textured gray leaves and
purple-blue flowers.
CULTIVATION Sow seed or propagate (easily) from cuttings. Leaves
dry well. Cut back straggling
branches or trim the plant in
late spring.
USE A pungent flavoring herb;
add chopped leaves to stuffings,
sausages, cheeses and other fatty
foods. Excellent general tonic
medicine. Infusion of leaves
makes pleasant tisane with a
valuable antiseptic, digestive and
cleansing action; use also as a
gargle for sore throats, mouth

ulcers, and as a revitalizing hairwash or rinse. Rub fresh leaves
daily on teeth and gums to cleanse
and strengthen.
VARIETIES There are several including *S.o.* 'Purpurascens', the
handsome purple or red sage, the
variegated gold-leaved *S.o.*
'Icterina' and the less hardy *S.o.*
'Tricolor', whose leaves are
splashed purple, cream and green.
There are also low-growing forms
with small, narrow, highly aromatic gray leaves, and the white-
flowered, half-hardy *S.o.* 'Laven-
dulifolia'.

S. pratensis Meadow clary
Perennial on grassland in N.
European climates. Grows about
80cm/32in high, with blunt, dark,
aromatic wrinkled leaves and
spikes of rich, purple-blue
flowers in midsummer.
CULTIVATION Sow seed or divide
root. Plant in sunny position.
USE Dark seeds contain mucilage
and were formerly soaked in water
until soft and swollen, then used
to cleanse and clear the eyes.

S. rutilans Pineapple sage
Half-hardy, shrubby perennial
thought to originate in Mexico.
Grows to 1m/3ft, with soft, ovate
pointed leaves that smell fruitily
of pineapple when brushed, and
red flowers in autumn and early
winter.
CULTIVATION Propagates easily
from cuttings. Grow in pots and
bring indoors in winter.
Note *S. grahamii* and *S. coccinea*
can be cultivated as *S. rutilans*.
Both are similar with red flowers,
but their leaves have different
scents.

S. sclarea Clary sage
Handsome biennial to 1.2m/4ft,
with large wrinkled dark leaves
and long spikes of mauve flowers

with pink bracts from midsummer. Whole plant has powerful, rich smell.
CULTIVATION Sow seed in sunny
position.
USE Seeds were used medicinally
as for *S. pratensis*, meadow clary.
Scented oil extracted to give
muscatel flavor to wines. Clary
wine formerly considered an
aphrodisiac. Oil also used in the
perfume industry.
VARIETY *S.s.* 'Turkestanica' is the
most ornamental with silvery
mauve bracts and similar scent.

Note The herbaceous perennial
Russian sage, *Perovskia atriplici-
folia*, has sage-scented leaves. The
handsome shrubby evergreen
Jerusalem sage, *Phlomis fruticosa*,
has downy, gray, aromatic leaves
and grows up to 1.2m/4ft high,
with whorls of hooded yellow
flowers in summer.

SAMBUCUS nigra

Elder, black elder
Caprifoliaceae
Hardy deciduous tree, common in
hedgerows and scrubland in temperate climates. Up to 8m/28ft
high, with strong-smelling leaflets, clusters of creamy, scented
flowers in early summer and dark
berries in autumn. There are
varieties with golden and
variegated leaves.
CULTIVATION Propagate from
suckers or cuttings. Grows easily
and fast in most situations.
USE Every part. Flowers make
fragrant light wine, flavor
jellies, and can be fried in
batter as fritters. Infusion of
flowers has soothing, cooling
properties and is a remedy for
fevers, colds, catarrh; use externally as an eye lotion and a
cosmetic wash. Berries (not eaten
raw) make good wine, delicious in
apply jelly; hot juice or syrup can

Santolina
chamaecyparissus

Santolina
neapolitana

Santolina
virens

Satureja
hortensis

Satureja
montana

be taken for coughs, bronchitis, etc., with slightly laxative effect. Leaves, used externally only in ointment or wash, have effective healing, soothing action; infusion acts as insect repellent. Bark formerly used as strong purgative. Tree is associated with magic and witchcraft.

S. ebulus Dwarf elder, dane-wort
An herbaceous perennial, natural-ized in Britain. It grows about 1.2m/4ft high, with similar leaves, flowers and fruit to *S. nigra*, but with a very violent purgative effect when taken internally.

SANGUINARIA canadensis

Bloodroot *Papaveraceae*
Native to N. American woodland, a creeping hardy perennial about 20cm/8in high, with broad, lobed leaves and beautiful white flowers in spring. A double-flowered form is commonly cultivated.
CULTIVATION Divide root after flowering and plant in moist, enriched soil in shady position.
USE Dried rhizome used by American Indians as strongly antiseptic stimulant, irritant and emetic. Has violent action and should only be taken under super-vision. Bright red sap from plant and especially root is strongly caustic and gives a good red dye.

SANGUISORBA minor

Salad burnet *Rosaceae*
Hardy perennial, native to grassy places on limestone in Europe. Variable height to 80cm/32in, with long leaves divided into leaflets and small heads of green flowers throughout summer.
CULTIVATION Sow seed in sunny position. Grows easily and self-seeds readily. Cut down coarse old growth to encourage fresh leaves.

USE Faintly bitter and nutty in salads. Usually available through-out the year.

SANTOLINA *Compositae*

Hardy evergreen shrubby herbs from S. Europe. Aromatic leaves and long-stemmed yellow button flowers from midsummer.
CULTIVATION Takes easily from cuttings. Plant in light, well-drained soil and sunny position. Cut back leggy growth and trim in late spring and summer. Most species make good hedging.
USE Scented, disinfectant leaves are dried and used as insect and moth repellent.

S. chamaecyparissus

Santolina, cotton lavender
Makes a good dense bush about 80cm/32in high and wide, with slightly downy silver toothed stubby leaves and rich yellow flowers.
S.c. 'Corsica' (*S.c.* 'Nana') is a compact dwarf variety, good for edging or knot gardens.

S. neapolitana

About 80cm/32in high and wide, with lighter, more feathery, silver foliage. *S.n.* 'Sulphurea' has pale lemon-yellow flowers.

S. virens

About 60cm/24in high, with narrow less aromatic rich green leaves and bright yellow flowers.

SAPONARIA officinalis

Soapwort *Caryophyllaceae*
A hardy perennial, native to Europe and a common garden escape. Grows up to 80cm/32in high, with sprawling jointed stems, smooth lanceolate leaves and pretty scented lilac-pink flowers in high summer. There is a double-flowered variety, 'Bouncing Bet'.

CULTIVATION Sow seed or divide creeping root. Plant in sun or light shade. Becomes invasive, so contain roots.
USE Decoction of root is used externally to treat eczema, acne and other skin conditions. Whole herb simmered gives thin, green, disinfectant lather with a cleansing action, good for washing fragile fabrics.

SATUREJA hortensis

Summer savory *Labiatae*
Native to eastern Mediterranean and Asia, an aromatic hardy annual about 60cm/24in high, with lilac-colored stems, narrow leaves and pale lilac flowers from midsummer. It has an elegant habit.
CULTIVATION Sow seed in spring and grow in sunny well-drained position. Pull up whole plant and dry before frosts begin.
USE Good peppery thyme flavor for bean dishes, sausages, stews and soups. Aromatic oils stimulate appetite, aid digestion and act as an antiseptic gargle. Was formerly considered an aphrodisiac.

S. montana Winter savory
Native to stony hillsides in Mediterranean regions, a hardy evergreen perennial with a woody stem. Grows about 40cm/16in high, with tough narrow leaves and white or lilac flowers in late summer. There are some lovely varieties with white or purple flowers and a creeping form with strongly aromatic leaves.
CULTIVATION Sow seed or take cuttings or layerings. Plant in well-drained soil and sunny position. Prune back straggling branches in late spring. Good low hedging plant, though some leaves may fall during frosts.
USE Similar to *Satureja hortensis*, summer savory, but has a slightly

coarser flavor. Rub leaves on insect bites to ease pain.

SCROPHULARIA nodosa

Knotted figwort
Scrophulariaceae
Hardy European perennial about 1.2m/4ft high, growing in shady places. Has square stem, ovate slightly fetid leaves and complex strange little red-brown flowers from midsummer, very attractive to bees and wasps. An odd rather than a handsome plant.
CULTIVATION Sow seed or divide root. Plant in shady corner.
USE Bruised root or whole herb can be used as a poultice for wounds and skin complaints, and, traditionally, for piles. Action on heart similar to that of related *Digitalis*, foxglove; must not be taken internally.
Note *S. aquatica*, water figwort, is taller with smoother leaves but has similar properties to *S. nodosa*. *S.a.* 'Variegata' is smaller but very ornamental with bright cream and green leaves.

SCUTELLARIA lateriflora

Virginian skullcap, mad dog skullcap *Labiatae*
Hardy perennial from N. America, about 75cm/30in high, with blunt-toothed leaves and curious blue, hooded flowers from midsummer, opening successively up long curving stems that straighten as seeds ripen. Seed capsules are like tiny lidded dishes and the plant has a neat habit.
CULTIVATION Sow seed or divide root. Plant in sun or light shade.
USE Formerly used as nervine, bitter tonic and remedy for hysteria, neuralgia and hydrophobia. Now considered unsafe to take without supervision.
Note *S. galericulata*, European skullcap, has slightly weaker medicinal properties, a looser

habit, and larger flowers growing in pairs. Found near fresh water.

SEMPERVIVUM tectorum

Houseleek *Crassulaceae*
Hardy perennial native to mountains in Europe, but long cultivated and often found as a garden escape, particularly on walls and roofs. Succulent multiple rosette of fleshy leaves and occasional stem of pink flowers in early summer.
CULTIVATION Detach little offshoots from parent and plant in stony soil.
USE Ancient protective and medicinal herb. Use bruised or pulped leaves to cool, soothe and heal minor burns and wounds.

SERRATULA tinctoria

Sawwort *Compositae*
Hardy European perennial, about 60cm/24in high, with wiry stem, cut leaves or leaflets and purple, thistlelike flowers in late summer.
CULTIVATION Sow seed or divide roots. Grow in full sun.
USE A wound herb and formerly an important dye plant giving a good green-yellow color.

SILYBUM marianum

Milk thistle *Compositae*
Native to central Europe but often naturalized elsewhere, a hardy annual or biennial with a rosette of large dark prickly leaves dramatically marked with white and purple thistlelike flowers in midsummer.
CULTIVATION Sow seed in sunny well-drained position. Self-seeds readily.
USE Shoots, leaves, stem and buds can be used as rather bitter potherbs and salads. A bitter tonic herb, it is taken especially to increase nursing mothers' milk flow. Seeds are emetic and not taken internally.

SINAPIS alba

White mustard *Cruciferae*
Originally native to the Mediterranean, a much cultivated, fast-growing hardy annual, up to 1m/3ft high, with deeply cut leaves, yellow flowers from midsummer and beaked pods bulging as seeds ripen.
CULTIVATION Sow seed in sunny position in rich soil.
USE Seeds have less pungent flavor but are more effective medicinally than those of *Brassica nigra*, black mustard; they have strongly disinfectant and preservative properties. Seedling leaves are good in salads. Useful as green manure for poor soils.

SMYRNIUM olusatrum

Alexanders *Umbelliferae*
Hardy biennial or short-lived perennial, native to Mediterranean regions but widely naturalized and generally found near the sea. A statuesque plant, up to 1.5m/5ft high, best in spring with glossy broad leaflets and yellow flowerheads.
CULTIVATION Sow seed in autumn and grow in sun and light soil.
USE Strong aromatic flavour. Formerly cultivated widely as a potherb. Add buds and leaves to salads; bitter stems are best blanched and stewed. Acts as a mild digestive. Crushed leaves make a healing treatment for wounds.
Note *S. perfoliatum*, perfoliate alexanders, a biennial, is particularly decorative with circular upper leaves. It has similar uses.

SOLIDAGO virgaurea

European golden rod
Compositae
Native to open woodland in Europe, Asia and N. Africa, especially on high ground, a variable hardy perennial, up to

1m/3ft high, with lanceolate leaves and ruffled yellow daisy flowers in late summer.
CULTIVATION Sow seed or divide root. Plant in open, sunny position.
USE Traditional wound herb, whole plant being astringent and containing healing oils. Use as a poultice or in strong infusion as a styptic wash. Flowers give a good yellow dye.
Note Many other *Solidago* species have similar properties, including those native to N. America.

STACHYS officinalis

Betony *Labiatae*
A hardy perennial, native to grassy places in Europe. About 50cm/20in high, with regular round-lobed leaves and spikes of purple flowers from mid- to late summer. *S.o.* 'Grandiflora' has more showy flowers.
CULTIVATION Sow seed or divide root. Plant in sunny position.
USE Legendary medicinal herb, formerly taken in infusion as a nervine, sedative, tonic and emetic. Astringent, bitter leaves are now usually used only externally as a poultice.
Note Several other *Stachys* species have similar healing properties: the wild woundworts and the garden donkey's ears with long, downy, silvered leaves, *S. lanata*, and its useful non-flowering cultivar *S.l.* 'Silver Carpet'.

SYMPHYTUM officinale

Comfrey *Boraginaceae*
Native to temperate Europe and Asia, naturalized elsewhere in damp places, ditches and riverbanks. A large lush hardy perennial, generally over 1m/3ft high, with prolific very long broad hairy basal leaves and bell-shaped flowers of white, pink or purple

in a spike in early summer.
CULTIVATION Easy to propagate from pieces of root or root division. It grows best in rich soil. For steady supply of leaves, cut whole plant down regularly throughout growing season. May need containing as it spreads rapidly.
USE Country names 'boneset' and 'knitbone' indicate long-established use as prime healing herb. Fresh-grated root and leaves contain much mucilage and allantoin, a healing agent. Apply a poultice of root or of leaves (briefly steamed or blanched to soften irritant hairs) to inflammations, cuts and bruises. Infuse leaves as a healing and cosmetic wash. Excellent composting plant and nutritious liquid fertilizer.
Note There are many smaller, decorative comfrey species for the garden: *S. caucasicum* with blue flowers, *S. grandiflorum* with pale yellow, orange-tipped flowers and *S. ochroleucum* with soft leaves and pure white flowers.

TAGETES lucida

Cloud plant, anise-flavored marigold *Compositae*
Native to Mexico, a tender perennial marigold growing about 45cm/18in high, with toothed lanceolate leaves and single orange-gold flowers in summer.
CULTIVATION Sow seed or take cuttings. Plant out after frosts are over, or grow in pots to take indoors for winter protection. Grow in sunny sheltered position.
USE Whole herb is sweetly scented. Use anise/tarragon-flavored leaves in soups or dry them to make a fragrant tea.
Note Other *Tagetes* species (African, French or Mexican marigolds) are valuable as companion plants in the garden: excretions from their roots deter nematodes and other pests.

TANACETUM parthenium (Chrysanthemum parthenium)

Feverfew *Compositae*
A bushy short-lived hardy perennial, native to E. Europe and a common garden escape. Grows up to 60cm/24in high, with strongly aromatic, divided, rounded leaves that may persist through mild winters, and pretty daisy flowers blooming from late spring to autumn.
CULTIVATION Sow seed or divide root. Foliage tends to be darker when grown in shaded position, but the plant is generally tolerant and self-seeds widely.
USE Ancient tonic and nervine. Recent research indicates use for migraine sufferers. The bitter leaf can be taken with bread and butter or as infusion. Eat only in small quantities. Bruised or infused, the leaves can be used externally as an effective healing, soothing wash.
VARIETIES There are several; especially decorative is *T.p.* 'Aureum', golden feverfew, with its bright leaves, and the darker-leaved, double-flowered 'White Bonnet'.

T. vulgare Tansy
Native to N. Europe, naturalized in wasteground elsewhere, a strong hardy perennial, up to 1m/3ft high, with feathery pungent leaves and yellow button flowers that bloom from mid- to late summer.
CULTIVATION Sow seed or divide creeping roots. Plant in a sunny position.
USE Bitter, aromatic leaves were formerly used as flavoring and as a digestive and vermifuge. Now used only as an insecticide, the leaves being bruised, dried or infused.
VARIETY *T.v.* 'Crispum' has decorative curled leaves.

TARAXACUM officinale

Dandelion *Compositae*
Very common hardy perennial weed of variable height to 30cm/12in, with long toothed leaves, golden flowerheads from spring and a 'clock' of silky-haired seeds.
CULTIVATION Grow cultivated forms for juiciest leaves. Sow seed in spring in open sunny position. Blanch under a pot or indoors (as for *Cichorium intybus*, chicory) for winter use.
USE Young tender inner leaves or blanched leaves are eaten as a rather bitter salad. Flowers make good wine. Roots are dried and ground as coffee substitute. Wholesome and highly nutritious, it is a good tonic herb. Decoction of flowers used as a cosmetic wash.

TEUCRIUM chamaedrys

Wall germander *Labiatae*
Hardy, shrubby evergreen, native to S. Europe, growing about 40cm/16in high. It has small dark glossy aromatic leaves with rounded teeth and spikes of bright pink flowers from mid-summer. There is also a creeping variety.
CULTIVATION Sow seed or take cuttings. Plant in well-drained sunny position out of the wind. Responds well to regular clipping and makes good low hedge. Ideal for knot gardens.
USE Formerly a medicinal herb for fevers, indigestion and gout. Its scent also made it a commonly used strewing herb.

T. scorodonia Wood sage
Hardy European native most common on acid soils. It grows 60cm/24in high on banks and in light woodland. Oval, aromatic leaves are closely wrinkled; spikes of green-yellow flowers from mid- to late summer have purple anthers and no upper lip.

CULTIVATION Sow seed or divide creeping root. Plant in dry soil.
USE Good bitter tonic herb. Take infusion of whole herb for fevers and to promote menstruation.

THYMUS *Labiatae*

There is a tremendous number of thyme species and varieties, all hardy, with small, variously and powerfully scented leaves, and tubular flowers from early summer. Bushy species are native to S. Europe while creeping species are widely distributed even in cold climates.
CULTIVATION All grow well from seed, cuttings or layerings. They need good drainage and a sunny position. Trim leggy plants, if necessary, after flowering.
USE One of the prime culinary herbs; the aromatic leaves (particularly of *T. vulgaris* varieties) give their strong, warm flavor to soups, stews, meats and vegetables. Their powerful oils, which include thymol, are very antiseptic and an infusion of the leaves is valuable for coughs, colds and bronchitis, as a gargle for sore throats and mouth ulcers, or as a disinfectant wash. The oil makes a strengthening rub.

T. azoricus
Low growing with compact, mounded habit, spiky leaves and a resinous scent.

T. × citriodorus Lemon thyme
Hybrid from *T. vulgaris*, with delicious lemon scent and pink flowers. The slightly less hardy *T. × c.* 'Aureus' has golden variegated leaves and *T. × c.* 'Silver Queen' has silvery variegated leaves.

T. drucei (T. praecox arcticus) Common wild thyme
Prostrate creeping thyme native

to open, grassy places. It has purple flowers. Strength of scent varies according to habitat and season.
VARIETIES Including *T.d.* 'Albus', very pretty with light green leaves and white flowers; and 'Annie Hall' with pale pink flowers. *T.d. coccineus* has strong crimson flowers and *T.d.c.* 'Doone Valley' is variegated and lemon scented. *T.d.c.* 'E.B. Anderson' has large, strongly scented leaves of variable golden-green. *T.d.c.* 'Elfin' has tiny rounded leaves. 'Lanuginosus' has pale, downy leaves and 'Pink Chintz' has pink flowers and forms a compact carpet.

T. fragrantissimus
Has a loose upright habit, white flowers and pale gray strongly fruit-scented foliage.

T. herba-barona   Caraway thyme
Prostrate, handsome, with red stems and dark, caraway-scented leaves.

T. pulegioides
Native to N. Europe, it has a low, spreading habit, large glossy dark leaves and purple flowers.

T. vulgaris   Common thyme
The most commonly cultivated and highly flavored thyme, with narrow leaves, pale mauve flowers and a shrubby habit. Grows up to 35cm/14in high. Responds to clipping and can be grown as a low hedge. The many varieties include *T.v.* 'Silver Posie' with silvery variegated leaves.

TILIA cordata
Small-leaved lime   *Tiliaceae*
Native to Europe, a hardy deciduous tree growing up to 11m/34ft high, with rounded leaves and

scented clusters of yellow-white flowers in midsummer.
CULTIVATION Sow seed or layer shoots in autumn. Grow in sun or semishade. Responds well to pollarding and training.
USE Young fresh leaves are edible and cooling. Infusion of dried flowers and bracts makes delicious scented tisane that is sedative, soothing and calming; also a treatment for fevers and, used externally, makes a beneficial wash. Nectar-rich flowers attract bees. Other lime species have similar properties.

TRIGONELLA foenum-graecum
Fenugreek   *Leguminosae*
Native to S. Europe and Asia, a tender annual widely cultivated as a fodder crop. About 75cm/30in high, it has trifoliate leaves, cream flowers in midsummer and stiff, beaked pods 15cm/6in long; these contain squared seeds. Scent of leaves increases as they dry.
CULTIVATION Easily grown from seed. Plant in sunny, sheltered position.
USE Use fresh leaves as a spicy salad ingredient or flavoring; sprouted seed as a bitter salad ingredient. Dried seed is a spice and makes a strongly aromatic and nutritious tonic medicine, especially for nursing mothers.

TRILLIUM erectum
Birthroot, bethroot   *Liliaceae*
Native to N. America, a hardy woodland perennial with broad leaves in groups of three and a solitary red-brown flower in late spring.
CULTIVATION Sow fresh seed (long germination period) or divide rootstock. Plant in shady, moist soil.
USE An astringent tonic, it has a powerful action. Acrid root is

used in cases of hemorrhage; a poultice of leaves can be applied to ulcers and wounds.

TROPAEOLUM majus
Nasturtium   *Tropaeolaceae*
Native to Peru, a hardy annual well known in gardens. It has scrambling pale stems up to 3m/10ft long, rounded leaves and spurred yellow, orange or red flowers from early summer.
CULTIVATION Grows easily from seed and self-seeds well. Plant in sunny position, in rich soil to encourage leafy growth or poor soil to encourage flowers.
USE Flowers are edible and young leaves have hot, pleasant flavor in salads. Unripe seeds can be pickled. Leaves are nutritious, also cleansing and antiseptic.

VACCINIUM myrtillus
Bilberry, whortleberry
Ericaceae
Native to Europe and N. Asia, a hardy deciduous subshrub 50cm/20in high, with glossy pointed leaves, drooping pink flowers in late spring and purple-black berries.
CULTIVATION Sow fresh seeds in autumn or take cuttings or layerings. Plant in moist, shady, peaty soil.
USE Eat juicy sharp-flavored berries raw, stewed, or in jellies and conserves. Astringent, antiseptic and vitamin rich, they are also a good treatment for all intestinal disorders.

VALERIANA officinalis
Valerian   *Valerianaceae*
Native to Europe and Asia, a tall, spreading, hardy perennial, 1.5m/5ft high, with graceful, pinnate leaves and clustered, scented, pink-white flowers from early summer.
CULTIVATION Divide root. It is

Thymus vulgaris

Thymus vulgaris 'Silver Posie'

Thymus drucei coccineus

Thymus herba-barona

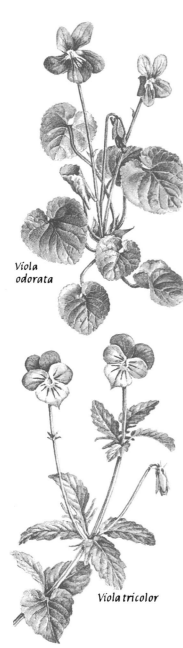

Viola
odorata

Viola tricolor

tolerant of most soils but grows best in slightly moist, semi-shaded position. Creeping roots may need containing.
USE Pungent scent of root increases as it dries. Used as a strong sedative, nervine and painkiller but take only under supervision. The roots of several other species are used medicinally and in scent.

VALERIANELLA locusta

Corn salad, lamb's lettuce
Valerianaceae
Widespread in temperate climates as weed in open ground, a small, lush-leaved, hardy annual or biennial with clusters of tiny mauve flowers.
CULTIVATION Sow seed throughout growing season, especially in late summer for winter crop, in well-composted, sunny position. Self-seeds prolifically. Gather leaves or whole plant before flowering.
USE Excellent, wholesome salad herb. Especially useful in winter and early spring.

VERATRUM viride

White or American hellebore
Liliaceae
Native to damp places in N. America, a statuesque hardy perennial, over 1.5m/5ft high, with broad, ribbed leaves and a strong spike of beautiful green flowers in midsummer.
CULTIVATION Sow fresh seed (which takes at least two years to germinate) or divide roots. Plant in moist soil and light shade, or keep roots shaded among other low-growing plants. Do not disturb.
USE All parts **poisonous**. Black rhizome has similar properties to *Helleborus*, and was formerly used as an emetic, sedative and analgesic.
Note *V. album* and *V. nigrum*

have a long history of similar medicinal uses.

VERBASCUM thapsus

Mullein *Scrophulariaceae*
Native to waste and open places in temperate climates, a hardy biennial of variable height to 2m/ 6ft 6in. Has a rosette of large pale woolly leaves and a downy spike of pale yellow flowers from mid-summer. There are many beautiful species and varieties.
CULTIVATION Sow seed in autumn or spring in well-drained, sunny position. Self-seeds well.
USE Emollient, sedative effect. Infuse leaves or flowers (strain to remove hairs) to soothe coughs, bronchitis, etc. Steam or blanch leaves and apply as an astringent poultice. Steep flowers in olive oil to use on bruises and aches.

VERBENA officinalis

Vervain *Verbenaceae*
Local to limestone soils in temperate climates, a hardy perennial of variable height to 1m/3ft, with toothed lobed leaves and stiff stems of pale mauve flower spikes from midsummer.
CULTIVATION Sow seed or divide root. Grow in well-drained sunny position.
USE Legendary sacred herb with astringent effect on wounds. Take the flowering plant in infusion as a tonic and nervine.

VIBURNUM opulus

Guelder rose *Caprifoliaceae*
Not the familiar garden variety with snowball flowers, but native to hedgerows, a small and decorative hardy deciduous tree growing up to 4m/13ft high, with maplelike leaves that turn purple in autumn, flat heads of creamy, scented flowers in late spring and translucent red berries in autumn.
CULTIVATION Sow fresh seed or

(more easily) take cuttings. Grow in good soil and full sun.
USE Fresh berries are toxic, but edible when cooked. Bark is prescribed as a nervine and sedative, and for uterine complaints.
Note The N. American *V. prunifolium*, black haw, has a similar habit, white flowers and blue-black berries. The bark has similar properties.

VIOLA odorata

Sweet violet *Violaceae*
Common on grassy banks and in shady places in many temperate countries, a small hardy perennial, about 15cm/6in high, with heart-shaped leaves and scented spurred violet flowers in spring.
CULTIVATION Sow seed, divide crown or detach runners. Plant in good well-drained soil and semishade.
USE Edible flowers can be added to salads or crystallized to decorate candies. Infused or as a syrup, flowers have a slightly sedative and laxative effect and are a remedy for headaches and insomnia. Use leaves as a poultice or ointment to soothe and reduce inflammations. Root can act as an emetic and purgative.

V. tricolor

Wild pansy, heartsease
Parent of the cultivated pansy and native to fields and open waste-ground in Europe, a hardy variable annual or short-lived perennial, up to 25cm/10in high, with yellow, purple or creamy flowers that bloom throughout the year and ovate or lanceolate leaves.
CULTIVATION Sow fresh seed in open sunny position.
USE Whole plant was formerly used as a tonic and a remedy for fevers; also as a healing herb for wounds and ulcers.

GLOSSARY

Acid Term applied to soil with few basic minerals, deficient in salts, pH content below 7.0.

Alkaline Term applied to soil containing salts, pH content above 7.0.

Alkaloid Plant constituent which acts powerfully on the animal system.

Annual Plant with a life cycle of one year or less.

Biennial Plant with life cycle of two years, generally dying after seeding.

Blanch Exclude light from a plant generally resulting in paler, sweeter, more tender leaves/stems.

Bract Modified leaflike organ at base of flower.

Bulb Fleshy underground storage organ.

Classification (of plants) Division into groups that share a similar structure or natural relationship. In descending order these are: families, genera, species and varieties.

Composite Member of the *Compositae*, the daisy family.

Corm Swollen underground stem used as storage organ.

Cottage garden A garden in which all the needs of a family are catered for – with a mixture of vegetables, herbs and flowers grown together rather than separately.

Crazy paving Irregularly shaped pieces of stone laid together to form a paved area.

Crown Upper part of root system of herbaceous perennial plants.

Crucifer Member of the *Cruciferae*, the cabbage family.

Cultivar A cultivated variety of a plant.

Cutting Piece of stem, root or leaf used for propagation.

Deciduous Shedding leaves in autumn.

Decoction Extraction of active principles of herb by boiling or simmering in liquid.

Dormant Term applied to resting period in life cycle of plant, when it slows or stops growing.

Drill Straight furrow drawn in soil in which seeds are sown.

Evergreen Retains leaves all year.

Floret Small flower, part of larger flowerhead.

Genus See Classification.

Habitat Area where plant grows naturally.

Half-hardy Applied to plants that will survive moderately low temperatures in a sheltered position.

Hardy Applied to plants that survive outdoors without protection throughout the year.

Heathland Open tract of ground, sometimes covered with shrubs.

Herbaceous Generally applied to perennial plants whose stems die down each winter.

Hybrid A plant created by crossing two separate varieties, species or genera.

Infusion Extraction of active principles of herb by steeping in liquid.

Introduced Term applied to plants that do not occur naturally in an area but are brought in by man.

Lanceolate Leaves that are narrow, tapering, spear-shaped.

Loam Fertile soil of good texture containing balanced mixture of nutrients.

Lobed Leaves/petals that are deeply cleft but not separated.

Mucilage Viscous substance obtained from certain herbs.

Narcotic Substance that, according to dosage, soothes pain or induces stupefaction and death.

Panicle Grouped cluster of stalked flowers.

Perennial Plant that lives longer than two years.

Pinnate Term applied to leaf divided into at least four leaflets arranged in opposite rows.

Principle Active chemical constituent of plant.

Rhizome Creeping underground stem, usually swollen and used for storing food.

Species See Classification.

Spike Long, unbranched flowerhead at end of stem.

Taproot Main plant root.

Tender Term applied to plant that cannot survive outdoors during the winter.

Tisane See Infusion.

Toxic Poisonous substance.

Tuber Fleshy, enlarged portion of stem used as storage organ.

Umbel Flowerhead with stalks that radiate from a central point:

Umbellifer Member of the *Umbelliferae*, the parsley family.

Variegated Leaves (or flowers) patterned with at least two colors.

Vulnerary Heals wounds.

GENERAL INDEX

PLANT INDEX

Italic type indicates illustrations; **Bold type** an entry in the Catalog of Herbs.